The Virtuous Marketplace

The Johns Hopkins University Studies
in Historical and Political Science

118th Series (2000)

1. Lu Ann Homza, *Religious Authority in the Spanish Renaissance*

2. Victoria E. Thompson, *The Virtuous Marketplace:
Women and Men, Money and Politics in Paris, 1830–1870*

The Virtuous Marketplace

WOMEN AND MEN, MONEY AND POLITICS IN PARIS, 1830–1870

Victoria E. Thompson

The Johns Hopkins University Press
BALTIMORE AND LONDON

The Johns Hopkins University Press
2715 North Charles Street
Baltimore, Maryland 21218-4363
www.press.jhu.edu

Library of Congress Cataloging-in-Publication Data
Thompson, Victoria Elizabeth.
The virtuous marketplace : women and men, money and politics in Paris,
1830–1870 / Victoria E. Thompson.
p. cm. — (The Johns Hopkins University studies in historical and political
science; 118th ser., 2)
Includes bibliographical references and index.
ISBN 0-8018-6414-3 (alk. paper)
1. Women—France—Paris—Economic conditions—19th century. 2. Paris
(France)—Economic conditions—19th century. 3. Paris (France)—Social
conditions—19th century. 4. Wealth—France—Paris—History—19th
century. 5. Money—France—Paris—History—19th century. 6. Free
enterprise—France—Paris—History—19th century. 7. Social status—
France—Paris—History—19th century. I. Title. II. Series.
HQ1620.P2 T46 2000
305.42′0944′361—dc21   00-021025

A catalog record for this book is available from the British Library.

Contents

v

Conclusion

170

Illustrations are on pages 119–130

Acknowledgments

Although scholars often like to think of the work that they do as being separate from the mechanisms and principles that drive the market, scholarship, like the market economy, consists of a series of exchanges: exchanges of ideas, information, encouragement, and inspiration. Since beginning this project, I have been the fortunate beneficiary of numerous such exchanges.

Many of these exchanges were made possible by the generous support of various foundations and institutions. The Mellon Foundation provided me with a pre-dissertation research fellowship as well as with a dissertation writing fellowship. A Pepper Fellowship from the University of Pennsylvania freed me from teaching duties for one year, allowing me to get a head start on my research. A year's research in France was made possible by a Chateaubriand Fellowship from the French government. As I worked to turn the dissertation into a book, a Xavier University Summer Research Fellowship and Research Sabbatical, as well as a grant from the American Philosophical Society, provided me with the means to continue researching and writing.

I have presented portions of this project at national conferences as well as at various colleges and universities. I have benefited from my exchanges with other scholars at these various forums and have appreciated their comments and questions.

While I worked on this project, first as a dissertation and then as a book, numerous individuals were generous with their advice, questions, and criticisms. Friends and colleagues from graduate school who read and commented on early drafts include Rose Beiler, Nan Dreher, Jim Heinzen, Ken Holston, Jeff Horn, Lara Iglitzin, Abby Schrader, and Eugene Weiss. In Paris, Ann Illan-Alter, Clare Crowston, Lisa DiCaprio, Nicole

Dombrowski, Charlotte Eyerman, Cheryl Koos, Sharon Marcus, Dan Ringrose, and Lynn Sharp all offered feedback, ideas, and friendship. Along the way, numerous colleagues have helped me turn my ideas into a dissertation, and my dissertation into a book. Many thanks to Elinor Accampo, Claudia Goldin, Gay Gullickson, Walter Licht, and Michelle Perrot, all of whom offered valuable advice at the beginning. Later on, Lenard Berlanstein, Suzanne Desan, John Fairfield, Roger Fortin, Casey Harrison, Maura O'Conner, Jeremy Popkin, Tip Ragan, Louise Tilly, Peggy Waller, and Whitney Walton were generous with their advice and encouragement.

A few individuals have been enormously helpful and supportive from the very beginning. Lynn Lees, a member of my dissertation committee, read numerous drafts of the dissertation, offering detailed and precise criticism and suggestions. I have greatly appreciated her willingness to continue to read and comment on drafts of chapters and articles in subsequent years. Rachel Fuchs, whom I met during my year of research in Paris, helped give direction to my research at a crucial time. Generously offering to read both the dissertation and the book manuscript, she has been unstinting in providing criticism, ideas, and support when I most needed them.

Lynn Hunt has gone above and beyond the call of duty as an advisor. She has discussed, read, and commented on countless versions of the dissertation and book manuscript. Her comments have always been right on target, helping me to formulate my ideas and clarify my arguments. Throughout this entire project, she has offered valuable advice and constant encouragement.

The support of my family has also been invaluable. I owe many thanks to Barbara, Jenny, Mary, and Ted Thompson for this as for so many other things. I also owe a debt of gratitude to Deborah Hamilton, who has been, for better and for worse, with me every step of the way. I hope that she will feel that this work is as much hers as it is mine.

Finally, I would like to dedicate this book to the memory of Jack Eugene Reece. Jack was my advisor at the University of Pennsylvania and a member of my dissertation committee. As I worked on this book, I thought often of his careful criticism and attention to detail, both of which greatly improved my dissertation. I also thought of his biting wit, his enormous love of history, and his generous heart. Jack was a fine scholar, an excellent teacher, and a man of integrity. Wherever you are, Jack, I raise a toast to you.

The Virtuous Marketplace

Introduction

This book addresses three questions. Why is it that French women, previously accepted as producers and consumers of wealth, became defined in opposition to the marketplace during the nineteenth century? How did making money come to be considered an honorable pursuit for men, especially men of the middle classes, during the nineteenth century? And finally, how did the French resolve the conflict between self-interest and the public good that they associated with the spread of market forces and market ideology? In other words, this study seeks to explain the attempted economic exclusion of women from public life, and its relation to the political exclusion of women first articulated during the French Revolution, by placing this process within the context of changing and sometimes contradictory views of the market as a model for French society.

During the Old Regime, work and the pursuit of profits were associated with the third estate—that part of the population that could make claim to neither ecclesiastical function nor aristocratic lineage. The aristocracy was of course concerned with questions of money—increasingly so over the course of the eighteenth century. Money was necessary to maintain a lavish lifestyle as well as to buy public offices. France during this time possessed a lively system of exchange in which "titles of nobility, judicial and fiscal offices, royal fiefs, seigniorial courts, local monopolies of trade, and the right to collect certain taxes were all bought and sold like so much beef on a butcher's scale."[1] Yet even though money was necessary to buy such offices, its pursuit was not perceived as a goal in its own right. As Kristen Neuschel has argued, "although honor found expression in and could be enhanced by material advantage . . . it was nevertheless not equivalent to it."[2] Furthermore, the accumulation of wealth, which was then put into offices that conferred privileges and authority, was not

1

perceived as an avenue for individual advancement but as a means to further the position of one's family and to cement social relationships. Rather than a manifestation of individual success and advancement, money was understood within a framework of patronage.[3] According to Jonathan Dewald, "money entered the nobles' lives independently of the market, indeed in ways that contradicted the assumptions of a market economy."[4]

Money was therefore not valued in itself, for in itself it conferred no direct power or status. It was useful to the extent that it could buy one's way into or up through the ranks of the nobility, but as soon as one "arrived," one tended to "forget" that it had been thanks in part to the size of one's purse. In marriages between wealthy members of the middle class and impoverished aristocrats, it was the person with money who occupied the lower rank and who was perceived as having "risen" in society. Money certainly did not confer the important trait of honor, which, as Robert Nye has argued, was maintained in the eighteenth century through lineage, comportment, and above all, courage.[5] Honor was a trait associated with the aristocracy, whose members lost their status if they openly engaged in increasingly lucrative activities such as commerce or manufacturing.

Although important as a medium of exchange in Old Regime France, money did not carry great ideological significance. While an overt concern with and pursuit of money could lead to loss of status for an aristocrat, money in and of itself was not determinant of hierarchies of rank, status, and power within French society. Indeed, as Albert Hirschman has argued, "the very contempt in which economic activities were held led to the conviction, in spite of much evidence to the contrary, that they could not possibly have much potential in any area of human endeavor and were incapable of causing either good *or evil* on a grand scale."[6]

By the late eighteenth century, however, doubts began to appear regarding the innocuous nature of money. Thinkers such as Adam Ferguson, a member of the Scottish Enlightenment, questioned assumptions that the pursuit of one's economic interests did no harm to the public good. In 1767, Ferguson warned that a society ruled by the pursuit of money was one in which "the bonds of affection are broken" and in which a man "deals with his fellow creatures as he does with his cattle and his soil, for the sake of the profits they bring."[7] Of course, the opposite point of view developed during this period as well. The work of Adam Smith in England and Jean-Baptiste Say in France sought to prove that the pursuit of individual economic interests contributed to, and indeed was necessary for, the maintenance and expansion of the public good. In 1796, Say associated the "improvement and happiness" of the country with the financial security of each individual, writing, "I should wish, in short, that in a great republic there should be not a single idler whose unproductive existence would be a burden to society, and not one poor person to complain that, by his work and good conduct, he cannot earn an easy subsistence or lead a life that the English would call 'comfortable.'"[8]

Whether they warned of its dangers or lauded its potential for good, commentators increasingly associated money with individual liberty. At the outbreak of the French Revolution, the third estate, arguing for its right to participate in the political process on an equal footing with the aristocracy and the clergy, emphasized the value of activities that contributed to the nation by producing wealth. The idea that wealth conferred freedom from the hierarchies of rank and status that had structured Old Regime society led revolutionaries to organize the new political system on the basis of economic qualifications rather than birth. During the Revolution, according to William Reddy, "France embraced money, gave it sovereign authority over all relationships outside of a few refuges—the family, the army, the prison—institutions, that is, whose functions could not be made to square with the liberal illusion [that money was a source of liberation] even in the 1790s."[9] Economic success was seen as a manifestation of individual merit and talent, and it was the basis for political participation for much of the first half of the nineteenth century.

This association of money with liberty, and with the Revolution, continued throughout the early nineteenth century. In the introduction to an 1828 *Dictionnaire Historique de Paris,* Antony Béraud argued that free economic exchange was at the heart of all forms of progress. "It is on the basis of the most absolute liberty," he wrote, "of the competition of all talents and all industries, that progress in science, art, and all other genres is established. The government has nothing to prevent or command in this domain; it has only to protect each citizen in the exercise of his liberty, against all acts of injustice and violence."[10] Up until at least the 1870s, when the outbreak of a serious financial and industrial crisis prompted a turn toward protectionism, political economists in France promoted the idea that a market free from government intervention, in which each individual was able to compete with others in pursuit of his or her individual interests, constituted the best road to political stability and economic growth.[11] The pursuit of money, they argued, was a beneficial force in human society.

By the late 1820s, however, concerns regarding the effects of market forces and market ideologies were beginning to surface with increasing frequency. These criticisms maintained that rather than promoting the public good, free competition destroyed social bonds. Individualism, defined as the self-interested pursuit of wealth, was said to overwhelm familial and national loyalties, creating a society in which each individual was concerned only with the satisfaction of his or her personal needs and desires. These criticisms became especially strong during the July Monarchy (1830–48), which expanded the tax-based suffrage system to include the upper ranks of the bourgeoisie. Under the leadership of King Louis-Philippe, financial and banking elites exercised unprecedented political power, while many members of the traditional landowning elites opposed the new government. To those members of the middle and working classes who complained that they too should be allowed to vote, government minister François Guizot replied, "get rich." At the same time, the introduction of new methods of production in manufacturing, including limited mechanization and an increased division of labor, combined with periodic economic and agricultural crises to depress wages and raise unemployment rates. Finally, the experience of repeated revolution and a constant threat of social unrest lent a negative cast to the equation between money, liberty, and revolution elaborated in the late eighteenth century.

Increasingly, therefore, the pursuit of wealth came to be seen as something that could undermine, rather than improve, society. In 1845, Honoré de Balzac suggested that the perversion of social relationships into economic relationships could one day lead to a violent "settling of accounts." According to Balzac, due to the endless competition for wealth and its trappings, "the needs of all the classes, devoured by vanity, have been overexcited . . . . When one perceives the *fluctuating debt* of the Treasury, and admits to oneself the *fluctuating debt* of each family that has modeled itself on the state, one is frightened to see that one half of France is in debt to the other. When the accounts are settled, the debtors will swallow up the lenders."[12] In opposition to political economists who argued that the pursuit of self-interest was compatible with the public good, many began to associate self-interest with unrestrained appetites, egoism, and debauchery and warned that it threatened the very foundations of French society.

It is difficult to assess the accuracy of French perceptions regarding the inroads made by market society and market ideology during the mid-nineteenth century. Although few historians would still argue that France's economic development was backward compared to that of England, most scholars agree that traditional methods, organizational practices, and outlooks persisted well into the nineteenth century.[13] In manufacturing, one can site in evidence of this argument the persistence of the handicraft trades, the preference for domestic piecework rather than mechanized factory labor, or the attachment of the working class to corporate ideals and corporate language.[14] French firms tended throughout the nineteenth century to remain small in size and to retain their family character. Even larger firms relied upon paternalistic practices and modeled the relationship between employer and workers on that between a father and his children.[15] The government retained a strong hand in economic growth; indeed this hand was strongest and most evident during France's period of industrial takeoff, the Second Empire (1852–70).[16] The persistence of traditional practices and outlooks seems to imply that the free-market model was not easily applicable to French society.[17]

Despite the persistence of traditional models of organization and practices, however, French society did undergo a number of significant changes that contemporaries perceived as sources of upheaval and associated with the incursion of market forces and the adoption of free-market ideology. The abolition of the guilds in 1791 effectively ended the ability of workers to exercise control over their wages or working conditions. In Paris, changes in production practices such as the increased division of labor or limited mechanization coincided with greater competition for jobs as the population of the capital swelled. Problems of falling wages were exacerbated during periodic crises of overproduction that repeatedly devastated the Parisian economy. Poverty became more visible in Paris as the specter of hungry mobs taking to the streets grew in the public's imagination. Indeed, repeated political unrest that rocked the capital, toppling regimes and keeping alive the memory of the Terror, was commonly held to be the result in part of the creation of a growing number of poor, the "dangerous classes" of Paris.[18]

At the same time as changes in manufacturing were contributing to the problem of poverty and the political unrest with which it was associated, new economic opportunities were enriching the bourgeoisie. Changes in government policy and public perceptions encouraged an increased investment in real estate, industry, and government bonds. Credit became easier to obtain and bankruptcy less odious as successive governments sought to free up capital for the creation of railroads, the promotion of industrial growth, and the renovation of the capital. Speculating on the stock market became another new source of wealth, and innovations in retail, such as the establishment of department stores, catered to a growing group of people with money to spend. Freed from the need to invest money in government offices, members of the aristocracy and the upper middle classes could now use their wealth to create even greater wealth through investment and speculation. In so doing, they also gained political power, since the right to vote or run for office was based until 1848 on the amount of taxes one paid.

Significant changes in production, investment, and retailing during the mid-nineteenth century drew attention to the structural transformation of the French economy. Increased awareness of these changes, as well as of their impact on society, partially explains the growing concern with the market that is evident in the mid-nineteenth century. At the same time, the transition from a social order based on blood and privilege to one based on money and talent created a situation in which the market became an increasingly attractive model for society.

Although the attack on blood and privilege had begun even before 1789, the July Monarchy inaugurated a new organization for society by encouraging the growth of speculation and by making wealth, regardless of birth, the only standard for political inclusion. The definitive rejection of the estates-based model of the Old Regime gave rise to a search for new models of the social hierarchy. Envisioning society as a market offered a new means of imagining the social order, one in which individuals and groups would be assigned a place according to their relationship to money rather than by their birth or their relationship to the king.[19] Since one's relationship to money could change (through an increase or decrease in one's fortunes), this model offered a measure of openness and flexibility that the estates model lacked.[20]

The egalitarian implications of this model were perceived with ambivalence, especially among the bourgeoisie. The market model allowed for the possibility that anyone, including members of the lower classes, could change their place in the social hierarchy by altering their relationship to money. Thus while members of the middle class considered the market the source of their political and social emancipation, they also feared its destabilizing potential. Martin Wiener's characterization of early nineteenth-century English attitudes toward the market holds true for the French as well: "early Victorians' feelings about the market were often uneasy and conflicted. Although it was sometimes seen as a 'civilizing' force, rewarding self-discipline and deferral of gratification, the market was also feared as *encouraging* impulsive, willful behavior."[21] Fears that the unfettered pursuit of self-interest dissolved social bonds, undermined hierarchy and authority, and encouraged a life of debauchery and vice repeatedly appeared in a variety of writings from the mid-nineteenth century. At the same time, contemporaries constantly stressed the importance of the market as an agent of modernization and civilization.

While contemporaries sometimes questioned the implications of the market model, they did not wish to abandon it. They sought rather to resolve these contradictory attitudes toward the market by reshaping the market model of society. Since this model was based in part on the awareness of and involvement in structural changes in the French economy, the process of reshaping the market model also often led to a reshaping of the economic structures of French society. The reshaping of the market model thus entailed a redefinition of both the meaning and practice of production, investment, and consumption, as well of the relationship among the three.

Concerns regarding the impact of the market, and attempts to define and shape the relationships of various groups and individuals to money and the market, permeate a variety of primary sources from the mid-nineteenth century. Memoirs, political brochures, newspaper articles, and studies concerning social problems such as the conditions of workers or prostitution all devote a great deal of attention to money and market forces. In their directives and correspondence, police and municipal authorities also manifested their interest in such matters. In addition, concern with money and market forces pervades popular literature during this period; not only novels and plays, but also the extremely popular works on Paris and the Parisians that were published in great numbers during the mid-nineteenth century reveal a great interest in the effects of the market on French society.

In the literature on Paris and the Parisians, authors who situated themselves along the entire political spectrum attempted to make sense of the changes French, and especially Parisian, society was undergoing by repeatedly describing, defining, and categorizing the city and its population. This literature includes the *tableaux de Paris* and the *physiologies.* The *tableaux de Paris,* taking their inspiration from Louis-Sébastien Mercier's 1782–83 *Tableau de Paris,* attempted to capture a complete view of all aspects of Parisian life. During the July Monarchy, these were usually collectively authored works sold in weekly installments by subscription, with each author treating a different aspect of Parisian mores, characters, and institutions. During the 1850s and 1860s, these works were more often sold in one volume and written by one author. The *physiologies* were inspired by the *tableaux.* These were smaller, shorter, and less expensive books that treated only one aspect of Parisian society, usually a specific social type, such as the journalist, smoker, or prostitute. The heyday of the *physiologies* was the 1840s, although they continued to be published into the Second Empire.[22] While the more expensive *tableaux* appealed to an affluent audience, the one-franc *physiologies,* of which half a million copies of over one hundred and thirty titles were sold, were widely read among all ranks of the middle class.[23]

According to Richard Terdiman, periods of social crisis and transformation give rise to an increase in "semiotic behavior": the attempt to define, distinguish, and classify so as to make sense of changes within society.[24] This concern can be understood as one of the major impulses behind

7

the development and popularity of the literature on Paris and the Parisians during the July Monarchy. This literature was devoted to creating an all-inclusive (or "panoramic"), orderly, and highly legible overview of the various inhabitants, institutions, and public spaces of the new Paris.[25] Urban institutions, public spaces, and inhabitants were, in this literature, reduced to a set of highly stereotypical characteristics that served to identify their place within a social order that appeared to be fixed and easily comprehensible. In addition, the creation of new social types served as a shorthand to identifying new segments of the social strata or new ways of being and acting in society. For example, the characteristics and behavior of the *flâneur,* the urban observer whose ability to move freely throughout the public areas of the city while remaining detached from the crowds around him, were developed in this literature. The *flâneur* provided a new model for male, middle-class authority, one based on disinterested observation and spatial mobility.[26]

Despite the ordering impulse of this literature, many conflicts and unresolved concerns regarding the effects of market forces can be seen in its pages. Descriptions of the social types and public spaces that filled this literature touched indirectly on many significant topics of debate, including conflicts between self-interest and the public good, speculation regarding the impact of economic change on society, critiques or endorsements of new economic theories, and discussions regarding men's and women's relationship to the market. The questions posed at the outset of this introduction were debated and resolved in the pages of this literature.

This literature was so popular in part because it helped contemporaries identify and debate many of the most significant transformations in Parisian society. Evidence of its widespread appeal can be found in the adoption of the descriptions and social types developed in this literature in a variety of other sources. The characters that peopled the literature on Paris and the Parisians often found their way into seemingly unrelated texts, such as police reports or legislative debates. The widespread use of characters made popular in this literature attests to its ability to both shape and reflect public opinion. The characters disseminated in this literature became fixtures of the Parisian imagination during this period, widely recognized and alluded to in a variety of contexts and for a variety of purposes.

Because this literature was so widely disseminated and exerted such influence, it forms the backbone of this study. However, just as the questions and answers, the debates and disagreements, found within this literature occurred within a larger context, this book combines an analysis of this literature with a variety of other sources to explore the myriad debates regarding the effects of market forces on French society. These sources reveal both disagreement and consensus: disagreement over the extent to which the market was undermining French society, disagreement concerning the best way to control the potentially damaging effects of the market, but also a widespread consensus that the market must not destroy virtue. How to create and maintain a virtuous marketplace—one in which making money would be seen as an honorable pursuit, one in which self-interest accorded with the public good, one in which freedom did not degenerate into license—were questions that preoccupied Parisians in the mid-nineteenth century.

Those questions were resolved in large part through the use of gender. During the French Revolution, a gendered division of society—one in which public, political functions were performed by men and private, familial functions performed by women—was invoked as necessary to the maintenance of political stability.[27] The 1804 Civil Code articulated this difference as one of women's subordination to men. Women were considered legal minors, who lost control of their children and their property. However, although most women lost the power to manage their assets, female merchants were granted an exceptional status, retaining the right to enter into contracts, to buy and sell at will, and to engage not only their own assets, but those of their husbands as well.

The exceptional economic status of the merchant stemmed in part from an awareness that her livelihood depended upon her ability to retain her freedom to act in the marketplace. It can also be seen, however, as part of a widespread acceptance of the important role played by women of the popular classes in manufacturing, consumption, and commerce.[28] During the early nineteenth century, the idea that most women of the popular classes worked for wages, to support themselves or their families, was accepted as a fact of life. Until the middle of the century, many middle-class women worked for wages as well. In Paris, women were especially prominent in commerce and retail; they made up the majority of the capital's merchants, and in every bar, café, or restaurant, women ran the cash register. Among the popular classes, women were in charge of consumption; it was women who bought the food and other necessities of daily life. Women also managed the family's cash flow through the negotiation of loans from neighbors or merchants as well as the regular pawning and recovery of the family's assets during hard times. Women, it was believed, were more likely to buy lottery tickets, just as among the aristocracy women were considered to be especially avid gamblers. Finally, women who were prostitutes were the ultimate manipulators of market forces, as they transformed themselves into commodities that were bought and sold, and reaped the profits generated by their own sexuality.

The regular and widespread participation of women in economic life was not considered a problem before money became a constituent component of political identity.[29] As the significance of money as a determinant of political authority and social status grew, however, the privileged relationship of women of the popular classes to money and the marketplace became a topic of growing concern. As the ability of women to earn wages, engage in commerce, and manage their assets was increasingly considered an anomaly, women's relationship to the marketplace came to be seen as a source of social disorder. Fears regarding the possible effects of market forces on French society, including the fear of popular revolution, were projected with growing frequency onto the image of the woman of the popular classes. Soon, calls for her exclusion from economic life were added to those justifying her exclusion from politics.

As in the case of production and consumption, however, women's participation in commerce, exchange, and investment was not so much denied as it was transformed. In all realms of the economy, women's activities and opportunities were redefined during the mid-nineteenth century, often in paradoxical ways. In manufacturing, women experienced falling wages and shrinking work opportunities during the nineteenth century.[30] At the same time, production became symbolically feminized by the mid-nineteenth century, as the working woman, or *ouvrière,* became the prototypical symbol of industrialization.[31] Similarly, consumption was increasingly "feminized" and "eroticized" as contemporaries expressed fears concerning women's supposed inability to control their behavior as consumers.[32] Women's relationship to commerce and investment was likewise both reinforced and called into question during the nineteenth century. Traditional associations between women and economic activity encouraged this "feminization." At the same time, long-standing views of women's double nature helped contemporaries work out a new understanding of the market and its impact. When identified with women's ability to act as a moralizing force, the market was seen as an agent of progress and civilization; associated with women's negative side—a propensity to disorder and sexual license—the market became a maleficent agent that encouraged social and gender disruption and moral corruption. Through the use of gender, then, contemporaries were able to distinguish between positive and negative aspects of the market.

Such a perspective demonstrates the importance of discussions concerning the market to the development and dissemination of the ideology of domesticity in the nineteenth century. As women became increasingly defined as beings who were unable to interact with the market in a positive or successful manner, measures were taken to limit their access to networks of commerce and exchange, production, consumption, and investment. At the same time, the centrality of feminine imagery to the creation of new models of the marketplace made women's access to the market a topic of intense public concern and actually opened up the possibility for women to act and speak in public on this matter. The model of the virtuous marketplace drew public attention to women's public and private relationship to the market; it also drew attention to men's public and private responsibilities. Studying the way in which gender was used to redefine the marketplace in the mid-nineteenth century thus helps to explain the rise of domestic ideology at the same time as it calls into question the neat divisions between public and private that are often associated with it. In this way, this study can be seen as part of a recent trend in feminist scholarship that seeks to complicate the model of separate spheres by capturing, as Ann-Louise Shapiro stated, "a more nuanced vision of the permeability of prescribed boundaries and the tensions and adjustments that were necessarily a part of this permeability."[33]

Contemporaries redefined the market in response to fears that unfettered self-interest threatened to destroy both public and private virtue. The redefinition of the marketplace affected the middle class as well as the popular classes, men as well as women. Debates and anxieties concerning the effects of the marketplace on French society resulted in the creation of new political and professional identities, influenced beliefs regarding proper behavior for men and women, and shaped assumptions regarding the proper use and organization of urban space and urban institutions.

Chapter 1 introduces these debates and anxieties, which occurred at a time when many still believed that it was possible to escape the damaging effects of the market altogether. This chapter focuses on the image of the prostitute as a metaphor for market society. Focusing on what was probably the most influential text of the nineteenth century on prostitution, Alexandre-Jean-Baptiste Parent-Duchâtelet's *De la prostitution dans la ville de Paris*, the chapter begins by exploring the ways in which the prostitute was associated with political liberty and popular commerce, but also with economic dependency and immorality. The chapter then discusses two attempts to redefine the image of the prostitute. Contributors to the Saint-Simonian newspaper, *La Femme libre*, all former members of the utopian socialist Saint-Simonian movement that attracted adherents from the popular and middle classes in the 1820s and early 1830s, argued that prostitution was the result of the incursion of market forces into the world of love and romance. They maintained that women could only escape the pull of the marketplace by becoming economically independent. Middle-class journalists and authors of popular literature were also concerned with the figure of the prostitute, since they were themselves frequently charged with "selling" themselves in an increasingly commercialized press. Like the Saint-Simonian feminists, they argued that it was possible to escape the pull of the market, not, however, through economic independence but through self-control, an argument that would take on growing importance throughout the period.

Chapter 2 turns to the debates concerning the effects of market forces on Parisian workers. During the 1840s, an articulate and increasingly politicized group of artisans began to agitate in print for widespread economic and political reform. They created the image of the male breadwinner to oppose middle-class critics who argued that workers' dependency stemmed from their inability to manage money. Workers used this image to justify their demands for higher wages, arguing in particular that their demands for higher wages were not driven by self-interest but rather by the need to care for economically dependent wives and children. Although feminists attempted during the 1848 revolution to argue that women also deserved higher wages and political recognition, the usefulness of the male breadwinner image for articulating a balance between self-interest and selflessness meant that women's demands, raised within the context of revolution, were perceived as dangerous.

By 1848, agreement concerning women's economic dependency served as the basis for a cross-class alliance that was manifested on the political level through the establishment of universal manhood suffrage. At the same time, however, female economic dependency was used to justify measures designed to control the presence of the popular classes in the city. Chapter 3 examines how this was done by addressing anxieties regarding the supposed disruptive nature of popular commerce. Fear about the effects of market forces and unease over the revolutionary potential of the popular classes combined to shape the approach taken by police and municipal authorities to the regulation of popular commerce within the capital. During this period, the Paris police increased their supervision and control over street merchants; it also presided over the renovation of the city's major markets, the *halles,* the central food market, and the Temple market, the used-clothing exchange. Both regulations designed to control merchants and the design of the new markets hurt merchant interests. Despite this apparent blow to freedom of commerce, police and departmental authorities justified the changes they made by referring to the figure of the prostitute as well as to that of the economically dependent woman. The control of popular commerce—perceived as a potential source of disruption, contagion, and immorality—was also an attempt to control the presence and conduct of the popular classes in public areas of the city.

Of all French institutions, nowhere was the potential of the market—for good or for bad—more evident than in the stock market. The Paris stock exchange took on an enormous importance during the mid-nineteenth century as a source of wealth, but also as a source of social and political identity. While some supported the "democratization of credit" that was said to accompany the growth of the stock market as a source of liberty and progress, others worried that as speculation spread to the popular classes it would undermine the bonds and erase the distinctions that structured the French family and the French nation. Concern regarding the potentially devastating effects of the stock market was expressed as a fear of female speculators. As in the case of the city's markets, attempts to limit access to the stock exchange were also attempts to control the forces of democracy. In distinguishing between the honest investor and the immoral speculator, contemporaries further articulated ideas concerning the proper relationship of men and women to money and the marketplace that had been circulating since the 1830s. They concluded that the defense of the French nation required male honor (understood as self-control in the face of market forces) and female virtue (understood as a withdrawal from the marketplace altogether).

Throughout this study, I have attempted to capture the complexities of beliefs and perceptions within Parisian culture. Rather than posit a model in which ideas move in one direction (from top to bottom or bottom to top), I have tried to show that systems of belief that gain widespread acceptance and use in a culture are the result of multiple articulations, challenges, and negotiations.[34] The widespread acceptance of female economic dependency by the late 1860s resulted from a variety of discussions among many different groups, centering on the relationship between gender and the market. By the 1860s, the model of the virtuous marketplace—of which the idea of female economic dependency was a part—provided a new perceptual framework. Linked to new practices, this framework shifted the grounds of debate, determining what was possible to imagine and experience, and was itself the object of new challenges and renegotiations.

I have also tried to demonstrate the way in which belief systems affected individuals' lives. Debates concerning the effects of market forces shaped the evolution of political and personal identities, and helped to determine the range of opportunities open to each individual. They put new pressures on men to measure their worth in terms of their economic success, while resulting in an even greater withdrawal of women from public life. The effects of continued anxiety regarding the marketplace can also be read on the landscape of the capital, as the result of decisions made regarding the use of public space in the city's markets or in the neighborhood of the stock exchange.

In 1834, Honoré de Balzac wrote in his preface to *La Fille aux yeux d'or* that "[in Paris,] there was no real relation but the thousand franc note, no real friend but the pawn shop."[35] Fifty-three years later, a character created by Emile Zola dreamed of a society in which there would be "no more money, and thus no more speculation, no more theft, no more abominable exchanges, no more of these crimes worsened by greed, girls married for their dowries, elderly parents strangled for an inheritance, passersby assassinated for their wallets."[36] While many during the mid-nineteenth century feared a society governed by money, few desired one in which it would be absent. Their challenge was to render the pursuit of wealth compatible with the maintenance of honor, to balance self-interest with the public good, to create, in short, a virtuous marketplace. This study explores the way in which the attempts of French men and women to meet these challenges contributed to the transformation of French society.

ONE

The Free Woman

FEMALE SEXUALITY AND
ECONOMIC LIBERTY

Eugène Sue's *Les Mystères de Paris,* arguably one of the most popular serial novels of the July Monarchy, opens with a scene that warns readers of the dangers of debt for women. La Goualeuse, a young prostitute who practices her trade in the dark, narrow alleyways of the *cité* neighborhood, is accosted by an acquaintance who threatens her with physical violence if she does not repay him for an *eau-de-vie,* a clear brandy. When the frightened girl protests that she has no money, her acquaintance replies that the owner of a nearby bar would "grant you credit on your pretty face." Within the next few chapters, the reader learns that the facility with which La Goualeuse could obtain credit caused her fall into prostitution. As a young girl, she was imprisoned on a false charge. When released, she spent all of her savings from work done while in prison on entertainment and pretty things. Broke, and with nowhere else to turn, the girl succumbed to the *ogresse,* a procuress who "rented" clothing and lodging in exchange for her wages from prostitution. When we first meet her, then, La Goualeuse is at the mercy of a debt she cannot escape, one that condemns her to moral degradation and economic dependency. "The clothes that I wear belong to the *ogresse,*" she states, "I owe her for my lodging and my food . . . I can no longer leave . . . she will have me arrested as a thief . . . I belong to her . . . I must repay her."[1]

The primacy of economics in the account of La Goualeuse's fall into prostitution is not accidental. Like so many of his contemporaries, Sue placed prostitution at the heart of the market economy. For numerous writers in mid-nineteenth-century France, prostitution was an institution that raised questions concerning the relationship between credit and consumption, production and speculation. The prostitute worked, yet produced nothing. She possessed a capital—her beauty and sexuality—and yet she was also a commodity. Although she was believed to serve a public function in acting as an outlet for men's supposedly uncontrollable sexual urges, contemporaries argued that self-interest drew her into her profession. For many writers of the mid-nineteenth century, the prostitute seemed literally to embody the conundrums of a society based on market principles. As writers struggled to come to terms with the impact of the market on French society, they worked to redefine the prostitute, to restore her "virtue." The redemption of the prostitute was a common theme in July Monarchy literature.[2] In *Les Mystères de Paris*, for example, La Goualeuse became the virginal Fleur-de-Marie, who spent her time helping others, took the veil, and finally died in expiation of her sins.

In creating his portrait of La Goualeuse, Sue drew heavily upon the work of Alexandre-Jean-Baptiste Parent-Duchâtelet. His two-volume *De la prostitution dans la ville de Paris* is the focus of the first part of this chapter. In addition to providing a coherent justification for the regulatory system established to supervise the behavior and health of prostitutes, this study reinforced the connection between women of the popular classes and prostitution. It also likened unregulated prostitution to unregulated commerce, implying that both were equally dangerous. Parent-Duchâtelet's study was thus as much about the impact of the free market as it was about prostitution.

The Saint-Simonian newspaper *La Femme libre* offers a second example of the way in which prostitution was used to explore the effects of market forces on French society, and on women in particular. Contributors to this paper used the image of the prostitute to discuss the relationship between economic emancipation and personal freedom. Saint-Simonian women argued that women's sexuality could be used as a positive force to change society for the better and consistently emphasized the necessity of women's economic independence. Only by earning a living wage, these authors argued, could woman escape the trap of prostitution, thereby escaping market relations altogether.

Male middle-class writers and journalists also wished to escape the pull of market relations. Critics frequently likened writers and journalists to prostitutes, charging them with allowing commercial concerns to taint their objectivity and creativity. Male writers and journalists thus sought to create a professional image that would emphasize their virtue and disinterestedness. They did this by redefining and popularizing the image of the grisette. "Grisette" was a nickname for a working girl. In the late eighteenth and early nineteenth centuries, the grisette as depicted in popular and libertine literature was frequently assimilated with the prostitute.[3] In the works on Paris and the Parisians published in the 1840s and beyond,

16

the image of the grisette was transformed, and she became a noble and selfless being motivated by love rather than the desire for gain. Writers were interested in the grisette because her life story offered a model of how to deal with the temptations of the marketplace. Journalists and authors of popular literature thus used the image of the grisette as a means of exploring their own professional and political identities.

In each case, concern regarding the relationship between sexuality, economic exchange, and freedom was a major component of these discussions. Although various authors held different views concerning the relationship between these issues, they all manifested a common interest in limiting the effects of laissez-faire principles on French society. Parent-Duchâtelet argued that the legal subordination of and police control over the prostitute would limit the ravages of self-interest inherent in prostitution. He justified this subordination and control by arguing that prostitutes were unsuccessful participants in the free-market economy. The Saint-Simonian feminists maintained that economic independence would create a realm outside of market relations, in which women would be truly free because they were able to act out of love rather than self-interest. Male journalists, taking the grisette as their model, argued that freedom from self-interest, so necessary to be able to translate public opinion, was the preserve of only a select few who possessed the self-control necessary to resist temptation. In each case, the authors under discussion in this chapter explored the relationship between female sexuality and the market economy, devising various strategies for rendering interactions with the market virtuous.

Regulating Female Capital: Prostitution and Legal Debate in the July Monarchy

In 1836, Alexandre-Jean-Baptiste Parent-Duchâtelet published his authoritative two-volume work on prostitution in Paris. A public-health expert who studied a variety of questions related to waste disposal, putrefaction, and disease, Parent-Duchâtelet turned his talents to the study of prostitution in an attempt to explain the causes of prostitution, to catalog information relating to the behavior, appearance, and beliefs of prostitutes, and to justify the police administration's system of registration and medical examination. Alternately sympathetic and severe toward the women he studied, Parent-Duchâtelet has remained famous for his proclamation that prostitutes, like sewers, were an unpleasant but necessary component of human society. And just as sewers allowed for the movement of waste products throughout a city, prostitution allowed for the circulation of female sexuality, which Parent-Duchâtelet implied was a specifically feminine sort of capital. Parent-Duchâtelet identified the circulation of female capital with a malfunctioning of market society. In order to counterbalance this malfunctioning, he argued, the civil rights of prostitutes had to be curtailed.[4]

Parent-Duchâtelet's study of prostitution must be placed within a context of growing concern with all forms of urban crime during the July Monarchy. The 1830s and 1840s were a tumultuous period in the capital. Growing numbers of both migrant and permanent workers came to the capital during a period of economic instability. The Parisian economy was changing as certain industries, such as textiles, moved out of the city to reduce overhead while others altered their production practices, favoring mechanization or domestic labor.[5] This second tendency was particularly apparent in the luxury trades, long the mainstay of the capital's economy. These trades were furthermore buffeted by swings in the economic cycles caused by speculation in real estate, canals, and railroads during this period. Profiting from the rapid increases in fortunes during an "up" period to hire more workers, these trades suffered during lean periods such as 1837–39 and 1846–47. While both men and women were vulnerable to such cycles, women often also faced the added burden of supporting a child. Many working-class couples cohabited rather than marrying; if couples separated, women were more likely to be left with the children. Furthermore, women who were newly arrived in the capital had little support and no recourse in case of abandonment or rape.[6] In hard times, some women did turn to prostitution to make ends meet. While the precise number of prostitutes in Paris cannot be known due to the fact that many escaped police control, scholars have estimated that the number of prostitutes nearly quadrupled between 1820 and 1850.[7]

Parent-Duchâtelet, aware of such trends, associated prostitution with a failure in the labor market. In particular, he argued that prostitution came about because wages received for accepted forms of work could not match those received for selling one's body. "Let one compare," he wrote, "in particular the price of [women's] work with the price of their dishonor, and one will cease to be surprised in seeing such a great number fall into a disorder that can be called inevitable."[8] The ability of women to earn more through the deployment of their sexuality than through any other type of work was, he believed, the greatest cause of prostitution. This "inevitable" reality of the labor market could be exacerbated by either systemic weaknesses within the structure of the Parisian economy or by personal failings.

Parent-Duchâtelet reported that the number of trades named by prostitutes in police records were "frightening" in their quantity and variety. No matter what trade a woman may have exercised before becoming a prostitute, he implied, she was still vulnerable to the upheavals of economic cycles. The periodic closure of workshops and the frequent slow periods in various trades, he argued, both contributed to diminishing women's already low wages. In becoming aware of such economic insecurity, "one frequently asks oneself," he wrote, "if it is possible, with such resources, to procure even the bare minimum."[9]

In addition to economic insecurity caused by cycles of production, women workers faced male competition in what had formerly been predominantly female trades. The abolition of the guilds in 1791 had thus allowed for "male usurpation of a great number of jobs that it would be more fitting and honorable for our sex to leave within the domain of the other."[10] Washing dishes in cafés or selling cloth, Parent-Duchâtelet believed, left men effeminate and women without sufficient employment.[11] The government's commitment to the principles of laissez-faire, he implied, meant that the question of proper occupations for men and women was for the most part ignored.

Systemic problems arising from the deregulation of the labor market were thus the greatest cause of female poverty, and female poverty, he believed, was one of the greatest causes of prostitution. Once women became aware of the economic advantages of prostitution, he argued, they frequently turned to this means to support themselves and their families. Because of these economic realities, women without other resources, such as those of a parent or husband, were particularly vulnerable to prostitution, even if they would have preferred to have come by their incomes "honestly." Other women, Parent-Duchâtelet believed, made more of a coldhearted calculation regarding the value of their labor power versus the value of their sexuality. Surrounded by the temptations of consumer goods, and with a disinclination for work, such women chose prostitution for the considerably higher wages it offered. Thus "vanity and the desire to shine in sumptuous clothing is, along with laziness, one of the most active causes of prostitution."[12]

This second interpretation of the prostitute's motives was by far the more predominant argument before the publication of Parent-Duchâtelet's study. In the libertine literature of the late eighteenth and early nineteenth centuries, prostitution was most often explained by women's desire for material goods. The case of the grisette is a good example.[13] The name "grisette" first appeared in the seventeenth century and came from the gray, or *gris,* cloth worn by women of the popular classes. Despite changes in clothing styles, the name stuck as a means of identifying a young working woman. Mercier was the first to describe in detail the characteristics of the grisette in his *Tableau de Paris:* "One calls a grisette the young girl who, having neither birth nor property, is obliged to work for a living, and has no other means of support than the product of her manual labor . . . . All these girls of the people, accustomed from childhood to working regularly in order to survive, leave their poor parents at the age of eighteen, rent a room, and live according to their whims."[14] The independence and economic vulnerability of the grisette made her easy prey for young men of the upper classes, for whom an important rite of passage was an attempt to *faire,* or seduce, a grisette.

The dividing line between the grisette and the prostitute in early-nineteenth-century accounts was unclear. The two were considered to be similar because of their presumed sexual availability, but were not identical. Contemporaries believed that the grisette was a woman of "easy virtue," who was employed in a trade, yet still chose to supplement her income by forming relationships with men in commerce or with the *jeunesse dorée,* whose haunts were the Palais Royal, the commercial and entertainment center of Paris, and the boulevards. These men came into contact with the grisette as she went to and from work, or they spied her through the glass of a shop window. According to the author of an 1830 brochure, "the title of grisette is given to any girl or woman with dubious morals, but who nonetheless declares a trade and who has not openly paraded the flag of libertinage in drawing her capital and her revenue from the traffic in her charms."[15] Unlike the prostitute, the grisette did not depend upon prostitution for her survival; rather, she used her sexuality to improve her standard of living.

The grisette was most commonly identified with the luxury trades situated on the right bank. She was thus found in areas of the city also identified with prostitution, another cause for confusion, although writers usually identified the grisette with a trade. Louis Huart, in his *Physiologie de la grisette,* stated: "You have certainly strolled around eight in the evening in the rue Vivienne, the rue Saint Denis, the rue Richelieu, or in any other street, provided that one meets there a crowd of young milliners, flowermakers, seamstresses, fringers, embroiderers and book decorators!"[16] The grisette was both a producer of luxury goods and an object of consumption by young men, who paid for her favors with items of clothing, dinners, and tickets to the theater. Many authors implied that grisettes did not accept money for their favors, another factor that distinguished them from prostitutes. The grisette did have a "price," however, which rose with her place in the hierarchy of luxury trades and was determined by increasingly expensive tastes in clothing or food. Authors of works treating the grisette in the early nineteenth century tended to depict the hierarchies of levels of venal sex (which included grisettes as well as prostitutes) as a mirror image of the hierarchies of women's work in Paris.[17] The 1826 *Dictionnaire anecdotique des nymphes du Palais Royal et autres quartiers de Paris*, for example, which served as a guidebook to Parisian prostitution, created a geography of venal sex in which sexually available women were ranked by quality (of performance or beauty), neighborhood, and trade.[18] In these early texts, authors did not focus on the question of poverty as an explanation for the grisette's behavior; rather it was assumed that the grisette—carefree, irresponsible, and desirous of tasting all the pleasures the capital had to offer—was making an understandable choice to "capitalize" on her youth and beauty. These early texts contained no moral condemnation of the grisette.

The image of the carefree grisette would persist into the July Monarchy. The association of prostitution with the pursuit of consumer goods, however, would be problematized by writers during the July Monarchy such as Parent-Duchâtelet, who saw it as a sign of the growing materialism and self-interest of French society. Yet although Parent-Duchâtelet condemned such behavior, he still believed that a woman's sexuality was an important form of capital that could be used to supplement or replace other forms of income. In addition, Parent-Duchâtelet argued that women could borrow against this capital. In entering into a brothel, for example, the prostitute received clothing and food for which she was indebted to the mistress of the brothel. This "debt" could only be paid off by working for the house. Female prostitutes were likewise said to be "indebted" toward male or female lovers who offered companionship and protection.

Parent-Duchâtelet put great emphasis on the prostitute's indebtedness and her consequent lack of economic independence. The prostitute acquitted her debt to a lover, especially a male lover, in part by supporting him economically. Rather than retain control over her money, however, the prostitute transferred control to her lover. According to Parent-Duchâtelet, "[the lovers of prostitutes] watch them all the time; they know if they have earned thirty or forty *sous*, and oblige them to come that instant to a cabaret to spend it with them." If the prostitute is in a brothel, the madam makes sure that she is unable to amass any savings. Madams, he wrote, "know by experience that their authority over a girl ceases the instant that this girl finds herself in possession of some [sum of money]." They thus attempted to keep their charges in a state of constant indebtedness to prevent them from leaving. Unlike the grisette of the early nineteenth century, who chose her lovers and reaped the benefits of her sexuality, the prostitute as depicted by Parent-Duchâtelet actually lost her freedom of choice once she decided to sell herself. Thus despite his insistence that the liberty of prostitutes, who entered into no formal contractual agreement with either lover or madam, constituted their "unique wealth," he consistently emphasized the way in which their economic dependency led to a gradual diminishing of their freedom.[19] Moving from an imperfect labor market to a brothel did nothing therefore to relieve their economic vulnerability.

Parent-Duchâtelet's concern with establishing the economic dependency of the prostitute reveals his deep sense of anxiety regarding the free circulation of female "capital." He feared the ability of the unregulated, unsupervised prostitute, the *insoumise*, to circulate freely through society, sapping bourgeois men of their wealth and granting them in exchange only a lasting dose of venereal disease. Indeed, Parent-Duchâtelet was not the only one to link unregulated economic exchange with prostitution. In a memoir submitted to the minister of the interior in 1841, Aimée Lucas called the attention of the administration to "certain boutiques that disguise the commerce that they carry out [prostitution] with a display of gloves, suspenders, and shelves of perfume."[20] Lucas warned that, in such shops, young girls hired to watch over the counter (girls who would have been considered grisettes) would soon find themselves embarked on careers as prostitutes, and he recommended that parents take great caution when placing their daughters in retail.

Despite Lucas's complaint that the administration was ignoring this problem, recommendations of the Special Commission for the Repression of Prostitution, established by the police in 1829, had resulted in a law forbidding prostitution in boutiques. In an 1840 meeting, the commission once again denounced shops where "the display that is presented announces a boutique that can in no way be distinguished from those of the same type whose commerce is real." The commission feared the effects of entering into such an establishment, especially for young girls. Whereas a man could shrug it off, even if he had been offended, "for a young girl the ordeal could be fatal and the damage irreparable."[21] Such concerns reflected a belief that women were especially vulnerable to the impact of the marketplace, perhaps because they were believed to be less able (or willing) to distinguish between different sorts of market interactions, for example, shopping versus prostitution.[22] That these concerns were expressed even after the 1829 law reflects a perception that controlling women's relationship to the market was extremely difficult.

The sometimes blurry line between commerce and prostitution that concerned Lucas and others also contributed to a law, passed in April 1830, that forbad prostitutes entry to the Palais Royal.[23] This area was well known as a site of prostitution, and the combination of sexual and other attractions found there made it a favored spot with both French and foreign libertines. Just before the 1830 revolution that established the July Monarchy, prefect of police Jean-Henri-Claude Mangin ruled that prostitutes would no longer be allowed entry to the Palais Royal. A spate of pamphlets protesting this measure quickly appeared on the shelves of the bookstalls of the Palais Royal.[24] Humorous in tone, these pamphlets were similar to the libertine literature regarding prostitution of the early nineteenth century, much of which was also sold in the same shops. The authors of these pamphlets posed as prostitutes or procurers, but their tone, as well as their underlying political message, leads to the conclusion that they were written not so much to defend the cause of the prostitutes as to support or criticize the government. The pamphlets also served to warn visitors that they would henceforth be required to address themselves to the neighboring brothels if they wished to hire a prostitute.

The climate of political unrest in which the pamphlets appeared caused them to raise, as one author put it, some "interesting questions concerning individual liberty."[25] By linking prostitution and popular commerce to make their political critique, the pamphlets addressed the issue of individual liberty within the context of a debate concerning the morality of economic exchanges. The pamphlets thus linked individual freedoms promised in the charter of 1814, freedom of commerce, and unregulated prostitution. Some of the pamphlets attempted to ridicule liberals by associating their support of political and economic freedom with a support of prostitution. One author declared, for example, "[t]he charter, this friend of the liberals, is just as valid for *filles* as it is for the gentlemen of the police; it in no way forbids these young ladies from loafing about on the streets."[26] Another pamphlet asked: "Cannot individual liberty, which exists for all French nationals, be invoked by a woman, when she bargains in exchange for money that which others bargain in exchange for cashmere shawls?"[27]

Such comments played upon the distinction in libertine literature between the prostitute and the grisette. Although meant in part as a political critique, the pamphlets also used this distinction to debate which economic practices were moral and which were not. The pamphlets thus raised the difficult issue of how one could determine which interactions with the market (in this case, a market in female sexuality) could be considered harmless and which endangered the public good. By associating the control of prostitutes with institutions considered by the French to be barbaric, such as the harem, some authors used the occasion of this conflict to criticize the government for its repressive nature, while at the same time making a bid for laissez-faire ideals. These authors argued that prostitutes, like any other French citizen, had the right to be free. They demanded that women be allowed to preserve the right to come and go as they pleased in public, rather than being "sequestered."[28] The pamphlets also explicitly linked the exclusion of women from public places and public view with financial hardship: "To forbid us from appearing in public is tantamount to wanting our ruin," one pamphlet proclaimed, "You are not unaware of the proverb that says that *one doesn't wish to buy a pig in a poke.*"[29] In accordance with laissez-faire beliefs, such statements implied that government intervention would prevent the optimal functioning of the economy.

Yet even some who "supported" the cause of the prostitutes seemed to do so only as a means to avoid a lesser evil. One author argued that regulating prostitution would deprive countless pimps of their source of revenue, driving them to a life of crime. Another implied that prostitutes would henceforth be forced to disguise their true profession. This pamphleteer, posing as a procurer, boasted, "I was the one who first gave Caroline *Belles Dents* . . . the idea to do herself up with a decent outfit and a hatbox in hand. It was Achille who convinced Elisa *Joli-Pied* to dress as a seamstress."[30] It was better, his pamphlet implied, to give prostitutes the freedom to exercise their trade in public, where they could be supervised, than to force them to carry it out in secret.

Here again, references to common types of grisettes—the seamstress or the milliner's delivery girl—played with the distinction between them and the prostitute to raise the question of how one could determine the meaning of various types of economic exchanges. These last examples, however, which occupied a place in between that of those who accepted laissez-faire ideals and those who rejected them outright, revealed the greatest anxiety regarding the functioning of the market. Might a man who expected to give only a shawl in exchange for sex be forced to hand over money? What was the difference between the two, and was one worse than the other? Pamphlets such as that quoted above did not necessarily answer such questions, but did imply that the problem lay in not knowing what one was getting into. Such pamphlets suggested that a balance of supervision and liberty could best limit the uncertainties of economic exchange.

The debate over individual liberty versus the role of the state in regulating prostitution was thus central to the political critique contained in these pamphlets. This issue plagued Parent-Duchâtelet as well, for he was well aware that the system of registration and medical examination used by the Paris police to supervise prostitution and check the spread of venereal disease did not have a firm legal basis.[31] In fact, in the absence of legislation outlawing or otherwise criminalizing prostitution, police regulations designed to limit prostitutes' access to public and commercial spaces appeared to infringe upon their legal rights. The ambiguous legal status of the prostitute provided an opportunity for the authors of these pamphlets to comment on the correct balance between individual liberty and government control. By highlighting the economic transaction involved in prostitution, authors linked the question of freedom to that of economic exchange in general, conflating economic, political, and personal liberty.

Parent-Duchâtelet justified the ambiguity of the prostitute's legal status by arguing that prostitutes, by their conduct, placed themselves outside of society. The prostitute belongs, he wrote, to "a class that separates itself from society, that renounces [society], that, by its scandalous customs, which are constantly and boldly public, declares its abandonment of this society and the common laws that govern it."[32] Yet although Parent-Duchâtelet's study opens by declaring the prostitute's separation from society, much of his work leads to the conclusion that prostitutes share many of the same emotions, goals, and beliefs as other women. Indeed, even upon close physical examination, nothing distinguishes the woman who prostitutes herself from her "honest" counterpart.

Much more than this supposed "otherness," it was, for Parent-Duchâtelet, the prostitute's constant state of economic dependency that both prepared her for and justified her subordinate legal status. The economic dependency of prostitutes, he argued, encouraged a constant and never satisfied desire to improve their economic status and to acquire material goods. Although some women might have begun prostituting themselves to support others, the ability to satisfy their appetites and desires that prostitution offered quickly seduced them.

Many believed that this appeal to self-interest was inherent in prostitution, and they considered it one of its most dangerous aspects. Former police commissioner F. F. A. Beraud warned of the power of self-interest in his 1839 work on prostitution in the story of Elise. Elise, a beautiful young girl, made the acquaintance of a certain Dame B., who entered into the good graces of Elise's family by bringing the girl work that was easy to execute but received a high price. Once she had gained the trust of the girl, the Dame B. made Elise aware of "the benefits that [she] could gain" through prostitution.[33] While the Dame B. appealed to Elise's desire to help her mother with her earnings, the girl in fact soon abandoned her family and went to live with the older woman, where she was employed as a prostitute. Parent-Duchâtelet also argued that madams attracted employees by appealing to their self-interest, their desires, and their appetites. To allow prostitution to remain unregulated, Parent-Duchâtelet implied, was to allow women the (ultimately unrealizable, in his opinion) hope of an avenue for an increased standard of living and for economic independence that they could rarely find in other areas of the economy.

While when looked at in this light prostitution could appear to be a powerful metaphor for the benefits of the free market, Parent-Duchâtelet made sure that his readers did not arrive at this interpretation. By strengthening the association between prostitution and the popular classes, and by placing the interests of the prostitute in opposition to those of the male bourgeois client, Parent-Duchâtelet avoided the implication that prostitution was a prime example of a mutually beneficial and self-regulating economic transaction. Although Parent-Duchâtelet's work repeatedly implied that women possessed a powerful form of capital in their sexuality, he ultimately argued that the deployment of this capital was either dangerous to society or without economic benefit to the woman involved, who remained economically dependent. Prostitution, Parent-Duchâtelet implied, was an example of a market with adequate supply and demand, but one in which the pursuit of self-interest by those involved did not lead to the greater good of the whole.

To allow prostitutes the freedom to capitalize on their sexuality, Parent-Duchâtelet maintained, would be to commit a great crime against society, since liberty could so easily slide into licentiousness. "[I]f individual liberty is one of the greatest goods one can enjoy," he wrote, "it is also one that is the easiest to abuse."[34] Left to their own devices, prostitutes would allow their self-interest to guide their actions. For this reason, Parent-Duchâtelet argued, "individual liberty is something to which prostitutes cannot aspire."[35] Indeed, in his study it is only once prostitutes have been deprived of the ability to sell themselves on the open market that their virtue reappears. In prison, altruism and shame replace self-interest and selfishness. While prostitution might be inevitable, Parent-Duchâtelet argues that by controlling it, one could temper its negative effects on society and even recapture some of the virtue of "fallen" women.

While the comparison between prostitution and the free market remains implicit in the work of Parent-Duchâtelet, later authors would make this connection much more explicit. Nonetheless, in his concern with the possible nefarious effects of self-interest, Parent-Duchâtelet provides a criticism of free-market ideals as propounded by liberal political economists. While Parent-Duchâtelet does not altogether reject the system of exchange that is prostitution, he does argue that this system would retain its usefulness, and even perhaps a measure of virtue, only if strictly controlled. Although immoral, prostitution in itself was not dangerous; the danger lay rather in the lack of regulation, the free market in female sexuality represented by the *insoumise*, the prostitute who operated outside the regulatory system. Parent-Duchâtelet's work had such an impact on contemporaries because he demonstrated how the regulation of prostitution could provide a model for the redefinition of the marketplace, one in which individual interests were controlled, or even denied, in the name of the public good. Furthermore, the denial of the prostitute's civil rights on the basis of her unsuccessful interaction with the marketplace provided a precedent for denying other groups in society complete and free access to the market on the same grounds.

Parent-Duchâtelet was not alone in his concern with the relationship between sexuality, economic exchange, and virtue. Both Saint-Simonian feminists and middle-class male journalists explored these linkages and their implications regarding questions of political and professional freedom. Yet whereas Parent-Duchâtelet had accepted prostitution, and the market relations it implied, as an inevitable if unpleasant aspect of human society, these others tried to resist the pull of market ideology. Both Saint-Simonian feminists and middle-class male journalists during the July Monarchy argued for the possibility of escaping market relations altogether. They did this through a redefinition of the figure of the prostitute.

Sexuality and Freedom in *La Femme Libre*

In 1832, a group of young women founded a newspaper that they called *La Femme libre*. This paper was their response to the decision made the previous November by the leader of the utopian socialist Saint-Simonian movement, Prosper Enfantin, to exclude women from positions of leadership until the arrival of a mythic female leader, whom he referred to as "the woman." During the 1820s and 1830s, the Saint-Simonian movement, which appealed to both men and women, both workers and the middle class, with its message of economic prosperity and social harmony, had offered a vision of a society freed from self-interest, in which men and women acted as equals out of love.

The contributors to *La Femme libre* kept this message alive, paying special attention to the conditions under which women would become free.[36] The paper's writers argued that women were especially vulnerable to the influence of market forces, which perverted their natural desire for love and companionship into prostitution. Criticism regarding the emphasis on sexuality in the paper led to ridicule and condemnation of the paper's name because of its sexual connotations. As a result, the paper went through a series of name changes, finally settling on the *Tribune des femmes*.[37] Despite the change in name, and the growing emphasis on maternity in the paper, its contributors continued to insist that women could escape the realm of market relations by gaining their economic independence.

The presence of women workers was very strong among contributors to *La Femme libre*. Two seamstresses, Désirée Veret and Reine Guidorf, founded the paper. Late in 1832, Suzanne Volquin, an embroiderer, took over as primary director of the journal.[38] However, despite the presence of so many women workers on its staff, the paper did not give much attention to the particulars of women's work. This can be explained in part by the fact that in the early 1830s, work had not yet taken on the importance it would have by the late 1840s as a constitutive component of social and political identity. In addition, many workers associated with the Saint-Simonian movement rejected work as central to their identities.[39] The authors were concerned with issues of women's economic dependency; however, discussions of this issue tended to be placed within the context of women's physical, sexual, and emotional vulnerability vis-à-vis men rather than within a class-based analysis. *La Femme libre* was therefore more concerned with issues of personal freedom, especially the freedom to love whomever one chose, rather than with those concerning women's work opportunities.

Representations of women in *La Femme libre* were shaped by the predominance of two very powerful images of women circulating in early July Monarchy culture. One image was that of the loving partner and tender mother made popular by the works of Jean-Jacques Rousseau in the late eighteenth century; the other was that of the working woman as prostitute. Both images highlighted for the contributors to *La Femme libre* the importance of sexuality in determining a woman's role in society.

Rousseau's exhortations regarding the necessity of mothers nursing and caring for their children had a significant influence on child-rearing practices in the late eighteenth and nineteenth centuries.[40] The image of the tender mother became a mainstay of nineteenth-century culture, when motherhood was promoted as the noblest calling possible for women. Yet as Mary Sheriff has noted, eighteenth-century artists such as Fragonard depicted motherhood as highly erotic.[41] Rousseau himself placed great emphasis on the erotic power of wives and mothers. In *Emile,* a manual for child raising, women's sexuality was portrayed as a powerful moralizing force. Female sexuality could be used, Rousseau argued, to incite men to a higher standard of self-control. Through her "many levers which may set the human heart in motion," and her "reign of gentleness, tact, and kindness," a woman could "manage" her lover by first inspiring desire, and then forcing him to respect her virtue. By thus learning to control his first passion—love for a woman—a man became "master of all the rest and [would] obey nothing but the passion for virtue."[42] Submitting to a woman's "gentle" mastery was thus portrayed in *Emile* as the crucial first step that later allowed a man to enter into the social contract that made him a citizen. The "sexual interdependence" of men and women thus laid a basis for social foundations and served as a brake to "narcissistic individualism."[43] Rousseau believed that while women experienced desire, they were also better able to subsume that desire to duty; they thus had a lesson to teach men about self-control.

Rousseau's view that female sexuality could serve to limit self-interest and thereby prepare individuals for life in society was further developed by the social reformer Charles Fourier and adopted by the Saint-Simonian movement. In his writings, Fourier laid great emphasis on passions of all sorts as the basis for cooperation among people. In developing his idea of the phalanstery, a cooperative of workers, artists, and capitalists, Fourier argued that in order for each individual to contribute his or her best, he or she must find the work attractive and a source of joy. "Happiness," he argued, "consists in having many passions and many means of satisfying them."[44] Likewise, the Saint-Simonians also saw the passions as a positive force. Henri de Saint-Simon, the originator of this movement, had been opposed to laissez-faire ideas. Although he supported industrialization, he believed that economic progress required strong leadership from the state and easy access to credit, so as to increase property ownership. His followers continued to support these ideas, but added to them a focus on sexual love as an important moralizing force. Following the footsteps of Rousseau, Saint-Simonian theorists emphasized the nurturing and loving characteristics of female nature, which they placed in opposition to selfish individualism, implied to be the province of men.[45] Saint-Simonians believed that fostering "feminine" qualities—in both men and women—would limit the impact of self-interest on society.

Following in this tradition, contributors to *La Femme libre* likewise made the moral force inherent in female sexuality a cornerstone of their arguments regarding women's role in society. In the first issue, for example, writers recommended that women use their sexuality as a source of moral persuasion: "use the irresistible charm of your beauty, the softness of your captivating voice for the benefit of society, [to] . . . make men march toward a single goal." Writers emphasized the value of the feminine, stating that contributors to the paper wished to remain "that being formed of grace, love and voluptuousness, that being born to charm and to please, . . . soft, suggestive and persuasive."[46]

Rousseau had linked the moralizing power of female sexuality to women's dependence on men. In his novel *Julie, or la Nouvelle Heloïse,* Julie reached her most sublime state only after entering into marriage with the paternal Wolmar. Likewise in *Emile,* Sophie, Emile's lover, was taught to bend to the wishes and needs of others, and easily gave herself to Emile. Yet at the same time, both Julie and Sophie entered into marriage of their own free will. This point was crucial, for it underlay Rousseau's entire theory regarding the formation of the social contract and the nature of political authority. For a government to be loved, for it to avoid the trap of despotism, those who placed themselves under its authority must do so freely and in full conscience of what that action entailed. Rousseau thus situated female sexuality at the center of contrasting forces of freedom and obedience. This tension between liberty and control, a tension that remained a fundamental characteristic of modern French political and economic theory, was thus from the outset associated with female sexuality.

Contributors to *La Femme libre* seized upon this aspect of Rousseau's theory to argue for greater autonomy for women. However, whereas Rousseau had portrayed liberty and dependence as inextricably linked, writers for the newspaper distinguished between the two by identifying the first as positive and the second as negative. Contributors made this distinction by associating female sexuality with economic exchange. Writers thus elaborated on the distinction between "giving" and "selling" oneself in love, arguing that only if women were allowed to "give" themselves freely would the moralizing force of female sexuality have a beneficial effect on society.[47] "Selling" one's love, on the other hand, was an indication of economic dependency on men; only wealthy women forced into loveless marriages or working girls who turned to prostitution to survive "sold" themselves. Sexual freedom thus became a metaphor for freedom in general. In a society in which women possessed true liberty, one writer promised, a young girl would be able to seek out and find "a heart that better responds to your heart's desires, a soul that better understands your soul, a wit that better grasps your wit, an organization that better harmonizes with your organization."[48] As this quote indicates, contributors to *La Femme libre* understood freedom within the context of relationships with others, rather than as a component of unfettered individualism. Writers thus presented the attainment of emotional, intellectual, and sexual fulfillment as an indicator of a society in which bonds between individuals were based on sympathy, rather than economic considerations.

Money and prejudice were, for the contributors to *La Femme libre*, the most significant obstacles to the fulfillment of their objectives. Early issues claimed that all women desired a relationship based on true love, but that rules regarding "proper" conduct for women condemned those who followed their hearts. Women of the popular classes were criticized by society for entering into premarital sexual relationships, while middle-class married women who sought love elsewhere were branded as adulterers. Focusing on the common prejudices surrounding the issue of female sexuality faced by women of both classes, writers for *La Femme libre* called for an end to all social hypocrisy and for a recognition that all women shared similar desires.

To lend weight to their arguments, contributors drew upon the stereotype of the prostitute as depicted in libertine literature from the early nineteenth century. Writers for *La Femme libre* repeatedly used this image of the prostitute, placing it within the context of their argument concerning the moralizing effects of female sexuality and extending the metaphor of prostitution to include middle-class marriage as well. Authors thus combined these two images of women (the loving partner and the prostitute), linking them to a critique of materialism, to argue for women's independence.

Writers for *La Femme libre* used the trope of prostitution to emphasize the commonality of women's condition. The newspaper depicted upper-class girls "sold" into loveless marriages in order to improve a family's wealth or status alongside images of girls from the popular classes who turned to prostitution in order to survive. Street prostitution and middle-class marriage were thus portrayed as two sides of the same coin, since in both cases economics replaced affection. They were, as one writer wrote, "those two camps, so opposed, of which one is as exclusive in its regularity as the other is in its disorder."[49] In their discussions of both types of "prostitution," authors revealed their unease with the growing importance of money as an indicator of social status and power. While they did not reject the market economy altogether, they argued that there were certain areas—in particular intimate relationships—in which its influence was nefarious.

Several of the contributors to *La Femme libre* knew from firsthand experience the dangers that faced a woman who entered into sexual relationships unsanctioned by society. Yet their concerns regarding the moral and economic obstacles to an independent sexual and affective life can also be placed within a larger cultural context. Like some of the authors of the Palais Royal pamphlets, contributors to *La Femme libre* expressed a sense of unease concerning the effects of market ideology by evoking fears regarding the ambiguous and uncertain nature of exchanges between individuals. Between lovers, for example, each party might attach a different meaning to exchanges of words of love or physical intimacy. Women were thus repeatedly warned against such lovers' exchanges, in which "men came to them, spoke to them of love, of happiness, they believed their words, they sold themselves thinking they were giving themselves, society rejected them . . . they were ruined!"[50] This statement offered a new perspective on the motives of the grisette as depicted in libertine literature, raising the possibility that she entered into a sexual liaison out of love rather than the desire to improve her standard of living. At the same time, by showing the folly of acting out of love it demonstrated the dangers women faced once market forces had invaded intimate relationships, transforming exchanges based on love and affection into calculations of self-interest. In such a world, women could survive only by renouncing love and embracing self-interest.

Like others who raised similar fears concerning the impact of the market on both social and intimate relationships, the contributors to *La Femme libre* wondered whether individualism and materialism were weakening communal bonds. As with the other groups discussed in this study, they linked gender and economics to promote a liberty geared toward the public good. Contributors to this paper thus argued that a truly virtuous society would be one in which a more equitable distribution of wealth would assure individual liberty for all.

To this end, writers for *La Femme libre* argued that women's economic dependency on men made them especially vulnerable to the sorts of misunderstandings described above. Low salaries were presented as a masculine invention designed to keep women economically dependent: "it is essential that our earnings be very modest, . . . this is one of the causes of our dependence on men, since we are obliged to resort to them for our material needs."[51] Writers argued that all claims to moral superiority were useless without an independent source of income. As one contributor warned Enfantin's anticipated Woman-Messiah, "before obtaining a throne, you need *bread of your own [un pain indépendant]*."[52]

Higher wages, the revision of articles in the Civil Code that rendered women legal minors, and associations for women were all presented by *La Femme libre* as changes that could improve women's economic situation. The paper did not provide much detail on these projects, presenting questions of economics as subordinate to the more pressing issue of emotional and sexual freedom. Economic independence was depicted as necessary only insofar as it would allow women to act as free and equal partners in social relationships based on trust, where, "He who tells you: 'I love you' will have no interest in betraying you."[53]

Special attention was paid, in this regard, to the girl of the people, whom writers seemed to believe revealed the link between moral hypocrisy and economic vulnerability in its starkest form. Writers tended to intertwine these two issues into a single vision of problems to be remedied by the establishment of a social order based on liberty. Addressing a girl of the people, one author promised that in this new social order "you will no longer be betrayed by your lovers, you will no longer be sold into debauchery . . . you will no longer be seen in the evening passing like a shadow along impure walls . . . . There will be delirious joys for you, love for you, real friends for you, and not brutal, jealous and despotic masters; . . . you will have no more regrets . . . you will no longer hold out your hand, because you will be paid according to your labor."[54] Low wages made such a girl vulnerable to men, who were presented in the pages of *La Femme libre* as untrustworthy, physically aggressive, and driven by self-interest.

While economic dependency isolated women, leaving them vulnerable to prostitution and encouraging them to embrace self-interest in order to survive, association could help women resist the more dangerous aspects of the market economy. The principle of association—cooperation among workers to protect or improve wages and working conditions—was a mainstay of nineteenth-century socialist thought. The emphasis on association in *La Femme libre*, as in socialist thought more generally, was consistent with the contributors' understanding of liberty as existing within a network of relationships with others. In particular, writers believed that association would allow women to protect themselves from men. In a letter elaborating a project of association, the authors justified their plans by evoking an image of female isolation and vulnerability: "A young girl, virtuous, living a Christian life, although accepting our ideas of liberty and emancipation, was recently the victim of a man. She was an orphan, and living from her own labor, hidden in a miserable hovel. A man lived below her, a strong man. She was pretty, and inspired desire in him. One day he climbed up to her room on an ordinary pretext, and there he abused his strength."[55] Arguing that the young girl's isolation made her vulnerable to both poverty and rape, the authors proposed association as a remedy for the twofold "brutality of man."[56]

Although association was presented as particularly important for poor girls, the idea was applied to all women, regardless of their class, since writers believed that although the particulars of a woman's experience might differ according to her class position, all women were physically, emotionally, and economically vulnerable vis-à-vis men. In addition, writers argued that women already belonged to an association of sorts in their common capacity to give birth: "the banner of women is universal, because . . . are they not all united by a single bond, MOTHERHOOD."[57] The mother was an important figure to Saint-Simonians, who conceptualized their movement as a family led by a mother and father (representatives of an androgynous God).[58] Motherhood was not incompatible with female sexuality for the Saint-Simonians, yet the two were becoming increasingly separated in French culture by the 1830s. Perhaps for this reason, as the paper toned down its emphasis on female sexual freedom in response to criticism, it placed an increasing emphasis on motherhood. Nonetheless, both motherhood and female sexuality were invoked to argue that association had roots in female biology and psychology. Authors thus urged readers to put aside their class biases and see in the woman of the other class a being like oneself. In the pages of *La Femme libre*, women were presented as possessing the potential to live in a world in which class divisions were no longer relevant. In this they could provide a model for "the people" (who were always depicted as masculine)—and indeed for society as a whole—of a community in which social bonds were based on love and sympathy because everyone's economic needs were provided for.

The class analysis employed by contributors to *La Femme libre* has been seen as "limited" since they did not identify themselves in opposition to employers and did not pay a great deal of attention to issues of working conditions, wages, and ownership of the means of production.[59] Yet as these examples illustrate, these writers were extremely sensitive to the relationship between money and power, and argued that economic independence was crucial if women were to be free. In emphasizing the commonality of all women, *La Femme libre* highlighted structural inequalities within July Monarchy society that kept women economically dependent upon men. Although not at the forefront of its analysis, the paper did make a connection between work (as a source of economic independence) and rights. In one issue, for example, a contributor asked why a merchant's wife, who shared her husband's work, did not also share his rights.[60] Yet for most contributors, economic independence was seen not as an end in itself but as a necessary factor, enabling women to love freely and, therefore, to use their moralizing influence on men. In this sense, writers for *La Femme libre* shared the critique of materialism that was evident in middle-class writings by men produced during the July Monarchy. Casting aside the trappings of power as "vanity," the contributors to *La Femme libre* celebrated instead the woman who was able to love freely.[61] A hero-ine and pioneer, this woman was portrayed as a "sublime creature," able to act according to her innate sense of liberty.[62] The *femme libre* was thus held up as a model for women and recognized as someone who "smoothed the road to our emancipation."[63] Defining female sexuality as a moraliz-ing force and basing their analysis on an opposition between women who "gave" themselves and those who were forced to "sell" themselves, con-tributors to *La Femme libre* used images of women, of working women in particular, to elaborate a vision of a society in which social bonds were based on choices made freely and cemented through love.

By distinguishing between self-interest and survival, contributors to *La Femme libre* separated female sexuality and prostitution, and used this separation as a basis from which to argue for a liberty free from self-interest. Critics ignored the distinction between the working woman who became sexually active out of love and the prostitute who did the same out of a desire for money (or consumer goods) that the authors of *La Femme libre* strove to elaborate. Instead, critics assimilated the image of the *femme libre* to that of the prostitute and used this image to ridicule women who argued for greater freedom and opportunity for themselves and others. However, while they may have rejected the argument for women's economic emancipation presented in *La Femme libre,* many crit-ics adopted the idea that women were associated with a realm free from market relations. While *La Femme libre* had made this argument to de-mand greater independence for women, these others used it to argue for women's economic, social, and political dependence.

With its emphasis on female love as a realm that needed to remain free from market forces, it is likely that *La Femme libre* influenced many who thought about how to create a virtuous marketplace. While it is impossi-ble to know whether the ideas expounded in *La Femme libre* may have influenced Parent-Duchâtelet in particular, there are certainly some sim-ilarities. Contributors to the paper associated prostitution with a lack of freedom and with the excess individualism of the free market, much like Parent-Duchâtelet would also do in his study. Its writers also enlarged the meaning of prostitution, arguing that all women who did not possess economic freedom were essentially prostitutes. While Parent-Duchâtelet stopped short of identifying all sexual relationships as potential forms of prostitution, he did imply that all working women were at least potential prostitutes because of their vulnerability to market forces. However, al-though *La Femme libre* held out the possibility of escaping the influence of the market through the paradoxical ability to earn a living wage, Par-ent-Duchâtelet implied that the market could at best be controlled—it could never be eliminated. Middle-class male journalists who transformed the image of the grisette drew upon both of these traditions. Whereas their depiction of the grisette seemed to imply the possibility of a realm free from market relations, it also posited the possibility that men and women understood and experienced the marketplace in different ways.

The Transformation of the Grisette

In his *Physiologie de la fille sans nom,* Charles Marchal explained that one of the most frequent reasons that women became prostitutes was to escape economic hardship and misery. Writers and artists, he argued, were subject to the same temptations, since the misery faced by the prostitute was "this misery that we have all felt to one degree or another, we young artists . . . the misery that we have fought, either with our pen, or with our brushes."[64] Authors of popular literature dedicated to Paris and the Parisians frequently evoked the similarities between the writer and the prostitute. They used the image of the prostitute, as well as that of the grisette, to explore their relationship to the marketplace during a period when both newspapers and book publishing were becoming increasingly commercialized.

The grisette was one of the most frequent characters in the literature on Paris and the Parisians. Each collection of essays published during this period had an obligatory chapter on the grisette; she also appeared in chapters as diverse as those concerning the student, the rue Saint-Denis, the Jardin du Luxembourg, the boulevard du Temple, and the Bal Mabille. The grisette was furthermore the topic of numerous smaller works such as *Physiologie de la grisette, Paris-grisette, Amours et intrigues de grisettes,* and *L'Invasion des grisettes.* Whole series of novels were written concerning the grisette, most notably those of Paul de Kock, and the grisette appeared in the work of almost every major author of the mid-nineteenth century, including Balzac, Sand, Sue, Flaubert, and Hugo. The time and energy spent on the grisette in these texts reveal a significant investment in her image.

Scholars who have discussed the cultural significance of the proliferation of the grisette's image in the mid-nineteenth century have assumed that this image was meant as a literal representation of the young working girls who served as sexual initiators for young men. They have thus interpreted the enormous attention to grisettes in works dedicated to describing Parisian life and mores, as well as the concern with the grisette's disappearance (a topic discussed in chapter 4) as a sign of an increase in "sexual misery," as the growing numbers of young, single men entering the capital outpaced the number of women who could serve as sexual partners outside of marriage.[65] However, while contemporaries certainly might have referred to a young working woman of their acquaintance as a grisette, the image of the grisette as developed in these texts must also be understood on a metaphorical level. Although sexual nostalgia or frustration may have colored representations of the grisette, the story of the grisette also offered a powerful model for discussing the impact of materialism and commercialization on French society. The sometimes blurry distinction between the grisette and the prostitute, a distinction that Parent-Duchâtelet lessened and the Saint-Simonian feminists strengthened, was often used to discuss the question of how to distinguish between moral and immoral economic transactions. Writers and journalists during the July Monarchy were obsessed with this question on both a professional and political level, as they sought to defend themselves from charges of venality while at the same time attacking the government for its focus on material wealth. The ability of the grisette to serve as a vehicle for exploring the issue of a virtuous approach to the marketplace, more than any interest in actual working girls who may have been called grisettes, explains her enormous popularity in popular literature during the July Monarchy and beyond.

During the July Monarchy, market forces made themselves felt in the literary world in an unprecedented manner. Technological advances and the growth of literacy spurred the development of new forms of literary and journalistic production.[66] In 1836, Emile de Girardin launched *La Presse,* a newspaper that sought to acquire a large readership through the dual strategies of halving the subscription price and broadening the subject matter of the newspaper to include gossip, theater and literary reviews, and fiction, in the form of the *roman-feuilleton,* or serial novel. Others quickly imitated Girardin's innovation. At the same time, the expanding market for popular literature devoted to descriptions of everyday life in the capital—the *tableaux de Paris* and the *physiologies*—encouraged the creation of new publishing houses and offered increased opportunities for writers who moved easily between political journalism and more popular and commercial genres during this period.[67] The 1835 September Laws, passed in response to continued unrest in the capital following the 1830 revolution, imposed strict censorship on newspapers. These laws further stimulated the growth of popular literature at the expense of "serious" journalism, as virtually all of the almost three hundred fifty newspapers published in Paris in 1835 either renounced their identity as "oppositional" or disappeared after the passage of these laws.[68] Due to the growth of popular literature, it became possible during the

July Monarchy for writers to win fame and fortune by their pen alone, and countless young men left their provinces and their studies to try their hand at writing.[69]

Most aspiring writers, however, faced enormous hardship. Competition among writers depressed wages. Book publishers, faced with competition from newspapers and high marketing costs, refused to pay high prices for works already published in serial form.[70] The decline of patronage also contributed to making writing a difficult career path, and forms of patronage that were still available, such as government pensions, were increasingly seen as a kind of charity rather than a sign of political favor and social prestige. Writers were thus reluctant to ask for, or accept, government pensions, preferring instead, like painters during this same period, to emphasize their independence from outside influences, even if that meant eking out a meager and uncertain living.[71] At the same time as writers were becoming, by choice as well as by necessity, less dependent on the state, they were becoming more dependent on market forces.[72] Thus while a select few found great wealth as writers, most struggled to get by. Even authors such as Honoré de Balzac or George Sand complained of the uncertainty and irregularity of their financial situations.[73] For more obscure writers, the situation was often much worse.

The effect of market forces also altered the public's perception of writers and journalists during this period. To offset increases in production costs, newspaper publishers increasingly generated revenues through the use of commercial advertisements.[74] The introduction of advertising, and especially the practice of accepting advertising for books and plays, led many critics to complain that journalists had lost their freedom of opinion and that the highest bidder would henceforth dictate their reviews. The *réclame*, which combined elements of both an advertisement and a book review, came under particular attack.[75] According to Saint-Beuve, "It was of no use wanting to separate that which remained conscientious and free from that which became public and venal in the newspaper; the line was soon crossed. The *réclame* served as a bridge. . . . In order to cash in on the advertisement, one was obliging toward new books; criticism thereby lost its credit."[76]

Honoré de Balzac, in his novel set in the world of journalism, *Illusions perdues,* put it in even harsher terms: "Outside the literary world . . . there's no one who knows the horrible odyssey by which one arrives at what must be called . . . the vogue, the fashion, repute . . . . This much desired repute is almost always an accomplished prostitute. Yes, in lowly works of literature, she represents the poor girl freezing on the street, in secondary literature, she's the kept woman who escapes the bad areas of journalism, in successful literature, she's the brilliant and insolent courtesan, who has furniture, pays taxes, receives great lords, and makes her avaricious creditors wait."[77] In this quote Balzac likened the career path of the journalist to that of the prostitute, each of whom was forced to sell him or herself at every turn in order not only to succeed but to survive. The growing commercialization of journalism and publishing, as well as the precarious economic situation in which many writers found themselves, made authors extremely aware of and interested in the play of market forces on their lives and their profession.[78]

The frequency with which journalists were compared to prostitutes prompted writers to defend their honor as disinterested interpreters of public opinion. One way in which they did this was through asserting their masculinity through a discourse concerning masculine honor, a discourse that often manifested itself in fighting duels to preserve journalistic honor.[79] By fighting duels, writers and journalists could assert that they were not looking for material gain in publishing their work since they were willing to defend this work with their lives. Within popular literature, however, writers also defended their honor by associating themselves with women of the popular classes, in particular with the grisette.

Like the Saint-Simonian feminists, male writers and journalists emphasized the distinctions between the grisette and the prostitute, and then drew upon the image of the grisette to craft a narrative for their own career path. Writers used the distinction between "giving" and "selling" one's sexuality to argue that it was possible to be in the market and remain virtuous. The image of the nonvenal, yet still sexual, grisette that they developed was meant to provide a countermodel to the story of the prostitute. Writers praised the transformed grisette for her selflessness, idealism, dedication to hard work, and moral fortitude; they then transferred these qualities to themselves, thereby distancing themselves from the prostitute and associating themselves with her now more virtuous counterpart. In their descriptions of the grisette, writers sought to prove that someone who was poor and faced with constant temptation to sell herself or himself (since this situation mirrored that of many journalists) could remain virtuous. Writers also used the image of the grisette to criticize the government. In the face of the censorship imposed by the September Laws, which forbad attacks on actual public figures, the "representative or symbolic type, which stood for a recognizable category of protagonists," became a favored vehicle for political and social critique.[80] Descriptions of the grisette thus served to transmit journalists' professional and political aspirations.

The grisette of the early nineteenth century was typically portrayed in popular and libertine literature as a young and attractive working girl, associated with the luxury and fashion trades located on the right bank of the Seine. The early grisette was depicted as sexually available, and although writers usually assumed that she would not accept money in exchange for sex, most accounts implied that she did accept, and expected, gifts. In these early texts, her lovers were most often assumed to be young fashionable men, living off their inheritances or investments, and pursuing grisettes in their considerable spare time. Both Parent-Duchâtelet and the Saint-Simonian feminists drew upon these common assumptions concerning grisettes even as they recast earlier lighthearted accounts to make serious arguments concerning the vulnerability of all working women to prostitution.

By far the most dramatic transformation of the grisette occurred, however, in the literature on Paris and the Parisians produced during the July Monarchy. Two of the most significant changes in the depiction of the grisette in this literature were her displacement from the right bank to the left and her association with the student of the Latin quarter. In part, this shift corresponded to a tendency evident in the luxury trades, which employed a great number of women, to move out of the neighborhoods near the stock market and the Palais Royal. When the increased use of home-based labor in these trades during this period is also taken into account, it is certain that young working girls who would normally be called "grisettes" were less in evidence by the 1840s, the period during which most of these accounts were produced. At the same time, however, the shift to the left bank in this literature is indicative of the association journalists wished to forge between grisettes and themselves. The luxury trades moved west, not south; the left bank never became an important center of luxury manufacturing. The left bank, however, and the Latin Quarter in particular, was the neighborhood par excellence of the student.

Beginning in the 1840s, and continuing well into the 1860s, writers and journalists produced a vast literature on students and grisettes; during this time they were probably the most popular pair in Parisian popular culture, meriting even an opera (*La Bohème*). In most of these texts, the student represented the writer in his youth; the grisette was in this way associated with the writer or journalist. Thus, for example, the vaudevillist Varin, in describing his humble beginnings, wrote, "I lived through the hardships of garret life, that life that has for counterpart only hope and the smile of grisettes."[81] Writers thus depicted the grisette as the love object of men who believed that talent and hard work would lead to success and recognition: "The grisette is the salvation of that race, beardless and apart, the honor, the spirit and the furor of our schools, that one can with reason call *the springtime of the year;* she is the smiling and disinterested love of poets without mistresses, of budding orators, of generals without swords, of Mirabeaus without rostrums."[82]

Writers transformed the image of the grisette at the same time as they attempted to develop a professional identity. They emphasized the similarities between grisettes and themselves, drawing upon the "rags-to-riches" narrative so often associated with early accounts of grisettes (and often with the prostitute in general), to craft a new vision of their own career path. Thus rather than downplay the possibility of social mobility that prostitution provided, as Parent-Duchâtelet had done, journalists celebrated it. Indeed the belief that women could improve their social status through prostitution might have been one of the reasons why writers, so interested in achieving fame and fortune, were drawn to the grisette. The life cycle of the grisette as portrayed in libertine literature of the late eighteenth and early nineteenth centuries seemed in many ways to replicate that desired by the writer. Works such as the *Histoire véritable d'une grisette . . . qui . . . est devenue . . . [une] baronne!!!* provided a model of social mobility based on innate qualities such as beauty.[83] Writers also hoped their innate qualities—talent or merit—would lead to success. Similarly, like would-be writers and journalists, and like the students with whom she was textually linked, the grisette was believed to be ambitious. She hoped to leave behind her humble beginnings and make something of herself. According to Alphonse Esquiros, "the majority of young girls who attach themselves out of love to the young men of our schools are women workers of a certain nature, who want to rise above their condition."[84] The grisette intended to use her beauty, like the writer intended to use his talent, to rise in the world.

Again, unlike Parent-Duchâtelet, writers were attracted to the grisette's independence. Whereas he had argued that women who were without husbands or families were prone to an inevitable fall into shame and degradation, journalists celebrated the grisette's desire to live on her own as a manifestation of her freedom as an individual. Her decision to break away from her family was said to be the "delicious privilege of the happy grisette, who emancipates herself with full powers."[85] Unhampered by family ties or parental surveillance, the grisette was free to make her way in the world entirely on her own merits. For most grisettes, this meant a life of hard work. "To speak of a grisette," wrote Jules Janin, "is to speak of a charming little being, content with what little [she has], who works and produces; a lazy grisette is an unnatural grisette."[86] The grisette's hard work barely brought her enough to survive; however, although poor, grisettes were always portrayed as happy and carefree. While this vision of "joyous poverty" may have been designed to excuse the low wages of women and their exploitation as sexual objects, it also undoubtedly made the grisette an attractive model for writers and journalists during the July Monarchy, many of whom also experienced economic hardship while trying to survive in the world of letters.

During the July Monarchy, authors of texts such as Louis Huart and Charles Philipon's *Galerie de la presse* developed a "rags-to-riches" narrative applied to journalists and writers that very much resembled the life story of the grisette. In the pages of this catalog, writers stated that they, too, like the grisette, possessed a desire for independence and a penchant for hard work. Félix Pyat, for example, was described as deciding to pursue a career as a writer despite the objection of his father: "deaf to the complaints of his family, nobly sacrificing the well-being of the paternal home and the favors that a concession of his principles could have led to, Félix, despite hard privations, resolved to continue this mission of courage, independence, and conviction."[87] Like the young grisette, these writers all began their careers, at least according to this catalog, lodged in attic rooms. Thus Jules Janin began his days, "housed in a humble garret of the Saint-Jacques neighborhood."[88] Janin, like his colleagues, endured material privation in order to safeguard his independence. Writers' accounts of their professional development, which consistently emphasized their modest beginnings and the hardships they endured, echoed the life cycle of the grisette.

Writers thus celebrated the grisette's ambition and independence, and identified with her need to earn a living. However, as both Parent-Duchâtelet and libertine authors argued, the difference between the grisette's needs or desires and her means made her susceptible to temptation. According to the anonymous author of one 1840 work: "Without birthright, without family, or at least without a rich family, the poor child, orphan of position and fortune, is consequently constrained to find in her industrial speculation a precarious and stormy existence, slippery and very thorny for her virtue."[89] Libertine texts, as well as tamer depictions of the grisette from the early July Monarchy, portrayed the grisette's "fall" as charming, but inevitable. While Parent-Duchâtelet also implied that this fall was inevitable, he, like the writers for *La Femme libre*, believed a woman's entry into prostitution was a sign of an imperfect market. Journalists and writers of the July Monarchy, however, who were themselves faced with countless charges of immorality and venality, preferred to deemphasize the issue of the grisette's fall altogether. Instead, they highlighted her ability to resist temptation and promoted the image of a virtuous, nonvenal grisette. Writers used this image of the grisette to argue that it was possible to resist the pull of the marketplace without abandoning one's hopes for upward social mobility.

In recasting the mirror images of the grisette and the man of letters, writers drew upon several currents in French society that valorized the feminine and associated femininity with moral progress. Writers such as Eugène Sue popularized the principles of the Saint-Simonian movement, including the belief in the moralizing influence of women, manifested in the character of Fleur-de-Marie, in *Les Mystères de Paris*. Sue and others who opposed the July Monarchy's emphasis on materialism were likewise influenced by the Romantic movement, which placed value on supposedly feminine qualities such as sentimentalism and closeness to nature, qualities that were opposed to the calculating mentality of the enlightenment.[90] At the same time, renewed interest in Catholicism, and in particular the cult of Mary, which exploded after 1830, encouraged an emphasis on "feminine" qualities such as nurturing and compassion.[91] All of these movements contributed to a strong focus on the positive aspects of female nature and opposed femininity, characterized by love and a concern for others, to self-interest.

These various beliefs were contemporaneous with, and no doubt promoted the popularity of, the ideology of domesticity. Rousseau first articulated the notion that women's moralizing mission was best accomplished when she limited her activity to the home and family. From the beginning, the ideology of domesticity assumed the withdrawal of women from politics and their subordination to men in both legal and economic matters, principles that were written into the French Civil Code (1804).

The transformation of the grisette during the 1840s coincided with a growing acceptance of domesticity in French society. In changing the characteristics of the grisette, writers both responded and contributed to this trend. During the 1840s writers de-emphasized the grisette's association with prostitution and instead increasingly portrayed her as representing the ideals of domesticity. Thus the grisette was portrayed as less fun loving and carefree, and more dependent upon the man with whom she had fallen in love. Although still specifying that she worked at a trade, representations of the grisette from the 1840s painted a much narrower vision of women's work. For example, in Huart's *Physiologie de la grisette*, the reader is told that the grisette is a young woman who "works, sews or embroiders."[92] Jacques Arago, in his *Physiologie de la femme entretenue*, identified her predominantly as a seamstress. Furthermore, Arago's grisette was portrayed more often keeping house for the student than working.[93]

In addition to losing a sense of the wide variety of trades in which Parisian women were employed, these representations of the grisette depicted a woman who was less independent and less mobile than her counterpart of the 1830s. The grisette of the 1840s was portrayed less and less often in the streets and public areas of the city. When she did appear in public, it was in areas associated with leisure, such as the public balls, rather than those associated with work. Emphasis was also put on her position of dependency vis-à-vis her lover; while the grisette of the 1830s had supported herself through work, by the mid-1840s most authors agreed that this was no longer possible. Although this change reflected a certain knowledge of falling wages for women in a time of economic crisis and restructuring of the Parisian luxury and clothing trades, it also served to create a grisette whose character better accorded with bourgeois notions of virtuous womanhood.

Given the growing influence of the ideal of domesticity in French culture, writers may have assumed that their reading public, a significant portion of which was composed of women, would not have appreciated or been entertained by the more "libertine" descriptions of the grisette that had dominated earlier literature. In transforming the grisette, writers thus responded to changed sensibilities regarding women's proper roles, while also promoting the ideals of domesticity. At the same time, however, writers diverged from the domestic ideal in one important aspect: aside from a very few exceptions, they portrayed the grisette as remaining sexually active outside of marriage. Thus the "domesticated" grisette was not, during the July Monarchy, a wife and mother, even if, in keeping house for the student, she often appeared to take on that role. Despite other changes that seemed to bring the grisette into accordance with domestic ideals, writers during this period did not abandon the convention that grisettes took lovers whom they did not expect to marry.

Writers did, however, change the meaning of the grisette's sexuality. Whereas earlier libertine accounts had linked the grisette to the prostitute by emphasizing her willingness to improve her style of life by taking lovers, writers who transformed the grisette during the 1840s insisted on her nonvenality. In other words, the grisette of the 1840s took lovers out of love, not money. In the words of Louis Huart, "Take note that the young grisette never gives in, in her love affairs, to a base calculation of interest; she always gives herself and never sells herself."[94] The belief that the grisette "gave" rather than "sold" herself was stated repeatedly in this literature. In constantly reiterating this sentiment, writers echoed the positive view of female sexuality, and its opposition to materialism and self-interest, promoted by contributors to La Femme libre. Unlike the Saint-Simonians, however, writers and journalists did not base this distinction on the assumption that certain areas of human existence should be free from market relations. Grisettes in these accounts still received shawls, dinners out, and tickets to the theater in exchange for sex and companionship. At the same time, however, they entered into these relationships of exchange out of love. Writers thus used this new image of the grisette to explore how one could act *in* the market without being driven by self-interest.

Along with the grisette's association with the student, signified by her move from the right to the left bank, the assertion of the nonvenality of the grisette's motives was the key transformation in her character. The grisette came to symbolize, in these texts, ambition without self-interest, social mobility based on the public good. Writers' interests in transforming the grisette in this way stemmed from their own concerns with the relationship between upward mobility and self-interest. In transforming the grisette, writers imparted to her traits such as self-sacrifice and disinterestedness that were believed to be the special province of women. Through association with the grisette, writers also transferred such traits onto themselves, thus appropriating characteristics increasingly equated with femininity in the early nineteenth century: the ability to resist temptation, modesty, self-sacrifice, and a moralizing influence.

In these texts, the image of the grisette and that of the man of letters reinforced each other; both were said to possess similar virtues and face similar problems. Like the grisette who, despite constant poverty, refused to sell her virtue, writers who were depicted as enduring material hardship without giving in to the temptations offered by their profession proved their dedication to its ideals. Defenders of journalism and journalists, for example, asserted that the "true" journalist, that is, the journalist who best represented the interests and the opinions of the public, always, like the virtuous grisette, turned away from temptation, no matter how difficult: "The journalist has his mission, but he must know what it is: because if he prostitutes himself to his passions, or to those of a party, or to those of a minister, [he] is no more than the son of Satan."[95] In order to remain true to one's ideals, one had, these writers warned, to guard against temptation, something that was true no matter how successful one became. Modesty could help in this battle. According to one author, the ideal journalist, "shows himself very little in society, does not make himself heard; he is not wasteful with his speech or his person . . . . His most meritorious actions are those that the public does not reward, and most often is not aware of."[96] A lack of modesty, in journalists as well as grisettes, led to danger: "Surrounded by pitfalls and illusion, [the journalist] must defend himself also from himself, from the heady sense of his own power. This renown that he distributes with open hands, with which

45

he feeds so much vanity and so many yawning ambitions, God preserve him from tasting it himself! He would be consumed by it. In this life of adventures and storms, wisdom is difficult."[97]

Just as the ideal journalist was supposed to hold back from acquiring the fame he created for others, so too the virtuous grisette had to resist the temptation of wearing the beautiful clothes she made for her clients. The grisette's carefree nature, according to Adolphe de Liancourt, was maintained only with effort: "Poor girl, whose dress is simply printed cloth, and whose agile fingers will trim tulle, silk and velvet on into the evening.—Next to this torture, that of Tantalus is nothing. To give one's life and one's intelligence to making others beautiful, when one is beautiful oneself; to work on the finery of great ladies when a word, a sign, would suffice to have [finery] just as dazzling . . . . But no, the grisette takes things philosophically."[98] The role of the journalist, like that of the grisette, was to make evident the talents or beauties of others, and thus to inspire others to greatness, all the while exerting an important moral influence. The grisette in these texts is the model who inspires the painter's brush, the young woman who writes the critic's theater reviews, even the willing subject of a medical student's experimentation.[99] Although the grisette was ambitious, the virtuous grisette acted not out of self-interest, but for the good of others and of society as a whole.

Likewise the writer who preserved his ideals in the face of all temptation became an important civilizing force, able to control the potential damage that a commercial press might pose if left in the hands of those guided only by greed and self-interest. Journalists were thus depicted as possessing a moralizing power, manifested by their lack of self-interest, which served to transform even the most commercial enterprises into a beneficial force. Emile de Girardin argued, for example, that when guided by the right principles, commercial journalism was not only a positive development but was in fact the only type of journalism free from self-interest, since a paper with a wide readership "erases all narrow party boundaries, and takes from each that which it possesses of useful viewpoints and national sentiments . . . ; the subscriptions of friends, the support of a coterie, will not be able to captivate [the greatest number of readers]—[the low-priced press] can only survive as long as it is the true and impartial organ of the country's opinion."[100] In Girardin's formulation, the success of the commercial press was a sign not of the corruption of journalists, but rather of the journalist's ability to interpret and articulate public opinion so as to reinforce national unity. Journalism, practiced with integrity, thus constituted a domain free from self-interest, where the public good could be articulated and defended. And similar to the virtuous grisette, whose gentle influence served to "civilize" the men with whom she came in contact, the virtuous journalist, in such accounts, escaped the pitfalls of the market and rose to success, his talent and principles intact. Through the image of the grisette, then, writers argued that social mobility and virtue were not incompatible. Personal success could be compatible with the public good, but only through constant vigilance and force of will.

Like Parent-Duchâtelet and the Saint-Simonian feminists, middle-class male journalists linked their discussion of female sexuality and economic disinterest to questions of freedom. Thus although the 1835 September Laws forbad writers and journalists from overtly criticizing the government or from professing loyalty to the republic, writers used the image of the grisette to call for greater political freedom and a renunciation of materialism in society. The passage of the September Laws corresponded with an enormous growth in stock-market speculation that served to increase the fortunes of the financial and banking elites of the bourgeoisie. Since the right to vote was based on taxes paid, these elites also gained in political power. Writers and journalists, most of whom did not qualify for the vote, were active in projects of political reform during this period. If they had not directly participated in the civil unrest that marked the years 1830 to 1835, many of them empathized with the efforts of those who had, and supported projects to widen the suffrage. For some, an expanded suffrage and a recognition of intellectual talent were linked, and they protested François Guizot's exhortation to "get rich" in order to obtain the vote as a sign of corruption. In this context, the story of the poor but hardworking, ambitious but self-sacrificing grisette posed a direct challenge to what writers and journalists saw as an overly materialist society.

The repeated assertion of the grisette's lack of venality can thus be read not only within the context of the professionalization of journalism but also as a political critique of a government that writers believed encouraged the pursuit of wealth above all else. As writers and journalists transformed the image of the grisette, they also began to express concern that the relentless pursuit of self-interest that they believed characterized July Monarchy society would lead to her disappearance. Writers sharpened this critique by associating the grisette with republicanism. Alfred de Musset's Mimi Pinson, for example, possessed a "republican heart" and fought on the barricades during the *trois glorieuses,* the three days that composed the 1830 revolution.[101] Several authors associated grisettes with the revolutionary and Napoleonic traditions. Thus included among the list of grisettes was the *vivandière*, a woman who followed the troops in order to sell them provisions, who, according to one author, "during the glorious period of the empire . . . appeared surrounded by an aura of glory."[102]

By associating grisettes with the Napoleonic era and with revolution, authors celebrated the ideals of public-spiritedness and careers open to talent. In contrasting the virtues of the grisette to the mores of a society that they saw as materialist and self-interested, writers and journalists criticized the regime they felt had betrayed them. This sense of betrayal is also reflected in descriptions of the grisette. Thus Louis Huart's lamentations concerning the tendency to replace delivery girls in the fashion trades, women commonly identified as grisettes, with delivery boys can be read as a remark concerning the fate of journalists and writers who supported the ideals of the 1830 revolution; the delivery girl, Huart wrote, "who emerged triumphant . . . from the revolutions of 89, 92, and even of 1830, has suddenly just been dispossessed of her job."[103]

Through the image of the republican grisette, writers and journalists reinforced their commitment to certain revolutionary ideals without, however, raising the specter of popular revolt. Through their textual association with the grisette, a girl of the people, writers indicated their commitment to the condition of the popular classes. However, whereas the grisette was one of the most popular stereotypes produced during the July Monarchy, the man of the people did not fare so well. With rare exceptions, men of the popular classes appear in these texts as either vulgar con artists or as potentially violent craftsmen and laborers. The identification of violent revolt and radical revolution as masculine may stem in part from the celebration of the symbol of Hercules during the Terror, when popular sovereignty was briefly associated with masculine rather than feminine models.[104] In addition, male workers were visible in greater numbers during the revolution of 1830, and by the 1840s they were once again organizing and pressing for reform. In creating the republican grisette, authors used feminine imagery to disassociate themselves from the potential violence of social and political revolution. Writers thus used female imagery to paint themselves as spokesmen for the people, without tainting themselves with the brush of radical revolution.

The grisette was thus an attractive subject for writers because her image allowed them to articulate, both politically and professionally, a balance between various extremes. Politically, the image of the grisette was used by writers to criticize the July Monarchy without seeming to condone the path of radical revolution. Professionally, writers focused on the image of the grisette to explore the ways in which one could participate in the market without being absorbed by "market values." In this sense, the focus on the grisette provides an interesting counterpart to other strategies of professionalization. In both France and England during the mid-nineteenth century, the process of professionalization that occurred among doctors, lawyers, government bureaucrats, and journalists included an attempt to deny or limit self-interest. Strict standards of conduct, adherence to a code of honor, and the necessity of obtaining advanced training were all methods used to promote "ethical" professional behavior, behavior driven by public-spiritedness rather than self-interest.[105] Most of these techniques demanded a complete distancing from the market and demanded a denial of any venal motives. In reality, however, professionals were constantly tempted by self-interest and by the lure of the marketplace. The image of the grisette offered a vehicle for exploring this contradiction and for thinking about how to be in the market without being dominated by self-interest.

Male writers thus embraced, even while recasting, the contradictions posed by the image of the prostitute, contradictions that were also believed to be inherent in the ideals and practices of laissez-faire. Parent-Duchâtelet had sought to resolve these contradictions through an emphasis on police surveillance and legal subordination, while the Saint-Simonians had attempted to reconcile them by positing dual understandings of women's sexuality: one determined by market relations (that of the prostitute) and the other free from them (that of the "free woman"). Male writers and journalists who transformed the image of the grisette, however, argued that just as women could be sexually active outside of marriage and yet virtuous, so too could they participate in the market without being consumed by self-interest. Like Parent-Duchâtelet and the Saint-Simonian feminists, authors of popular literature during the July Monarchy used female imagery to explore the ways in which the market might be rendered virtuous.

The authors of popular accounts of grisettes and journalists put great emphasis on the importance of self-control in creating a virtuous marketplace. At the same time, they implied that not everyone could exercise self-control. Both women and the members of the popular classes who attempt to enter the world of letters come off badly in these accounts, in both cases because they are described as being driven by purely materialist motives. Unlike male journalists whose lack of self-interest was indicated through their association with the feminine, the woman writer, or "bluestocking" was repeatedly rendered masculine in the literature on Paris and the Parisians.[106] Her inability to check her desire for fame and fortune and devote herself to others led to her complete immersion in the marketplace. As the enormously successful Frédéric Soulié wrote of his female competitors, "at the least *réclame* that she writes and inserts, at the price of ten francs per line, in any newspaper, her primitive innocence takes flight."[107]

Writers from the popular classes were also associated with the commercialization of the publishing world, as indicated in anecdotes of working-class fathers who pushed their sons into the writing profession when they saw the wealth that it could bring to the fortunate few. Writers warned that the incursion of women and workers into the world of letters threatened to unleash dangerous forces of ambition and greed, forces they signified by blurring class and gender boundaries. Women who wrote for money became "men" in these accounts, while working-class writers lost their class identity, becoming "scholars without knowledge, aristocrats without fortune."[108] Repeatedly, authors warned that "a position in literature and the arts is not such a simple thing to obtain, even for a man of wit and talent, often even for a man of genius."[109] For a man, or even worse, a woman, who could not resist the siren's call of fame and fortune, embarking on a writing career would be a personal, as well as a social, disaster. Writers used the image of the grisette to illustrate the perils of the marketplace—perils that included poverty, greed, self-interest, and ambition—and then argued that only a few possessed the force of will necessary to negotiate such perils successfully.

The image of the grisette was an image of an ideal—an ideal of sacrifice and selflessness, of hard work and talent. It was an ideal that served as the basis for a professional identity for journalists, as well as a critique of July Monarchy politics and society. As the reflection of an ideal, the story of the grisette was a vehicle for men of letters to develop and disseminate the virtues and qualities that they believed were important not only to their profession, but to French society in general. Writers were not always certain they could live up to this ideal; nonetheless, the story of the grisette, with its message of the triumph of virtue over the forces of the market, was a powerful narrative in a society seeking to understand the impact of economic and political change.

The grisette of the late eighteenth and early nineteenth centuries had been considered a woman of easy virtue, close to the prostitute in her willingness to sell her sexuality, even if her price might be nothing more than a cake or a shawl. While some during the July Monarchy continued to consider the grisette as little more than a prostitute in the disguise of a working woman, others redefined the image of the grisette so as to emphasize her virtue, selflessness, and patriotism. This transformation of the grisette's image explains her lasting popularity. While the heyday of writings concerning the grisette was the 1840s and early 1850s, her popularity was so enduring that in 1903 the city of Paris commissioned a statue of her. This statue, bearing the legend, "La grisette en 1830," can still be seen at the intersection of the rue du Faubourg du Temple and the Boulevard Jules Ferry. Throughout the nineteenth century, an appeal to the memory of the grisette became an appeal to a time when love, rather than materialism, ruled society, when individuals acted according to their principles, rather than to fulfill their interests.

The grisette embodied the ideal of resistance to the marketplace. The notion that such resistance demanded a superior willpower, identified with honor and sacrifice, would remain a powerful current in French popular culture. The use of feminine imagery to convey this ideal left open the possibility that women could also aspire to such a status, despite male writers' attempts to deny this. Over the course of the 1840s, another model of sacrifice and selflessness, this one decidedly masculine, was developed in the pages of the working-class press. While this model drew upon many of the elements discussed in this chapter, it implied that although women could practice the virtues of self-control and the denial of self-interest they could not do so in relation to the market. Within the context of the upheaval of 1848, this difference would prove to be crucial.

TWO

Work, Wages, and Citizenship in the 1840s

During the 1840s, the effects of changes in the organization of the French economy, changes associated with the adoption of laissez-faire principles, had begun to make themselves felt in ways that many considered frightening and incomprehensible. Although these changes are most commonly referred to as part of the process of industrialization, in the Parisian economy, where the handicraft industry persisted well into the nineteenth century, few large factories were established and an industrial proletariat did not develop until the end of the century. Nonetheless, during the 1840s, craftsmen and women were under tremendous pressure. New processes of production such as the rise of piecework and limited mechanization, competition from provincial workers who had migrated to Paris, and fluctuations in both domestic and international markets resulted in increased job insecurity and falling wages. The abolition of the guild system in 1791, the affirmation of the employer's authority over the worker in the Civil Code, and repeated restrictions concerning freedom of assembly left workers feeling that they had little control over their livelihoods in this new economy driven by the principle of free competition.

While many praised the legal and cultural adoption of the principles of laissez-faire, others worried that lessened government intervention and the erosion of institutions such as the guilds, which had served to regulate hiring, wages, and production, would lead to a general loss of control over the French economy.[1] This loss of control was imagined in very personal terms. A printing worker writing in 1847, for example, depicted this loss of control as a loss of professional status. As a result of unfettered competition, he wrote, "[t]omorrow—to live—you will fall among the ranks of the *bohemians;* you will add to the number of these thieves who encumber our intersections with chemical matches and coupling chains

. . . ; or else, you will be domestics, messengers, . . . or street sweepers,—that is, if you are strong and if there's a need for you."[2] Others, and especially middle-class writers, imagined this loss of control as a loss of distinctions within the working-class family, where a confusion of personal and familial relationships was believed to lead to licentious and disorderly behavior. Relationships among family members became a prime topic of concern, as both working- and middle-class writers explored the effects of the market economy on family formations.

[margin handwriting: Indust → concerns about family & poverty, but must recast poverty as not self-interest]

Just as familial relationships came under increased scrutiny, so too did the question of poverty, one of the most visible manifestations of the changes in the French economy. While middle-class writers tended to ascribe the causes of poverty to the moral character of the poor, champions of the working class identified the problem of poverty as one of insufficient wages. Wages were thus a crucial issue in the 1840s; however, to demand a higher wage in and for itself was to risk accusations of self-interest and venality. To avoid such charges, literate and politically active artisans recast their arguments concerning work and wages so as to deny charges of self-interest.[3] They did this in large part by redefining men and women's relationship to work and to the marketplace. By the late 1840s, writers for the major organs of the Parisian working-class press, *L'Atelier* (1840–49) and *La Ruche populaire* (1839–48), had developed a coherent argument concerning the masculine nature of wage earning.[4] While the revolution of 1848 would bring challenges to this model, it would also reaffirm the usefulness of gender in creating a vision of a virtuous marketplace.

Laissez-Faire and the French Family

During the July Monarchy, changes wrought in the French economy were associated with new economic doctrines, in particular with the adoption of laissez-faire principles. Middle-class writers differed in their opinions of these principles. Some criticized laissez-faire on the basis that it encouraged egoism and weakened communal bonds, while others insisted that allowing the free operation of the "natural laws" governing the market would lead to economic and social progress. In his two-volume work on poverty in France and England, for example, Eugène Buret asked, "because the birth and development of industry is only possible in the light of liberty, can we conclude that liberty is everything?" Liberty, he argued, must be balanced by order and restraint, for "absolute *laisser-faire* is no more valuable in industry than in politics; its true name is anarchy."[5] On the other hand, a critic of Buret's study insisted that "our century is less egoist than a few morose philanthropists take pleasure in repeating it is," arguing that the benefits of industrialization and economic modernization outweighed the disadvantages.[6]

Critics of laissez-faire focused much attention on the way in which new economic practices seemed to be transforming working-class families. Reformers took great interest in the dilapidated state of working-class housing, citing it as proof of both workers' primitivism and society's failure to provide for its poor. According to Buret, in the poor quarters of London, "the shanties are crumbling, half rotten; there is no drainage system, no regular service for the collection of rubbish, no lighting, in short, nothing that announces a civilized city; it is the most absolute *laisser-faire* that one could imagine." In descriptions such as this, critics like Buret associated a lack of regulation with an erasure of distinctions—between inside and outside, clean and dirty, as well as between families who shared the same living quarters. While Buret believed that the situation in France was better, he still noted that in cities like Mulhouse, "the population is squeezed to the point where two families often sleep in the same room."[7]

In addition to blurring the lines between families, reformers argued that industrialization and the acceptance of laissez-faire ideology led to a confusion of roles within families. Dr. Louis-René Villermé, for example, described his visit to a working-class family home that revealed "individuals of both sexes and of very different ages lying together, most of them without nightshirts and repulsively dirty. Father, mother, the aged, children, adults, all pressed, stacked together."[8] Such confusion, critics believed, weakened the moral fiber of the working class. Thus Buret wrote, "[m]isery and big industry, which pile together in any which way all ages and both sexes, the first in narrow lodgings and sometimes in the same bed, the second in workshops, directly elicit the illegitimate and premature union of the sexes."[9] Consonant with their belief that the new economic principles encouraged individualism at the expense of communal bonds that served to define and maintain social hierarchies, critics portrayed working-class families as subject to a loss of differentiating boundaries.

Critics focused in particular on gender confusion among workers, which they perceived as a precondition for vice and crime. H.-A. Frégier's 1840 study of the "dangerous classes" of urban centers, which painted a bleak and frightening vision of a world of underground crime, deprivation, and degradation, repeatedly noted the lack of differentiation between different categories of "workers" as well as between the sexes. While Frégier believed that female criminals, for example, were "recruited from every rank of the social hierarchy . . . [and] embraced every variety of depravation," his work also implied that the confusion of categories that char-

54

acterized working-class life created a powerful precondition to a life of crime and debauchery. Frégier thus condemned factories as "huge gatherings of workers where the sexes are ordinarily mixed" and proposed the separation of the sexes as a measure necessary to prevent crime, vice, and poverty.[10]

The work of labor historians has shown that industrialization often did alter the organization of working-class families. However, studies by Elinor Accampo, Gay Gullickson, and Tessie Liu, among others, have argued that changes associated with the new modes of production heightened rather than diminished the importance of gender distinctions within the family.[11] Liu has shown, for example, that weavers emphasized masculine and paternal control within the family to compensate for a loss of control over the work process. Middle-class authors writing during the 1840s, however, emphasized the leveling of gendered distinctions within the working-class family as a means to indicate the leveling effects of laissez-faire. Their work must therefore be seen as driven in large part by ideological concerns, and in particular by the desire to point out what they considered to be the dangers of a doctrine that gave primacy to the individual. In these texts, then, the working-class family became a model of society as a whole, the changes wrought in familial organization a metaphor for the possible disintegration of social bonds.[12]

The flow of money throughout the family was a topic of great concern to middle-class writers. Frégier's work repeatedly emphasized the inability of workers to manage their money. In one such passage, for example, he stated, "[n]ot content to dissipate their salaries with the most rash eagerness, a great number of workers contract debts that they do not pay."[13] Like Frégier, many were convinced that the problems faced by working-class families stemmed from their misuse of money. Both Villermé and Buret, for example, realized that many workers did not even earn enough to cover the basic necessities of life, let alone to set money aside for the future. Both agreed, however, that even with higher salaries, workers would need to be taught better monetary habits if they were to improve their condition and status in French society. "As to those who gain the better salaries," Villermé argued, "almost all could save and be comfortable in their old age, if their conduct were better. But the extravagance of their clothing, improvidence, and a taste for costly pleasures do not permit the majority [to save money]."[14]

Such beliefs led middle-class reformers to put great emphasis on budgeting as a means of both moral and financial improvement.[15] Reformers focused on the link between family morality and the dispensation of economic aid, helping only the "deserving" poor, those who could demonstrate that they would use the funds they received wisely. Many argued that an "immoral" understanding of the relationship between money and family was the cause of social ills such as prostitution. In both popular writings and in studies of prostitution, the story of the mother (or, less frequently, father) who sold her (or his) daughter into prostitution was a common cautionary tale meant to illustrate the way in which self-interest could pervert family relationships within the popular classes.

Working-class writers similarly used family imagery to criticize the doctrine of laissez-faire. In the early 1840s, their criticisms focused on what they argued was the egoism of the bourgeois nuclear family. Like their middle-class counterparts, workers argued that the problem with the economy was not so much industrial progress as a growing spirit of speculation and profit seeking at the expense of the public good. According to a printing worker writing for *La Ruche populaire,* "our age is a truly golden age. The fashionable motto is the sordid [']every man for himself.['] All who own anything want to double what they've got."[16] This constant search for wealth was designated as the cause of industrial disorder since it led employers to search for ways to lower workers' salaries. In addition, employers were said to encourage the development of an ethic of self-interest among workers by creating a system in which each was forced to compete with all others for work.[17]

Workers argued that the bourgeoisie's adherence to a political and economic regime driven by self-interest was reflected in the organization of its families. Worker-journalists thus emphasized the isolation of the bourgeois family from the larger community. In the fourth issue of *L'Atelier,* for example, writers argued that the economic self-interest of those in power was replicated in their desire to retire to a private sphere in which comfort and wealth was neither exposed to nor questioned by the poverty of others: "The men who govern today, are by science and sentiment the enemies of the fundamental principle of France. For these men, nationality is a word without value. According to them, society is no more than a collection of individuals, with diverse interests . . . . All actions of these men of state, all their laws are marked with this false and individualist spirit. They've formulated their ethic as *chacun pour soi, chacun chez soi* [every man for himself; every man in his own home]."[18]

Worker-journalists thus depicted the private, nuclear family as the foundation for an economic self-interest that destroyed communal and national bonds. They warned that the ability to take refuge in the private sphere of the nuclear family would eventually erode the moral fabric of French society. In July 1841, a tailor described the consequences of individualism in the pages of *La Ruche populaire,* arguing that it would make the French "a people in which each individual would make himself the center, would have to defend his little property, his little shop, his little workshop, his little political rights, because everything then would be infinitely little . . . . What could we expect from a people for whom every man in his own home, every man his own law would be the sacramental axiom of his individual egoism? from a people . . . without morality, without religion, a living cadaver, without soul, without passion and without love?"[19] Writers interpreted the primacy given to the nuclear family by middle-class reformers as a sign of self-interest in both politics and the economy. They argued that the search for profits, the denial of political rights to workers, and the valuation of the private sphere were inseparable elements of a new era of egoism and materialism. In opposition, writers emphasized productive labor, political equality, and an ethic of association.

In the early 1840s, working-class writers contrasted the role of women in middle-class and working-class families to emphasize further the differences between the two groups. When the Saint-Simonian *Globe* criticized *La Ruche populaire* in October 1841 for including a woman on its staff, Pierre Vinçard, the editor, justified women's participation in journalism by referring to their role in the family. "What," he asked, "is there that is so unusual among workers who appreciate the . . . respect they owe to their women, their mothers, their spouses, or their sisters that they manifest it and make it a moral example in honoring themselves with the patronage of one of them? We would be sorely affected to learn that the author of the article to which we are responding is still so *backward* as to believe that women are out of place anywhere other than in the home, the ball or the theater?"[20] In evoking the ball and the theater, Vinçard implicitly criticized the exclusion of wealthy women from public, political life, contrasting their limited public role with that of working-class women. Vinçard thus argued that it was *because* male and female workers were members of the same family that they should participate together in actions and institutions designed to better the welfare of the class as a whole.[21] Vinçard's vision of women's role accords with that of the Saint-Simonian "social mother," whose energies were to be devoted as much to the good of the community as to that of her own family.[22] In contrast to this vision, the isolation of the private, domestic sphere and bourgeois women's lack of meaningful public role symbolized the bourgeoisie's lack of communal spirit.

Whereas the middle-class advocated budgeting and the restriction of financial aid to the deserving poor as a remedy for the "confusion" of working-class life, working-class writers promoted the ideal of association as the best solution to a rising tide of self-interest that had already engulfed the bourgeoisie.[23] The associationist model of social organization appealed to workers in part because of its link to corporatism, as William Sewell has argued.[24] By restoring a means of regulating the economy, association was seen as a powerful counterweight to the competition engendered by the adoption of laissez-faire principles. The idea of association further appealed to workers because it seemed consistent with a long tradition of mutual aid, in both the workplace and the neighborhood, practiced by working-class families. In opposition to the nuclear family of the bourgeoisie, working-class writers emphasized the importance of what could be called the "communal" model of the family. The communal family was one rooted in the community, where friends, neighbors, and even institutions (such as the church or the pawnshop) played a vital role in the survival of family units within the neighborhood. The community thus helped to resolve disputes between spouses, raise children, contribute to the care of the sick or elderly, and provide aid in the form of money, food, clothing, and so forth, for families experiencing hard times.[25] By linking association to a model of family organization that would have been familiar to many, writers for the working-class press helped reinforce the value of association for workers.[26]

Both middle- and working-class writers used family imagery to criticize the new economic doctrines and to propose alternatives. Middle-class writers emphasized the need to teach workers how to use money wisely and morally, to save and budget, and to think of the future rather than of immediate appetites and desires. This emphasis on slow and steady improvement through work and savings constituted a central component of bourgeois identity in the nineteenth century.[27] Reformers thus countered workers' demands for greater control over the work process and for political inclusion by arguing that until they learned to manage their money, they could not hope to participate in public life. According to Frégier, "The improvement of the worker's condition depends to a great degree on his own will. Before demanding the regeneration of the rich, let him begin by regenerating himself; in showing himself to be thrifty, sober, temperate, he will have come halfway."[28] Reformers believed that "the 'moral economy' should exist first at the level of the family. Not until this task was accomplished could workers' families be truly integrated into a moral community at the societal level."[29]

Workers in the early 1840s, on the other hand, used the model of the communal family to emphasize the values of association. In opposition to a bourgeoisie that promoted working and saving to further the fortunes of immediate family members, workers emphasized the ethic of mutual aid among an extended group of coworkers, neighbors, family, and friends

that allowed the whole community to survive. Whereas middle-class reformers focused on saving, workers, especially those influenced by the
ideas of Fourier and Saint-Simon, emphasized the need for credit. Money,
they believed, should not be hoarded by the family to the benefit of its
immediate members alone, but should move easily through society for the
benefit of all. The Saint-Simonian Philippe Buchez, for example, argued
that equality could best be achieved by making credit easily available to
workers to allow them to establish cooperatives.[30] Buchez's enormous
influence on the contributors to L'Atelier in particular can be seen in its
constant recommendation of association as the ideal countermeasure to
laissez-faire principles. Associations financed by all (through credit), owned
by all, and benefiting all (through profit sharing) promoted economic
growth and at the same time reinforced the importance of communal
bonds. Associations would thus foster a healthy competition, while limiting competition workers considered "unfair" or "immoral," such as the use
of piecework to lower wages.[31]

Inspired perhaps by Parent-Duchâtelet's observation that prostitutes
practiced mutual aid, some middle-class reformers recognized the importance of the "communal" family to working-class survival. "The poor,"
wrote Buret, "bestow amongst themselves more aid than public assistance
can accord them."[32] Yet even those like Buret who were sympathetic to
the idea of association did not see this exchange of goods and services as
proof that workers could enter into a communal financial venture. For
example, although Buret was attracted to many aspects of Fourier's phalanstery, he found its goal of uniting "capital, work, and talent" unrealis-
tic. Buret argued that workers needed to learn to manage their own capital
(proof of which, he believed, would be their ability to purchase property)
before they could be trusted with that of others.[33] Frégier was even more
negative, arguing that allowing workers to manage associations would be
a financial disaster, as their inability to manage money and their tendency
to spend it on parties and "debaucheries" would lead to their eventual
ruin.[34]

Despite such criticism, workers never abandoned their support of associations. They did, however, attempt to address the widely held belief that
they were fiscally irresponsible by demonstrating their ability to support
their families. The communal family, with its ethic of mutual aid, had been
the dominant model of family life in the working-class press in the early
1840s. As workers attempted to assert their sense of economic responsibility, however, they turned increasingly to the nuclear family model, one
headed by a responsible male breadwinner.

While the adoption of the nuclear-family model entailed a redefinition of men's and women's relationship to the market, it did not indicate an unthinking acceptance of middle-class beliefs. Similar to middle-class reformers, workers by the end of the 1840s decried the effects of laissez-faire on the nuclear family. Unlike middle-class writers, however, they maintained, even reinforced, the importance of hierarchies of age, and especially of gender, within the working-class family.

An 1847 article by the printing worker Jean-Baptiste Coutant provides a good illustration of this new model of working-class family life. In this article, Coutant penned a description of working-class family life that emphasized the isolation and alienation of family members: "The father goes to his workshop in the morning, the mother to another; the children are placed, one in the factory, another in nursery school, a third in day care. From then on, no more intimate existence, meals in common . . . . Each one lives separately isolated."[35] The sorrow expressed by Coutant over a loss of community life may have in part reflected changes occurring in working-class communities. The slow disappearance of working-class networks through the demolition and increased regulation of popular neighborhoods, growing economic recession, and a partial dissolution of Old Regime sources of charity all contributed to making working-class family life more precarious by the late 1840s.

This new representation of working-class family life may have also reflected a change in strategy. By portraying the working-class family as disorganized, Coutant may have been trying to speak to middle-class critics in their own "language."[36] Yet it is interesting to note that Coutant chose not to emphasize confusion (of sex or age distinctions) in his description of the working-class family. Instead, he focused on the isolation of family members, their separation from each other rather than their undifferentiated mixing. It was this same isolation from the larger community that working-class writers criticized in their depiction of middle-class family life. In this article, Coutant argued that efforts to encourage women's work as a means of reducing labor costs were destroying the working-class family and creating among its members the bourgeois ethic of *chacun pour soi*.[37] He maintained that in forcing women to work, the middle class was promoting self-interest by turning each member of the working class family into an individual wage earner.

In making such an argument, Coutant restated, in a different form, Louis Blanc's fear of a society of rootless bachelors. In Blanc's 1840 *L'Organisation du travail,* he worried that the growth of competition and a subsequent decrease in wages would discourage marriage by making raising a family prohibitively expensive.[38] Coutant took Blanc's admonition to middle-class employers one step further by warning that, even within the bonds of marriage and family, unfettered competition and low wages could create a society of self-interested individuals devoted to nothing but their own survival. Coutant's description seemed therefore to imply that the disorganization of the working-class family was not rooted in the workers' lack of understanding or disrespect for hierarchies and distinctions but was instead the inevitable product of a society driven by self-interest.

The dislocation of working-class families became a major theme in working-class writings in the late 1840s. Such descriptions maintained the earlier critiques of bourgeois self-interest. However, whereas earlier descriptions opposed the middle-class nuclear family to the working-class "communal" family to establish the selflessness and public-spiritedness of the working class, later descriptions created this opposition between self-interest and the public good by focusing exclusively on the working-class family, a family increasingly portrayed as a smaller and more isolated unit. As a result of such changes, gender took on an importance as a means to create oppositions that it did not have in earlier descriptions of working-class family life. In Coutant's article, for example, gender roles within the working class were distinct and clearly defined, and the family was identified as a "feminine" space. Thus, he argued, the masculine sphere was that of work—"in regards to men, one should first consider work, second the remuneration of this work"—while that of women was limited to the family. In fact, for Coutant, the family did not exist without the presence of women at home. In replying to his own question, "Is there a family where the woman is absent?" Coutant stated that if both men and women worked there was no family.[39]

The emphasis on female domesticity in the working-class press was an innovation of the second half of the 1840s. Whereas reformers such as Villermé or Frégier had criticized mixed-gender work spaces, they did not oppose women's work. Likewise, Parent-Duchâtelet pointed to women's low wages and lack of job opportunities as problems, but did not propose their withdrawal from the labor market as a solution. Even middle-class journalists, who strengthened the grisette's association with interior spaces and with the home to render her more compatible with models of middle-class domesticity, never completely denied her identity as a working woman. Despite the spread of domestic ideology, during the 1840s even many middle-class women were still active in the workplace. Within the working class, where survival of the family depended on both members bringing in an income, the acceptance and recognition of women's work was even greater.

This new emphasis on female domesticity within the working-class press corresponded with the emergence of new definitions of masculinity and femininity, and with a restructuring of each sex's relationship to the marketplace and to money. These changes were prompted by a reconsideration of the relationship between wages, virtue, and self-interest. Thus while the emphasis on female domesticity helped to forge a bond with middle-class readers and commentators based in shared values and ideology, it was only one aspect of a larger discussion of workers' relationship to the marketplace that developed in the working-class press. Whereas earlier writers had used consumerist arguments to emphasize workers' humanity, worker-journalists of the late 1840s developed a different model of identity that allowed workers to assert both their individualism and their lack of self-interest. This model was founded upon the presupposition of a gendered private sphere, as male workers were only able to argue that their demands for higher wages were not driven by self-interest when they presented these demands in the context of supporting a family.

By the late 1840s, then, the working-class press had created as the core of its political and economic argument the image of the male breadwinner.[40] This figure was defined as rational, self-sufficient, and independent and was therefore presented as worthy of a voice in the polity. In creating this masculine image, workers writing for *L'Atelier* and *La Ruche populaire* defined it against a feminine image that was dependent and victimized. Women were increasingly portrayed as unsuccessful participants in the marketplace, while women's work was criticized not because it threatened to place women on an equal footing with men but because it denied male workers a way to claim economic disinterest. In making such an argument, working-class writers made explicit the different relationship of men and women to the marketplace that was only implied in the work of middle-class writers and journalists.

Wages and the Regendering of Work

In the working-class press of the early 1840s, women were depicted as relatively equal actors in movements to better workers' status. Often, women's concern for the survival of the family, her own or others, was invoked to explain or promote women's involvement in politics. In response to an unfavorable account of women's actions during the Revolution of 1789, for example, writers for *L'Atelier* defended women's political leadership by arguing that food shortages were most strongly perceived by women, who were usually in charge of shopping for the family. Women's role in the family economy thus gave them a leading role in expressing discontent; during the *journées* of 1795, for example, "[o]nce more, it was women who gave the signal for insurrection . . . . And who would dare say that the complaints of these unhappy women were unfounded . . . . The exasperation of the women was shared by the men." Calling on this tradition of political activism among women, working-class writers of the early 1840s called for men and women to "unite in order to demand guarantees against exploitation."[41]

Likewise, arguments for higher wages, which constituted one of the major issues for workers during the July Monarchy, were not based on gendered imagery in the early part of the decade. Instead, consumer desires, shared equally by men and women, were used as an argument for higher wages. Writers for the short-lived *L'Artisan*, which appeared for a few months in 1830, decried the injustice of a system in which workers could not afford the products they produced. Raising wages, they maintained, would help the economy by allowing workers to buy consumer goods. This critique was reproduced in early issues of *La Ruche populaire* and *L'Atelier*. In the July 1841 issue of *La Ruche populaire*, for example, a contributor wrote: "It is necessary that a seamstress could at least have the means to buy herself a beautiful dress; that a cabinetmaker could . . . have a few furnishings; that a milliner could honestly acquire a pretty hat; a tailor, a fine coat."[42] Repeatedly, criticism of the economy focused on worker's inability to participate as consumers. In 1841, for example, *L'Atelier* argued that the ability to consume was as necessary for the working class as education: "Yes, we need an education; we need good precepts and examples . . . ; we also need bread and clothing."[43]

The consumerist argument was a central component of early working-class discourse, and it tied into a number of characteristic themes of this early discourse. The consumerist argument emphasized workers' humanity by stressing their desire for comfort and pleasure.[44] In an 1833 brochure, a tailor linked recognition of workers as individuals and pleasure, complaining, "to us alone it is forbidden to taste the least pleasure . . . . Pleasure! but *we are not men like the others*." Workers would only achieve happiness, he continued, when they became "the artisans of their fates."[45] Workers presented the ability to experience pleasure, to be comfortable, and to enjoy what was beautiful in life as central characteristics of humanity, essential to their recognition as individuals with needs, emotions, and desires.

The consumerist discourse granted women an important role. In the first place, it did not distinguish between male and female desire; a tailor might covet a jacket as much as a milliner would a hat. It also recognized the important role played by women as managers of consumption for the working-class family. In establishing this consumerist argument, the early working-class press did not criticize materialism so much as it did the self-ishness of the middle class, which was depicted as hiding its profits away in the private sphere of the family rather than sharing them with the workers who had contributed to their generation.

By the mid-1840s, however, consumer desires were devalued as these papers, especially the more widely read *L'Atelier*, responded to middle-class accusations of worker materialism. During the 1840s, middle-class writers, arguing for political and social reform based on a critique of materialism, portrayed consumer desire as a dangerous thing. In the story of the grisette, for example, the intrigue of her struggle to maintain her virtue stemmed from the fact that she was constantly surrounded by consumer goods. "Barely descended from the fifth floor where she lives," Jules Janin wrote, "the grisette is introduced into the most expensive stores, the most sumptuous houses." Forced to maintain her virtue in the face of constant temptation, the grisette either succeeds, a "noble heroine," or "quite simply she becomes mad."[46] For middle-class journalists, the temptation of consumer desire tested one's ability to resist the pull of the marketplace. Journalists made the ability to resist such desires, which they depicted as an indication of a lack of self-interest, a central component of their professional and political identity.

As middle-class writers called into question the relationship between consumerism and virtue, workers' emphasis on material possessions seemed to undermine their cause. The belief that poverty and vice resulted from workers seeking pleasure from their wages, rather than saving their money, became a constant theme among those who opposed workers' efforts at economic and social reform. Even those who were friendly to the workers' cause questioned the validity of the consumerist argument for higher wages. For example, an 1845 article published in the liberal *National* forced *L'Atelier* to articulate its stance on the desire for material goods. In this article, *Le National* questioned the moral fiber of a working class that demanded "well-being, physical pleasures." *Le National* considered workers' emphasis on the insufficiency of salaries a sign of emanation "in the inferior classes [of] this poison of egoism that has corrupted everything above them."[47] Warning that a working class that sought only pleasure and wealth would lose the patriotic élan that had been the glory of revolutionary France, *Le National* implied that a working class in pursuit of material gain did not merit a place in the polity.

In responding to the criticism of *Le National*, *L'Atelier* articulated a distinction between economics and materialism: "We pray those who take the pain to read us to remark on the way in which we pose the question. We are speaking here of the enfranchisement [of salaries], and, although it concerns economics, we are not pleading the case of appetites, but that of the dignity and freedom of workers."[48] *L'Atelier* faced the challenge of finding a way to argue for higher salaries that would not seem self-interested. Its solution was the development of the male breadwinner image, which allowed workers to argue for increased salaries without appearing greedy or selfish. According to this argument, men required higher wages because they were responsible not only for themselves but for a family as well. Women's presumed inability to contribute in a meaningful financial way to the working-class family's well-being necessitated higher wages for men.

The development of the male-breadwinner argument, or family-wage argument, entailed a redefinition of male and female roles within both the workplace and the family, as well as a reconceptualization of the relationship of each sex to money and the marketplace. With its emphasis on the male wage earner and the economically dependent female, the male-breadwinner argument constituted a fairly radical departure from depictions of men and women as equally responsible for the well-being of the family and the community that appeared in the 1830s and persisted into the early 1840s. In particular, this argument depended upon a greater differentiation of gender roles than was manifested in early working-class writings.

Several factors may have made workers more aware of, and more willing to articulate, gender difference by the late 1840s. In the first place, changes in production practices often took on a gendered component. In the printing industry, the limited mechanization of the trade during the July Monarchy coincided with an increase in the number of women hired. Some of the new typesetting machines, such as the pianotype, which, as its name implies, resembled a piano, were designed specifically for women. Male workers associated the mechanization that cost some men their jobs with the entry of women into the trade. Likewise, in the clothing industries, the rise of confection and the greater importance of piecework were accompanied by a growing feminization of the trade. Printers and tailors, both very active in working-class politics and in the working-class press, were thus becoming increasingly aware of the importance of gender.

Ideological influences may have also played a role in sensitizing male workers to the role of gender in shaping political beliefs. From the very beginning, the Christian orientation of *L'Atelier* may have helped to explain its greater reluctance to argue, as did *La Ruche populaire*, for "equality between men and women."[49] On the other hand, the greater inclusion of women on the staff and in the pages of *La Ruche populaire* could be attributed in part to the participation of many of its contributors in the Saint-

Simonian movement. While each of these perspectives took a different view of female leadership, both made the difference between men and women a central component of their belief systems. As the working-class press faced increasing challenges from middle-class papers on the question of women's participation in both the marketplace and politics, gender difference was given more prominence in the arguments of both papers.

The issue of women's relationship to the marketplace through wage earning was treated differently by middle-class journalists and working-class feminists. Contributors to *La Femme libre* had argued that women needed wages in order to protect their sexual relationships from becoming economic transactions. Middle-class, and mostly male, journalists, on the other hand, over time paid less attention to the grisette's identity as a worker. Although this identity never completely disappeared, she was described less often in relation to a specific trade over the course of the 1840s. Instead, prominence was given to her relationship with the student to whom she "gave" herself without a hint of self-interest.

The diminishing importance of the grisette's identity as a worker and wage earner in popular literature may be a reflection of the influence of liberal political economists, who argued that the wages earned by women were "naturally" insufficient to support a family.[50] Political economists attempted to explain the disparity in men's and women's wages by arguing that this was a result of natural laws. Women's wages, they believed, were designed to act as "supplementary" income for the family economy; they were never meant to be the main source of economic support. Middle-class writers thus questioned the implication within the working-class press that men and women contributed equally to all areas of working-class life. *L'Atelier* in particular, which had several middle-class subscribers and was considered a "moderate" paper, entered from the beginning into a dialogue with bourgeois newspapers concerning women's work and women's public roles.[51]

Twice in 1841, writers for *L'Atelier* cited an article in the influential *Journal des débats* that had stated unequivocally that men alone should support the family. *Le Journal des débats* had linked low wages for workers, women's work, and the threat of revolution, writing, "as long as a worker does not gain a sufficient salary to meet his and his family's needs . . . the revolutionary volcano will remain active."[52] Writers for *L'Atelier* agreed with their bourgeois colleagues that the moral and economic condition of the woman worker was particularly troubling. At the same time, however, they did not automatically adopt the stance that women should be excluded from the workforce. While not all political economists adopted this position either, the author of this article in *Le Journal des débats* proposed the exclusion of women from the workforce as a means to limit competition that was bringing down wages. Rather than women's exclusion, however, *L'Atelier* advocated "agricultural colonization." *L'Atelier* called on "families of workers," both men and women alike, to leave the cities to pursue what *L'Atelier* believed would be a more productive, healthy, and moral lifestyle. In another article, *L'Atelier* argued that the problem of low salaries, for men as well as for women, could best be resolved by establishing a system of association; specifically, it proposed better education for women, higher wages, and the establishment of set tariffs for specific jobs as solutions.[53]

While *L'Atelier* did not agree with *Le Journal des débats* that the exclusion of women from the workforce was a measure sufficient to reestablish a decent wage level for men, the article in *Débats* raised what was to become a troubling issue for the writers of *L'Atelier*. The paper responded to the article by launching an investigation into women's work. It urged its readers to contribute what information they possessed, and published in the following months several articles on the topic.[54] In this way, special attention was drawn to the status of women within the working class.

This focus on women sometimes appeared to contradict the inclusive program of association. The difficulty of reconciling these two positions is evident in a December 1842 article on women's work that is worth quoting at length:

> One could improve the condition of women workers in calling them, with a few modifications, to the system of association, which we have explained several times and which we defend every day. We are persuaded that this would have positive results; however, we believe that the condition of women will not truly improve until male workers earn enough to support their families, as is only right [*comme cela est de toute justice*]; woman is so linked to man that the position of one can only improve with the position of the other; it is therefore necessary that the worker conquers his place, that he makes his true rights in society understood, and women can help him even in this work; our conviction is that we will only arrive at this mutual improvement through association.[55]

This paragraph reveals the difficulty workers experienced when attempting to reconcile the communal model of working-class life with an ethic of female domesticity. Slipping back and forth between the inclusion and the exclusion of women, the author ultimately seems to come down on the side of women's involvement in working-class life and politics. However, by singling out women as the group that best typified the problems of industrialization, *L'Atelier* laid the groundwork, however unintentionally, for the eventual acceptance of the idea that male and female workers should be treated differently.

Before arriving at the male-breadwinner argument, however, worker-journalists experimented with different family imagery. In the early 1840s, writers for the working-class press tended to place the issue of women's wages within the context of discussions concerning the overall organization of work; women were presented as only the most troubling instance of a problem with wages that affected all workers, male and female. Despite low wages, women workers were often depicted, in mid-decade, as going to heroic lengths to support a family. An 1845 article in *L'Atelier*, for example, told the story of Félicité D., who raised her own illegitimate child as well as two orphans all alone. Working day and night, eating little, never ill, Félicité finally seemed to have a chance for happiness when the father of her child returned. He demanded, however, that they abandon the two orphans. Rather than abandon the children, Félicité preferred to reject the offer of marriage and continue on her own. Perhaps influenced by the growth of the cult of Mary during the July Monarchy, *L'Atelier* presented this story as an example of the "treasures of heroism that God has placed in the heart of women, to whom he has destined the most noble and holy ministry that any of his creatures can hold in this world:—that of Mother!"[56]

This story and others like it dating from the middle of the decade celebrated the heroism of women who supported children on their own, emphasizing sacrifice and a dedication to the family. These women did not work in order to buy ball dresses and drink champagne, they worked to support their children. Like the grisette, heroic mothers were used to indicate the selflessness of the working class as a whole. Worker-journalists thus also used the image of female selflessness to argue for their own lack of self-interest. That these images were meant to resonate with middle-class readers seems evident, since workers specifically played with the image of the grisette in their articles. Coutant, for example, stated that "maternal love gives itself, it doesn't sell itself."[57] In the tale of Félicité D., the author first asserted a commonplace in regards to grisettes, that "they live on so little, . . . so little! . . . like the birds," and then corrected it: "But no, the comparison is false: birds sing . . . and you, you cry,——while your son is sleeping!"[58] In using the image of the grisette as a model for the heroic mother, workers sought to emphasize the nonvenality of the working class as a whole.

While this image certainly would have resonated with middle-class readers, its use was problematic for workers whose demands included not only higher wages but also a voice in the polity. While maternal sacrifice would remain a popular theme in working-class writings, lauding the ability of these women to support themselves and their children, even if only through heroic measures, did not add weight to arguments for higher wages. Such arguments instead echoed the criticisms of middle-class reformers who argued that worker immorality and an inability to budget, rather than low wages, were the causes of social problems. Furthermore, male workers often made a very poor showing in these stories, appearing most often as seducers and abandoners of women. Such images echoed many similar depictions of male workers in middle-class popular literature, which portrayed male workers as brutal drunkards and irresponsible louts. These stories thus reinforced middle-class perceptions that male workers were unworthy of a place in the French polity.

By the late 1840s, a new vision of the male worker was appearing in the working-class press. This worker was consistently portrayed as a responsible family man, whose willingness to sacrifice for his wife and children was compared to that of the soldier's commitment to serve his country. An 1847 article, for example, emphasized the heroism of a worker who exposed himself to industrial accidents in order to support his wife and children by comparing work to warfare: "—If I left, [the worker] said, this workshop because I run a risk, who would support my wife and children?—Heroic words! That go almost unnoticed, and that attest nonetheless to a force of love and courage at least equal to that of the soldier who fights valiantly for his country and dies on the field of battle."[59] By employing the image of the soldier, workers linked wage earning to sacrifice and duty rather than self-interest and pleasure.

This emphasis on male sacrifice was strengthened through an increasing insistence that women were unable to compete successfully in the marketplace. By portraying women as unable to earn a living wage, no matter how hard they tried, workers justified demands for higher wages for men as well as for women's exclusion from the workforce, an argument that became more popular by the end of the decade. Increasingly, women's role as mothers was invoked not to explain the heroic lengths to which women would go to support a family but rather to justify relegating women to the private sphere. Coutant, as a printer and writer for *La Ruche populaire,* was well aware of the way in which the mechanization of his trade was linked to the employment of women. He thus argued that women's maternal duties necessitated her withdrawal from the workforce, asking whether "a woman who is lactating and who receives insufficient and bad food, can without danger for her and her child give herself in hard work, for the most part in unhealthy workshops?" Coutant answered with a resounding no, and he "condemned absolutely" anything that might facilitate the mother working outside the home.[60]

By the end of the decade, women increasingly appeared as weak, victimized, and unable to earn a living wage in the pages of the working-class press. For example, an article published in September 1849 painted this picture of a female street merchant: "[She] is badly dressed; she covers herself with poor pieced-together rags, she has no shoes, she has no linen. Poor woman! . . .There is . . . a child on her cart, a tiny infant who sleeps in the open air, freezing in the rain or blinded by the dust, who is hungry and who pushes away the bit of hard bread he is given to suck, who is thirsty and finds nothing in the dried-up breast of his mother. Poor mother!"[61] Although the author assigned this woman a trade, her abject poverty and the hunger of her child implied that she could not support herself; indeed, she appeared as little more than a mendicant, waiting for the sympathy of passersby. By the late 1840s, female poverty was indeed on the rise in Paris, and such sights must have been increasingly common. This image was, however, more than a simple reporting of the reality of working women's lives in 1849; it was also an image meant to invoke sympathy in middle-class readers. This description played upon a rich repertoire of philanthropic imagery that emphasized the economic dependency of the poor—their utter inability to produce and manage wealth—as a means of rejecting their political and economic demands.[62]

While images depicting the inability of women workers to participate in the marketplace invited sympathy, male workers were portrayed as physically and morally unable to receive charity. Working-class writers thus rejected philanthropic imagery that tended to infantilize men, emphasizing instead their dignity and independence. The story of Bertrand, which appeared in L'Atelier, is interesting in this respect. When he lost his job, Bertrand was driven to begging on the streets in order to feed his wife and child. He found this so demeaning, however, that he fainted from shame when trying to address a passerby. The stories of Bertrand and of other heroic male workers thus illustrated the necessity of masculine participation in the marketplace. L'Atelier was critical of those who encouraged charity as a remedy to poverty: "That which we find detrimental, is that instead of taking time to organize work so as to cut the evil at its source and increase the dignity of the working class, time is spent organizing handouts that, once again, cannot heal the sore [of poverty], humiliate those who receive them, and degrade those who become accustomed to them."[63] L'Atelier rejected the helplessness implied by charity for men, and although they encouraged the notion that women were helpless, they

argued that male workers, not the state, the church, or middle-class philanthropists, were best suited to care for working-class women.

Both Saint-Simonian feminists and middle-class journalists imagined a
society in which both men and women would be able to free themselves,
to a certain extent, from concern with money and material goods. In contrast, writers for *L'Atelier* and *La Ruche populaire* came to argue by the
late 1840s that male participation in the market and female withdrawal
from the market were both equally necessary to the creation of a just and
virtuous social order. The central importance of the question of wages to
working-class writers meant that male workers were not able to celebrate
poverty or total economic disinterestedness without undermining their
own demands. By making wage earning the province of men, justified by
the economic dependency of women, workers were able to argue that
making money could in itself be seen as a sign of sacrifice to the greater
good.

Once this argument was in place, it could be used to justify not only
higher wages, but political recognition as well. By arguing that working-
class men, like their middle-class counterparts, could earn and manage
enough money to support their families, workers sought to cast off the
mantle of dependency that had been used to deny their political recognition. Writers for the working-class press thus increasingly emphasized
gender distinctions, and the dependency of women, in their arguments
for universal manhood suffrage. The author of an 1847 article on female
suffrage argued, for example, that while "it would be a million times absurd to think that the electoral body, composed solely of adult men, would
dream of passing laws prejudicial to women and children . . . , it is the
contrary of absurd, it is the truth even, justified by too long experience,
that if suffrage belongs only to one class it will abuse it in respect to
the excluded classes."[64] While the dependency of women justified their
exclusion from the polity, the independence of men demanded their
inclusion.

Just as arguments concerning female economic dependency could be
used to emphasize similarities with the middle class, they could also be
used to express class-based antagonism. The theme of female abandonment was thus often used to criticize the morals of the middle class.
While earlier accounts of victimized mothers often identified her seducer
as a worker, by the end of the decade the villain of choice was more commonly someone from the middle or upper classes, and very often a student. This moral tale was the workers' ending to the story of the grisette's
affair with the middle-class student. While he "fled the capital in order to

put on magisterial robes," the grisette, now a mother, was left to work day and night to support their illegitimate child.[65] Often in these stories a single male worker would meet the woman, take pity on her, and marry her. In this way, workers were portrayed as righting the wrongs of society through their willingness to take on the responsibility of supporting a wife and children.

During the 1840s, worker-journalists transformed the image of the male worker as drunken buffoon, kind-hearted child, or violent revolutionary, putting in its place the responsible and caring father and husband. In so doing, they recast their relationship to the market. Images of drunken and violent fathers who sold their children into prostitution implied that working-class men dealt with money in an irresponsible manner. Philanthropic imagery led readers to believe that working-class men were incapable of handling money, and representations of working-class men that presented them as violent revolutionaries warned that they had no respect for either private property or the nation's economic health, both of which were jeopardized during periods of revolutionary upheaval. The male breadwinner, on the other hand, was a working-class man who sought to make a living so as to support a wife and children. He mastered the market not in order to advance his own interest but rather to protect those who depended upon him, the weak and vulnerable.

This redefinition of the relationship of working-class men to the market necessitated a redefinition of that of working-class women as well. Whereas in the early part of the decade women were portrayed as active in work, the family, and politics, by the late 1840s women appeared almost exclusively as victimized and dependent mothers. In creating this new, highly gendered vision of working-class family life and in placing themselves at its head as breadwinner and protector, male workers were able to argue for their essential humanity, and thus for the right to be recognized as men and citizens. They were also able to argue for their right to produce and accumulate money (in the form of wages) and material goods. The desire to participate successfully in the marketplace, workers argued, was a male prerogative justified by the need to support a wife and children. This view that men and women related to the marketplace in very different ways would be challenged by a second wave of feminist writing during the revolution of 1848. However, the association between women's economic independence and revolution made by both feminists and their critics would serve to reinforce the usefulness of the highly gendered view of market relations developed by the working-class press.

Women's Work and the 1848 Revolution

In February 1848, revolution once again broke out in Paris. As Louis-Philippe and his government abandoned the capital, workers and middle-class republicans came together to proclaim the establishment of a Second Republic. Foremost among the actions taken by the new regime were the establishment of universal manhood suffrage and the declaration of the right to work. Joyous journalists, who like their male working-class counterparts had just gained the suffrage, emphasized their fraternity with working-class men through images of work. "Workers of Paris," proclaimed *Le Charivari* less than two weeks after the 1848 revolution, "we are workers like you, working at piece rates or a daily wage, at home or in the workshop called a newspaper."[66] Work and citizenship were to be the two pillars of identity in the new republican regime.

The concept of work had come to connote by the late 1840s a certain relationship to the marketplace. When men identified themselves as workers, they also implied their ability to negotiate successfully the pitfalls and temptations of the market so as to earn a living wage and support their family. The equation between work and citizenship implied a relationship to money that was increasingly believed to be outside the reach of women. In 1848, it was unclear whether the equation of work and citizenship would be made for women. The law that extended the suffrage to all the "French" (*tous les Français*) could apply to women as well as men, and the new government directed attention to both women's and men's work. However, when pressed to clarify its stance, the government denied women the vote and adopted a very narrow definition of appropriate work for women.

The feminist newspaper *La Voix des femmes*, founded by Eugénie Niboyet in March 1848, was born out of both exasperation with women's place in the republic and exultation over the promise of the new regime. Niboyet was joined by Jeanne Deroin and Suzanne Volquin of *La Femme libre*, as well as by Désirée Gay. Other women, such as Adèle Esquiros, wrote for the paper on an occasional basis, as did some men. Several of these women had backgrounds in journalism; the paper counted among its staff former contributors to *Le Conseiller des femmes* (Lyon), *L'Ami des familles*, *La Paix des deux mondes*, and *L'Avenir* (the last three, Paris).[67] While not all contributors were workers, issues of women's work received considerably more attention in this paper than they had in *La Femme libre*, written by women who identified themselves as workers. This emphasis on work was due in large part to the privileging of the concept of work and its link to citizenship by the late 1840s. By emphasizing women's identity as workers, *La Voix des femmes* staked a claim to women's right to inclusion in the polity. Although the masculine definition of work that had come to take a dominant place in French culture by 1848 would create problems for the paper's contributors, its writers rejected popular images that tended to define women as invalid or inferior workers in order to argue for women's political rights.

The background of several contributors to *La Voix des femmes* also contributed to the paper's focus on women's work. Many were active in organizing working-class women during the revolution, and several had ties to both the Saint-Simonian movement and to the early working-class movement. Jeanne Deroin and Suzanne Volquin had both been active Saint-Simoniennes, and Désirée Gay was one of the founding members of *L'Union,* an offshoot of *La Ruche populaire.* Even those not directly involved in the working-class movement had probably been exposed to the work of Flora Tristan or to female members of the worker-poet movement such as Reine Garde.[68] Contributors to *La Voix des femmes* thus shared in the general tendency, prominent in Parisian culture by 1848, to privilege work as a central aspect of identity. At the same time, however, images of women workers had tended over the course of the 1840s to become increasingly reductive. Ascertaining that "the question of work for women has been little understood until now," *La Voix des femmes* actively fought against images of women workers that emphasized their economic dependency.[69] They did this by including information concerning a diverse cross section of women's work in Paris; by allowing women to speak for themselves through articles, letters, and in the meetings of the *Club des femmes;* and by offering women alternative models of sacrifice and devotion.

Whereas *La Femme libre* had contained virtually no information regarding the concrete details of women's working lives, *La Voix des femmes* was very much concerned with reporting on and discussing the working conditions of Parisian women. From the going piece rate for a man's shirt to the reasons for conflict between merchants of the *halles* and street merchants, *La Voix des femmes* lived up to its name by providing an open forum for discussing women's work in Paris. With the establishment of the *Club des femmes,* contributors to the paper expanded the scope of this forum. Minutes to the club's meetings were often published in the paper; these minutes, articles written by a variety of contributors and numerous published letters gave voice to women in many different trades.

In reproducing some of the diversity of women's work in Paris, *La Voix des femmes* was presenting an image of women's work that had not been widely available to the general reading public since the publication of early accounts of the grisette. As such, it provided an antidote to the increasingly narrow view of women's work presented elsewhere. In a context in which women had been excluded from the vote in a regime that linked work and citizenship, this move had direct political implications. This was all the more true since contributors used discussions of women's work to argue against male control of women's lives. The paper's demand for a direct voice in politics, for example, was underscored by repeated assertions that women should have a direct voice in the management of the National Workshops, which were established by the government to relieve unemployment. One writer thus protested, "Women workers . . . do not want to complicate the government's task, but they want to be consulted in that which concerns them."[70] In making such a comment, the author implied that the inability of women to make a decent wage in the National Workshops did not stem from an inherently inferior relationship to the marketplace, but was the result of women not being allowed to participate freely in decisions concerning their working conditions and wages.

Much like male workers of the 1840s, contributors to *La Voix des femmes* presented the question of wages as central to the creation of a just and moral society. In a letter to the paper, a contributor who signed herself "P. G., *ouvrière*," invoked the image of the poor working girl forced into prostitution because of low wages: "A poor young girl struggles at length against misery, she holds fast against the seductions that surround her; but the day comes when she has no work, and not having been able to put anything aside during the busy season . . . she gives in to the demands of necessity, in accepting dishonor in order to hide her intolerable misery." Another writer, this time linking female poverty and popular unrest, used the image of the street merchant, "who, at all hours, under the pretext of selling matches or paper, pursues passersby with plaintive cries that become abusive if one gives [her] nothing."[71] These contributors adopted the strategy of *La Femme libre,* explaining female misery and crime by women's disadvantaged relationship to money and the marketplace. Higher wages for women, they implied, would remedy many of the capital's social ills. Thus rather than argue, as male working-class journalists had done, for male protection and economic support, contributors to *La Voix des femmes* maintained repeatedly that women needed to earn a living wage.

One of the solutions proposed by contributors to *La Voix des femmes* was for women to form associations. The editors supported, for example, the attempts of a group of women who gathered at the Vendôme column with the intention of marching on the Hôtel de Ville (city hall) and asking for the government's "protection" for their newly formed association. This "legion of young women from fifteen to thirty years of age, poor disinherited workers, who organized a community whose goal was the improvement of their condition" carried in its midst "a beautiful banner in the national colors upon which one read in golden letters this sole word: *Vésuviennes.*"[72] While the term "Vésuvienne" was frequently used to deride women's political and economic ambitions, these women chose it as an apt metaphor for the strength of women united in association. Jeanne Deroin in particular valued association as a means to raise women's wages; in *La Politique des femmes*, a paper she edited after *La Voix des femmes* folded, association would receive much greater emphasis.[73]

The close ties of Deroin and others to the working-class movement explain their support for association as a remedy for female poverty. And like their male contemporaries, the contributors to *La Voix des femmes* linked independent wage earning and political activity. Indeed, their numerous protests against women's double exclusion made this linkage even more explicit than it had been in the male working-class press of the 1840s. At the same time, contributors to *La Voix des femmes* faced the common problem of needing to justify their demands for higher wages and political inclusion by reference to a greater good. Like working-class men, they turned to the image of the soldier to do this.

In articles and letters published in *La Voix des femmes*, writers used the image of female soldiers to underscore women's varied contributions to the republic. In one article, the author told of a woman who brought dinner to her husband at his National Guard station. While he ate, she "took the rifle and acted as sentinel."[74] A letter recounted another woman's exploits during the February revolution: "Citizen Julie Brgniard [*sic*], a poor working woman, residing at 33 rue Coquillière, after having worked on the barricades of her street and those of the rue du Bouloy, went to the Palais National [Palais Royal], where there was furious fighting." She joined the battle, but soon noticed that a station containing fourteen national guardsmen was on fire. In the midst of opening the door to rescue the men within, she was shot in the hand. Still, she did not stop, but went to a first-aid station, where she spent two days and nights caring for others who were wounded. The author closed by emphasizing that it was a woman who did all this: "I thought that you might be so good as to publicize this story, which confers glory on our sex."[75]

Images of female soldiers implied women's willingness to sacrifice for the public good. In an April 16 article, one author spoke of the readiness of women workers, whom she referred to as "amazons of peace," to "come together, in numerous columns if necessary, in order to prove, by an energetic demonstration, that they also know how to devote themselves to the good of humanity." Through the use of such images, contributors hoped to prove that women were justified in demanding a public role. Images of armed struggle were so common that the paper noted in April 1848, "We've been asked if by the words[,] *rights of women,* we mean that each of us, *taking up a rifle,* will mount guard and patrol?"[76] The perceptive reader who asked the question no doubt realized that contributors to the paper used accounts of working women who risked their lives for the republic to illustrate women's lack of self-interest. Such images implied that women would adopt this same selflessness in questions of wages.

Working-class women needed higher wages to support their children, but what of middle-class women? Their devotion to the public good was illustrated through their desire to protect working-class women. Thus, for example, Niboyet attempted to diffuse criticism of the public and political role taken by writers for *La Voix des femmes* by insisting that they were engaged in helping women workers. To add extra weight to her argument, she used language of struggle and sacrifice: "France suffers, commerce is dying, and when we defend work, we are opposed with impudence and irony! What do we want, if not to do for women what justice and right do for humanity? What we ask for them is the right to live working."[77]

By invoking the slogan of the Lyonnais silk workers, "live working or die fighting," Niboyet underscored women's willingness to sacrifice their lives for a common cause. Yet Niboyet's insistence that working-class women needed the help and support of middle-class women tended to undermine arguments made elsewhere in the paper that the working woman was essentially independent. This ambiguity in *La Voix des femmes* concerning the relationship of working women to the market and politics indicates the difficulties feminists faced when attempting to create a "female breadwinner argument." Like male worker-journalists, Niboyet evoked the dependency of working-class women to attract sympathy and to justify demands for women's political and economic recognition. This would become a common tactic among middle-class feminists in the 1860s, who often introduced their demands for greater professional and educational opportunities for all women by employing images of weak and victimized working-class women. A good example is Julie-Victoire Daubié's prize-winning work *La Femme pauvre au dix-neuvième siècle* (1866).

Daubié, like male writers of both classes, drew upon images of working-class women to assert her authority and justify her demands. In her introductory comments, for example, Daubié evoked the vulnerability of working-class women to prostitution when she described "one of the *ouvrières* (working women) who says she has been brutalized by misery, because she tried in vain to live on her wages the same way others lived in shame." However, unlike contributors to *La Femme libre,* Daubié implied that such women needed protection to improve their situation. She thus wrote that the woman worker "lifted up her crestfallen head: the serenity of hope shone on her forehead and sparkled in an eye dulled by late nights and tears, when I told her that powerful protectors had arisen to defend our cause."[78] In this passage, Daubié implied both that the working woman and she were similar (referring to "our cause") and that she was among the powerful protectors bringing the poor woman the good news of a better future. While it lends moral legitimacy to Daubié's cause, this depiction of working-class women implies that they cannot improve their situation on their own. This same ambiguity was reflected in Niboyet's comments in *La Voix des femmes.*

Like their male counterparts, middle-class women may have used images of dependent working-class women because it allowed them to argue for a greater public role and wider opportunities on a basis other than that of self-interest. Working-class women, on the other hand, were increasingly unable to make such arguments without risking charges that they either usurped men's position as breadwinners or that, as single mothers, they were immoral. Working-class women could only make the argument that their efforts were necessary for the protection of society as a whole, rather than their husbands or children. This explains the enormous popularity of military images in *La Voix des femmes.*

Just as male workers had argued for a linkage between the wage earner, the soldier, and the citizen, so too contributors to *La Voix des femmes* portrayed women's activism in one realm—that of defending the republic—as justification for her recognition in the other two. However, whereas male workers maintained that the pursuit of higher wages was a noble and righteous cause because it was carried out in the name of weak and dependent women, women's assertion of their status as independent breadwinners seemed to many to imply a reversal of gender roles.

When contributors to *La Voix des femmes* used military metaphors to emphasize their willingness to take action to defend the republic, they raised concerns regarding the role of women in public. They attempted to avoid this danger by arguing that the revolution had not done away with "femininity," but had encouraged its redefinition. According to Amélie Praï, "the citizeness is less like the elegant and gracious French woman than the simple and austere Spartiate; and without renouncing that which harmonizes so well with women's nature, elegance and grace, we ought to henceforth turn our intelligence and our abilities toward a serious and moral end."[79] However, to assert in 1848 a woman's role as citizen was implicitly to assert her role as primary breadwinner and head of household. Critics of *La Voix des femmes* seized upon this image of the domestic world turned upside down. Revealing the linkage between women's wage work and their revolutionary political demands, critics focused in particular on the image of the Vésuvienne.

According to Laura Strumingher, the term "Vésuvienne" was first used by a chemist named Daniel Borme, who was taken with the use of military images in *La Voix des femmes*. In a wall placard that appeared in Paris in early March 1848, Borme called for the formation of a legion of unmarried female soldiers.[80] Male journalists and caricaturists quickly seized upon the image of the Vésuvienne, whom they assimilated to the *lorette*, or courtesan. The Vésuvienne of the caricaturists was portrayed as part of a female legion formed to keep men in their place. Rather than sacrificing for the new republic, the Vésuvienne was shown as profiting from the confusion caused by political upheaval to abandon her family and responsibilities. In one of Edouard de Beaumont's drawings of Vésuviennes that appeared in *Le Charivari,* the Vésuvienne was shown, in masculine dress and armed with a rifle, making a gesture of derision toward her (presumed) husband, left at home in his dressing gown with two small children. Yet although husbands in these illustrations took on sole responsibility for household chores, Vésuvienne wives were not depicted as selfless and dedicated breadwinners. Rather, other illustrations informed the public regarding the activities of the Vésuviennes outside the home: they played cards, lounged about, and harassed those bourgeois who in earlier days (when they were courtesans) would have been their lovers. In their illustrations, critics implied that Vésuviennes did not engage in any form of productive labor; instead they skirted dangerously close to the world of prostitution. Their ambiguous financial status, like their attitude toward the family, indicated their immorality.

Through images that linked women's military service with selfishness, frivolity, aggression, and prostitution, opponents of women's rights undermined the use of military metaphors to connote women's ability and willingness to sacrifice for the public good. Furthermore, the role reversal within the household of the Vésuvienne and her husband soon came to be identified with the upheaval of the revolution and, for middle-class writers, with the dissolution of social boundaries.

By linking women's economic status and women's political action, contributors to *La Voix des femmes* as well as their critics associated revolution with women's participation in the marketplace. As revolutionary unrest continued, sapping public confidence, attacks against women's demands escalated. With growing frequency, male writers called for women's retreat into the domestic sphere as a way to restore order. In an article published in *La Liberté*, for example, the author condemned the emancipation of women by arguing that a woman who was obedient, silent, and devoted was "much more attractive than the woman-elector, the woman-national guard, the woman-discourse, the woman misunderstood and in revolt."[81] Each attempt by *La Voix des femmes* to argue that the proclamation of universal rights with the February revolution mandated the political and economic inclusion of women was met by a response designed to reinforce gender distinctions and silence women. When Jeanne Deroin wrote a letter of protest to *La Liberté*, the paper refused to print it, out of "respect" for her as a woman. Such strategies sought to silence women by associating them with traits such as obedience, devotion, and dependence (traits that many wished an increasingly unruly populace would embrace as well). Repeated attacks against *La Voix des femmes* and the cause of women's rights thus served to establish limits to the radicalism of the Second Republic. A contributor to *La Voix des femmes* emphasized this policing function when she stated, "the time of terror has passed; the torture of our days is sarcasm."[82]

"To sing the Marseillaise, to plant trees of liberty, to vote in elections, to discuss in clubs or at the Constituent Assembly, and to let your wives become bored at home, this is their republic."[83] By the end of April, it was already evident to many contributors to *La Voix des femmes* that women's place within the new republic was going to be in the home. In the early 1830s, the romantic preoccupation with a utopian vision of a society free from market relations had allowed writers for *La Femme libre* to associate femininity with virtue and selflessness so as to argue for women's economic independence. In contrast, contributors to *La Voix des femmes* were writing at a time when female difference had increasingly come to be associated with passivity and economic dependency. Although these writers attempted to offer an alternative understanding of women's relationship to money, their efforts were perceived as upsetting a gendered balance that denoted the marketplace, and the political arena, as a masculine domain.

Given the attention to work in general, and to women's work in particular, during the 1848 revolution, the image of the woman worker became a prime arena for the reimposition of both gender and class difference following the government's brutal suppression of the June 1848 workers' uprising.[84] With its emphasis on passivity, the image of the economically dependent woman worker took on new allure in the second half of the nineteenth century. The *ouvrière*, as she was most commonly called, largely replaced earlier images of active, self-sufficient, and independent working-class women, such as the grisette.

In popular literature destined for the middle-class, this transition was striking. Early portrayals of the grisette assumed that she could support herself on her wages (however low those wages might have been), and the association between different types of grisettes and different trades was very strong. In Ernest Desprez's 1832 text, for example, the grisette was, "a metal-burnisher, book-binder, chamois-leather dresser, ornamenter, laundress, glove-maker, lace-maker, dyer, rug-maker, haberdasher, toy-maker, breeches-maker, vest-maker, linen-maker, flower-maker."[85] His list continues, naming thirty-nine possible professions in all and concluding that there were doubtless more that were unknown to him. During the 1840s, grisettes were less frequently associated with specific trades; more often they were shown doing a little sewing at home while their student-lover was away (or asleep on the nearby couch). In general, as the grisette's association with the student grew in importance, her identification with a specific trade diminished. Nonetheless, even during the 1840s, some authors identified the grisette as the primary breadwinner; her willingness to support her lover financially was, for these authors, one more sign of her devotion. By the end of the decade, however, the grisette's wage-earning ability began to be seen as dangerous, and she was increasingly associated with prostitution. In Alfred Delvau's *Grandeur et décadence des grisettes,* written on the eve of the 1848 revolution, the grisette "has nothing left of what made her a woman, except the body that she offers—in exchange for a salary—to each passerby who wishes to grant himself the pleasure of spitting upon her."[86]

This association of the grisette with prostitution continued to appear in popular literature written during the Second Empire. Other authors, however, transformed the grisette into the virtuous ouvrière. Indeed, while serious doubts would remain throughout the century regarding the ability of male workers to resist the pull of self-interest, the gendered model developed in the working-class press—in which men participated in the market in order to protect women from market forces—would become widely accepted throughout French society during the Second Empire. New images of working-class women in middle-class writings reveal the influence of this model, as throughout the 1860s the ouvrière replaced the grisette in the literature on Paris as the prototype of female virtue. Thus in 1866 former police commissioner Eugène Bruncamp wrote, "We saw Lisette [a common name for a grisette] become a wife and mother, and she was an attentive wife and courageous mother."[87] In an 1865 work, the

writer Henry de Kock, whose father was famous for his depictions of grisettes, wrote that the grisette of old had become either a prostitute or a
virtuous ouvrière.[88] Novelist Maximillien Perrin published several books
whose heroine was the new grisette/ouvrière. The heroine of his 1861
novel, *La Fleur des grisettes*, was a seamstress who worked at home, going
out only to pick up or deliver her work. She was kind, selfless, and a hard
worker.[89] Unlike the carefree grisette, she was often saddened by her life;
like the female victims in the working-class press, she was shown crying,
weighed down by the difficulty and monotony of her existence. In the end,
as in the moral tales in the pages of *L'Atelier*, the ouvrière was rescued
from despair by marriage. Once married, she gave up her work and devoted herself to home and family.

Although the ouvrière was, by definition, a worker, her work was not
financially remunerative. For reformers such as Jules Simon, who developed one of the most celebrated and influential portraits of the new
ouvrière, the low wages earned by women workers were proof that they
should retire to the domestic sphere. Like Parent-Duchâtelet before him,
Simon argued that women's low wages made them more vulnerable to
temptations, including prostitution, that could destroy them. Simon argued that to prevent attacks on their virtue, women needed to remain "isolated" in the home. While he stated that within the home, a little paying
work would not hurt a woman, he was vehement in his insistence that if
a woman earned as much as her husband, there would no longer be any
justification for his authority in the household, something Simon believed
to be indispensable. "It is necessary," Simon wrote, "that the head of the
family can exert the tutelary power granted him by God and nature." In
order to maintain women's position of dependency within the household,
Simon recommended that in addition to limiting their earnings, women
should not be allowed to enter into contracts or be involved in business
affairs in general.[90] For Simon, then, women's low wages and their withdrawal from the marketplace ensured the maintenance of masculine authority. Only in this way could the working class as a whole, and its women
in particular, retain its virtue. Reformers of the 1840s such as Villermé or
Frégier had proposed the segregation of work spaces by gender and the
inculcation of responsible financial habits as a solution to working-class
immorality. For Simon and his contemporaries of the 1860s, the ability of
the working class to retain its virtue depended upon the withdrawal of
women from all forms of public work, if not from remunerative work
altogether.

Belief in the vulnerability and dependency of woman workers could
serve as a springboard for the legal and economic emancipation of male

workers. At the same time, this belief also laid the groundwork for increased government intervention in working-class family life. During the Second Empire and beyond, concern for the working-class family was focused on images of weak and helpless women.[91] In the 1880s, when economic recession coincided with a fear of depopulation, the idea that the government should actively intervene in both the economy and in family life gained greater acceptance. The earliest policies of the nascent "welfare state" of the Third Republic addressed these two issues by focusing on the working woman, intervening in both her productive and her reproductive life. Ironically, these policies tended to weaken male authority in the working-class household by replacing, as provider and protector, the father with the state.[92]

The emphasis on female economic dependency and women's subsequent need for protection, whether on the part of the male worker or the state, served as a reassurance that women were somehow separate from the marketplace and could thus serve as guardians of those values and behavior most threatened by market culture. The need for such reassurance was especially strong following the revolution of 1848, and especially the bloody June Days, when the specter of a working class willing to destroy both private property and the nation's economic health frightened the middle classes.

Joan Scott has indicated how a study of Parisian industry undertaken by the Paris Chamber of Commerce reflected this sense of anxiety. The survey, published in 1849, repeatedly asserted that women's work was not "really" work but a cover for prostitution.[93] At the same time, the survey attempted to reassure readers by demonstrating the insignificance of women's work and by exaggerating the extent to which Parisian industry was organized by sex. In the introduction to this report, the authors presented an image of women's work that their own statistics largely contradicted: "men are employed," they wrote, "almost exclusively in construction, leather, metals, mechanics and ironmongery. Women left in the family interior and employed or occupied by housework [travaux de ménage] naturally escape the industrial inventory."[94] Despite this attestation that women did not participate in the labor market, even a cursory examination of the survey reveals that Desprez's description of the extent and variety of women's work in Paris was still largely accurate for the late 1840s.[95] The authors of the Chamber of Commerce survey, however, tended to see women's wage work as a sign and symbol of social and political instability, and therefore attempted to disguise its presence.

This tendency to deny the importance and even possibility of women's work and women's wage earning could be discerned as early as the 1840s.

Before the mid-nineteenth century, however, women's work was not perceived as threatening or dangerous, but was considered instead as an inevitable and necessary part of women's lives. The 1848 revolution, during
which participants discussed the link between work and citizenship in the
context of social and economic upheaval, seems to have served as a turning point in public attitudes regarding women's work and women's wage
earning. The politicization of women's work in 1848 made it difficult subsequently to separate the question of women's wage earning from the
major political and social debates with which it had become entwined.

Ironically, the denigration of women's work also indicated a new acceptance of the marketplace and its definition as a public and masculine
realm, participation in which was not only necessary for survival but was
linked to one's status as a citizen. The redefinition of the grisette as a
mother thus went hand in hand with the valorization of paternity in
French middle-class popular culture. Before 1848, an emphasis on paternity seems to have been more common in conservative discourses (especially those based in religion) than in liberal discourses, which tended to
stress individual achievement over any type of family-based model. Part
of this may be explained, as Lynn Hunt has argued, by a desire on the part
of liberals to reject the image of the father so as to imagine a society composed of (and represented by) male individuals.[96] During the July Monarchy, the bachelor, in the image of the student or the journalist as urban
observer (the *flâneur*), was the prototype of the liberal male. However, as
middle-class writers became more concerned following the uprising of
June 1848 with the consequences of equality, familial images became
more attractive to them.[97] The common usage during the Second Empire
of images of victimized mothers and protective fathers created a discur-
sive meeting ground between working- and middle-class writers and readers, while debates concerning the class identity of both the ouvrière's vic-
timizer and her rightful protector kept alive a certain measure of class
conflict.

The plight of the ouvrière became one of the most discussed issues in
the second half of the nineteenth century.[98] The ouvrière was defined by
her low wages, her isolation from the public sphere (she was most commonly portrayed at home), and her generally miserable outlook and de-
meanor. The ouvrière incarnated a number of trends developed since the
1830 revolution. As an unsuccessful participant in the marketplace, whose
"rightful" place was increasingly identified as the home, the ouvrière symbolized a sphere free from market relations. Her purity, selflessness, and
virtue were in fact said to depend on her distance from the marketplace
and her inability to produce economic wealth. While serving as a symbol

for public virtue and purity, the ouvrière also justified male participation in the market, since the alleviation of her condition was believed by most to depend upon the man's ability to compete successfully in the market-place and produce wealth. The ouvrière thus allowed for a reconciliation of the marketplace and its mores of competition and self-interest with concern for the public good, self-sacrifice, and devotion.

At the same time, the ouvrière's vulnerability, her precarious state, and her proximity to the world of prostitution served as reminders of how easily the market could invade all aspects of French society, how easily self-interest could overwhelm the public good. Protecting the ouvrière thus also meant protecting France's moral character in the face of an expanding market society and market culture. Paradoxically, then, while women as workers were increasingly portrayed as unable to earn a living from their labor, women as prostitutes were believed to possess the ability to unleash the corrupting influences of market forces on French society.

Repeated attempts to distinguish between the prostitute and the ouvrière in mid-nineteenth-century writings can be read as an attempt to create in French society a distinction between unfettered competition, perceived as a cause and consequence of social unrest, and a regulated liberalism that would promote order and economic growth concomitantly. The slippery boundary between the prostitute and the ouvrière thus served as a constant reminder of the fragility of social bonds designed to promote the public good and control self-interest. Following the unrest of the 1840s and the revolution of 1848, the need to reinforce these bonds was especially strong. In such a climate, women who worked in public spaces as well as women who worked in commerce became increasingly suspect. In the case of the female merchants of Paris, beliefs concerning the problematic relationship of women to the market encouraged the perception that popular urban space had to be controlled in order to avoid social unrest, or even, revolution.

THREE

Policing the Free Market

GENDER, CLASS, AND THE CONTROL OF URBAN SPACE

In the 1840s, mastery of the marketplace became an important theme in the creation of new social and political identities, as well as in the construction of new models of masculinity and femininity. With the revolution of 1848, female economic dependency served as a cornerstone of a new cross-class masculine alliance, manifested on the political scene by the establishment of universal manhood suffrage. Women's purported inability to participate successfully in the labor market, typified by the low wages of the ouvrière, justified, even necessitated, men's search for greater wealth. Consensus regarding female dependency could encourage unity between the classes. It could also, however, be used to justify the control and exclusion of the popular classes.

Despite the optimism of those who participated in the formation of the Second Republic, workers' power remained limited after 1848. Cultural unity and political recognition did not translate into social or economic equality. The principle of female dependency became a powerful tool used by authorities and elites to limit participation in the public sphere. Part of this public sphere was the urban landscape, which came to be considered a manifestation of the social order. During the nineteenth century, urban architecture, geography, and institutions were designed to support the growing dominance of the bourgeoisie by reflecting its worldview.[1] In Paris, repeated revolution and popular unrest as well as intermittent outbreaks of cholera, which hit the poor especially hard, served to increase middle-class awareness of working men and women in the capital.[2] During this time, police authorities, urban health experts, and middle-class journalists and writers expressed growing concern regarding the presence of the popular classes in public areas of the city. Just as assumptions concerning gender and money were important in the con-

struction of new social and political identities, they were also central to
the reorganization of urban spaces and institutions.

While those who study the renovation of Paris that occurred in the
mid-nineteenth century have offered different explanations of the motives
behind this massive undertaking, most agree that the result was a city
designed to reflect and support bourgeois dominance. As such, the city
could also be assumed to reflect bourgeois anxieties. One area of particular concern during this period was the effect of market culture on French
society. While the slow and steady accumulation of wealth through saving
was still a central component of the bourgeois ethic, members of the middle class were becoming increasingly aware that it was possible to make
money quickly and easily by engaging in speculation. The first widespread
and widely discussed opportunity to speculate since the failure of John
Law's system (which attempted to reduce government debt by allowing
investors to buy shares in banks and trading companies) in the eighteenth
century was intimately linked to the disposition of the urban landscape.
During the 1820s, a building boom in the northwestern section of the city
prompted a rapid rise in the cost of land as hardy entrepreneurs fought
each other to participate in the creation of new neighborhoods including
those of l'Europe, Poissonnière, and Saint-Georges. A banking and finance crisis that began in 1825 and worsened after 1827, when it was combined with a crisis in agricultural production, caused the bottom to fall out
of the real-estate market, leaving many builders with handfuls of empty
apartments. An even more visible manifestation of this crisis of speculation and overproduction were the unfinished building sites that dotted the
Parisian landscape until the early 1830s.[3] While the market eventually
recovered, this event heightened bourgeois anxiety regarding the effects
of the market. Coming as it did on the eve of the July Revolution, it served
to emphasize the dangers of the market to both individual wealth and public order.

The relationship between the urban landscape and the workings of the
marketplace remained a topic of concern throughout the July Monarchy
and into the Second Empire. Scholars have argued that urban renovation
during this period aimed in part at expanding middle-class wealth by creating a city designed to facilitate commerce. According to David Harvey,
changes to the capital during the Second Empire were part of "a phase of
striving for adjustment to a burgeoning and demanding capitalism."[4] On
a smaller scale, this was true for the July Monarchy as well. During this
period, the opening of new streets and widening of old streets allowed for
the rapid movement of goods and people throughout the capital; the creation of new shopping districts, characterized by arcades in the 1820s and

1830s and department stores by the 1850s, encouraged the growth and spread of a consumerist ethic; and the construction of railroads brought in tourists and shoppers and carried out goods to both the provinces and the colonies.[5]

Renovation did not, however, encourage the growth of all forms of commerce. A distinction between bourgeois commerce—characterized by the establishment of thoroughly enclosed boutiques, fixed prices, and a fashionable clientele—and popular commerce arose in the late eighteenth century.[6] During the nineteenth century, "bourgeois" commerce was encouraged and glorified as an agent and symbol of French civilization, while "popular" commerce was increasingly viewed as disruptive and dangerous. Bourgeois commerce was said to serve a public need and enrich the national economy, popular commerce was assumed to be ruled by an ethic of self-interest. Remaining areas of popular commerce such as the Palais Royal, the central food market of the *halles,* and the Temple market for used clothes became targets for renovators and popular writers, who depicted them as sites of fraud, prostitution, and insurrection. Street vendors, who for centuries had circulated throughout the capital selling their wares, also came under growing scrutiny. Popular commerce was depicted as the dark underside of the virtuous marketplace, whose nefarious influence continually threatened to erupt into the heart of bourgeois society. And just as gender was used by feminists, middle-class journalists, and male workers to indicate the difference between public good and private interest, so it was used to define the difference between popular and bourgeois commerce. Female merchants in particular were increasingly assumed to embody all the worst aspects of popular commerce; as such, they demanded special control.

While the presence of female ambulatory and street merchants in the city was a long-standing tradition, by the 1820s authorities and observers of public life began a process of questioning the suitability of their presence in public. Police and public health authorities, as well as writers and journalists, were increasingly concerned during the July Monarchy with the regulation of public commerce and the presence of women of the popular classes in the city's public spaces. Female merchants, at the intersection of these two main areas of concern, were suspected during these years of engaging in fraud, fomenting revolution, spreading disease, and corrupting the morals of others. Authorities responded to these fears by attempting, through regulation and renovation, to remove female merchants from public view. Police surveillance and regulation in the early part of the nineteenth century gave way by the 1850s to concerted attempts to "hide" merchants from public view through renovation of the city's primary markets.

The growing surveillance, increasing regulation, and eventual enclosure of female merchants mirrored that of another type of "public" woman, the prostitute. According to Michelle Perrot, the problematic place of women in the bourgeois public sphere, which she defines as both the realm of public opinion and the collection of rights and duties that constituted citizenship, created a tendency to conflate the woman in public with the *fille publique,* or prostitute. "The public man," Perrot writes, "eminent subject of the city, must embody its honor and virtue. The public woman constitutes its shame, the hidden area, dissimulated, nocturnal, a menial object, territory which one passes over, appropriated, without individuality."[7] By the mid-nineteenth century, such negative views of women in public constituted a staple of regulatory and medical discourses, even though women in public had not always been considered dangerous, immoral, or shameful. Increasingly, concern over the stability of the political order (expressed as a fear of revolution and popular unrest), unease with the growth of capitalism (demonstrated in suspicion of unregulated commercial transactions), and the influence of the ideology of domesticity (encouraged by a growing assumption of women's economic and physical dependency upon men) combined to problematize the presence of female merchants of the popular classes in the city's streets, markets, and open spaces.

In thinking about regulation and renovation, police and departmental authorities tended to imagine merchants in stereotypical terms, drawing much of their "knowledge" concerning female merchants from accepted notions regarding women's relationship to money and public life. At the same time, attempts to control the presence and actions of female merchants in public reinforced cultural attitudes. The physical alteration of the capital's landscape was thus accompanied by a change in perception regarding female merchants. As in the case of middle-class writers and working-class journalists, police and departmental authorities used, and transformed, images of women in their attempts to reorganize both the physical layout of the city and the public sphere it was meant to represent.

A "Scandalous Scene"

On the evening of 18 June 1841, at 8:30 P.M., two merchants in *nouveautés* and perfumes with stalls under the peristyles Valois at the Palais Royal started arguing. Adelaide Mazard, twenty-two years old and working as a sales girl (*fille de comptoir*) for another merchant, slapped Jeanne Jacquin, a former prostitute and now merchant at the Palais Royal, calling her "Whore, *Slut.*"[8] Jacquin, who also went by the name Rey, apparently yelled at Mazard, "You'll pay, Bitch! Whore!"[9] The Rousseau sisters, Virginie and Eleonore, who had stalls in the same area, came to the defense of Mazard and started yelling insults at Jacquin. A crowd, estimated by observers at somewhere between sixty and five hundred people, gathered around the women. Onlookers later said that respectable people had been shocked by this "immoral spectacle," although many young men in the crowd had egged the women on.[10] Eventually, the booing of the crowd and the arrival of officials charged with keeping order caused the merchants involved to close up shop and flee the scene, pursued by cries of "ah! ah!" coming from the crowd.[11]

This "scandalous scene," as the police inquiry labeled it, prompted an investigation into the activities and moral character of the thirty-one women working at stalls in the Montpensier and Valois peristyles of the Palais Royal. Police officials questioned those charged with maintaining order in the Palais Royal, other merchants, and the *concierges* of the buildings in which these women lived. This massive investigation, prompted by the public behavior of these women, was an attempt to prove that they were prostitutes and could therefore be expelled from the Palais Royal by virtue of police ordinances of 1 April 1829 and 7 January 1840.[12]

This police investigation into the activities of the Palais Royal merchants touches upon a variety of bourgeois fears and strategies for control when faced with an apparently disorderly popular commerce. Female merchants were feared because of their exceptional independence, their access to public knowledge, their presence in public, and their relationship to money. In response to such fears, observers and authorities redefined female merchants as either mendicants or prostitutes. By redefining what it meant to be a female merchant, authorities were able to justify measures designed to limit access to the trade of street vendor and remove merchants from public view. By recasting the relationship between women and money, authorities justified measures designed to control urban public space that might otherwise be considered violations of the principle of freedom of commerce.

Just as damage to both private property and the national economy was one of the most feared consequences of revolution, so too the fear of female merchants was part of a larger concern regarding the presence of the people in the capital. Disturbances that drew an agitated and vocal crowd, such as that caused by the merchants of the peristyles Valois, always possessed the potential of taking a more dangerous turn. Police ordinances regarding street merchants reveal a constant fear of popular unrest, which was often portrayed as a popular "invasion" of the city's streets and public spaces. This fear became especially evident after 1830. In October 1830, Prefect Girod de l'Ain justified measures designed to control the presence of street merchants by stating that "public thoroughfares are invaded daily at the most frequent points of the Capital by street merchants [*Marchandes Etalagistes*] who establish themselves without permission . . . ; as a result of this abuse, the freedom and safety of circulation are compromised at every moment."[13] Due to such concerns, public areas devoted to popular commerce such as the Palais Royal, the *halles*, or the Temple market were kept under close surveillance.[14]

As Girod de l'Ain's statement indicates, the belief that street merchants posed an obstacle to circulation was one of the greatest concerns of the police. While authorities rarely specified that by the term "circulation" they meant the movement of members of the middle class through the city, the literature on Paris and the Parisians clearly distinguished between bourgeois circulation and popular commerce. In an 1840 work, J. C. Maldan described the many obstacles popular commerce posed to the *flâneur*, arguing that the tendency of merchants to spread their wares out in streets and public spaces made middle-class movement throughout the city virtually impossible.[15] For Balzac, popular commerce was more than an annoyance, it was potentially dangerous, as this description of the Boulevard du Temple reveals: "In the evening, it is frighteningly animated. . . . Fifty open-air merchants sell food and furnish nourishment for the people. . . . It's the only place in Paris . . . where one can see the swarming populace in its rags that would astonish a painter, with its looks that would frighten a property owner!"[16]

As the quotation from Balzac indicates, observers and authorities expressed concern over the crowds that habitually gathered around merchants selling interesting or much needed items. Early nineteenth-century literature on Paris repeatedly warned newcomers to the city to keep track of their watches and other valuables when part of a public crowd so as to avoid being the victim of a pickpocket. Such warnings blurred the line between popular commerce and theft; police authorities also feared the possibility that congregations around merchants might quickly become public disturbances. The crowd surrounding the merchant thus became a source and symbol of danger, as well as a manifestation of the extreme instability of market values.[17]

Bourgeois circulation implied the efficient and rational flow of wealth throughout society; it was associated with middle-class mobility in both the city and society. The tendency of popular commerce to be situated in one place and to attract a crowd of customers and spectators, associated as it was with fears of fraud, theft, and insurrection, was seen as impeding the proper flow of commerce and endangering public wealth. In an attempt to minimize the perceived dangers of popular commerce, police authorities attempted to prevent popular gatherings around merchants. An 1830 regulation, for example, restricted merchants to areas with little foot traffic. Authorities also encouraged their agents to reprimand merchants who lingered too long in one spot; an 1851 ordinance stipulated: "Ambulatory merchants cannot remain standing [*stationner*] on any point of the public way, except for the time strictly necessary for the sale and delivery of merchandise."[18]

Regulations designed to limit public gatherings hurt the commercial interests of the merchant by separating him or her from his or her potential clientele. Such regulations could therefore be considered violations of the principle of freedom of commerce. Authorities grappled with this problem; one prefect even submitted proposed regulations to a lawyer to determine if they violated the free-market principle. Police authorities ultimately resolved this issue by distinguishing between the private interest (of the merchant) and the public good. In their ordinances, prefects repeatedly justified restrictions regarding the movements of merchants in the city by referring to the potential threat these merchants posed to public circulation. Such statements implied that the orderly movement of the public through the city, like the well-functioning market, had to be protected from the effects of disorderly "private" interests. As a police inspector wrote in an 1825 daily bulletin, "the sacrifice of a few unimportant [*légers*] private interests, of a few vicious habits will bring about a great improvement in the public way [*la voie publique*]."[19]

Private interest, as we have seen, was associated with revolution and vice; it was also associated with women. While police records indicate that there were approximately the same number of men and women working as street merchants, certain types of sales were almost invariably identified with one sex or the other. Flower sellers, for example, were always portrayed as female (by police as well as in popular literature), while chestnut merchants were usually assumed to be male. Fruit and vegetable merchants (*marchands des quatre saisons*) were almost always depicted as female, as were milk, oyster, and fish merchants. In addition to selling primary food items (as opposed to prepared foods), women were identified with the sale of women's clothing and hats as well as men's toiletries. What evidence there is indicates that these categories were often accurate, although there were exceptions. For example, according to tax surveys for the *halles,* fish and oyster merchants were female; however, judiciary records indicate that a number of men worked as fruit and vegetable merchants. Nevertheless, assumptions concerning the sex of merchants determined which merchants were targeted by police, as well as what arguments were used to justify the regulation of their commerce.

In general, regulations governing all sorts of merchants increased in the early nineteenth century. Merchants assumed to be female, however, such as milk and oyster merchants, were particularly affected by the increase in police surveillance and control. Both milk merchants and oyster merchants were actually removed from public view during this period. Fears regarding the exact nature of female commerce, the dangerous potential of female public gatherings, and mistrust of female economic power dictated the exclusion of these merchants, like those of the Palais Royal, from public areas of the city.

Repeated charges that milk merchants made excessive profits by watering down their milk rendered them particularly suspect. Such charges often appeared in the pages of the literature on Paris and the Parisians. An anonymous 1828 work, for example, contained a telling description of an early morning street scene: "You will first encounter milk merchants surrounded by a circle of gossips, who are too busy with the news of the neighborhood to notice that the cream resembles bad milk, and the milk whitened water."[20] The belief that milk merchants altered their wares took on a new dimension with the outbreak of cholera in 1832. At this time, the government, fearing that the disease was caused by contaminated food, warned people of the dangers of buying from street merchants. Rumors, such as that investigated by the Council of Public Health in 1841 that milk merchants were thickening their watered-down milk by mixing in brain matter from horses slain in the Montfaucon slaughterhouse, continued to cast suspicion on merchants.[21] In this context, the purported dishonesty of milk merchants took on a more sinister aspect.

Anxiety regarding the effects of market culture also heightened concern regarding this traditional association of milk merchants with fraud and contributed to a growing suspicion of their activities during the turbulent beginning of the July Monarchy. Such fears led authorities to issue repeated regulations designed to increase police control over merchants by restricting their sphere of activity. In a circular of 20 January 1832, for example, prefect of police Henri-Joseph Gisquet specified that no milk merchant would be allowed on the street after 10:00 A.M. Further restrictions on the public presence of milk merchants were issued under the prefect Gabriel Delessert. In a circular of 27 January 1837 he wrote, "in streets where the population is considerable, milk merchants are so close together that the circulation of passersby is hindered and public safety compromised."[22] Delessert noted that since his memo on this subject the previous fall, several agents had placed milk merchants "in the inside of properties," for example, under the arch of a *porte cochère*, the large arched doorways designed to allow carriages to enter and exit the courtyards of Parisian buildings. The prefect's recommendation to follow this example became an article of law in August 1837, when Delessert ordered that all milk merchants find places inside within three months.

Delessert justified his decision by emphasizing female vulnerability, stating that merchants henceforth "would have a shelter against abuses of the weather, and will no longer fear being harassed for either the hour of departure or for the fruit and other provisions that they might display." Milk merchants, however, did not respond favorably to the prefect's decision. As if to demonstrate that they needed neither protection nor shelter, milk merchants made their presence in the city unmistakable. Approximately two months after the decision to place all merchants in enclosed spaces, Delessert wrote, "I have been informed that since the milk merchants were informed that they can no longer remain on the public way, a fairly large number of them are circling in handcarts the area of their clients, whom they call with a trumpet or with cries."[23] With their actions, milk merchants demonstrated that police regulations hurt them by limiting access to their clients. By referring to female weakness and vulnerability, however, Delessert was able to sidestep the issue of restricting freedom of commerce, highlighting instead the milk merchants' supposed need for protection.

In addition to fraud, milk merchants were believed to engage in illicit forms of commerce, acting as clearinghouses for information that could corrupt other women and eventually lead them into prostitution. Writers expressed the fear that the crowds that gathered around female merchants were sources of moral contagion when, with their stories and jokes, the older, more experienced women exposed the younger and more innocent to tales of debauchery. As she listened to these stories, a young girl also risked being accosted by passersby seeking to seduce her. A moral tale written by Théodore de Banville in 1867 dramatically illustrated this danger. Lucille was sent by her mother one morning to buy milk: "she carries her four *sous* and the milk container in her right hand; her left hand picks up her skirts . . . the milk merchant is opposite, and it doesn't take long to cross the street. But what devil of a path did Lucille take . . . ? She doesn't remember very clearly, and there she is in a dressing-gown of quilted silk . . . , in an apartment hung with gilded paper."[24] Banville implies that Lucille had become a courtesan; in setting out to buy milk, she literally became a "public woman," or prostitute.

Likewise, in the case of merchants of the Palais Royal, witnesses cited their behavior as a group as proof of their moral corruption. According to a hairdresser asked to testify, "every morning, they seem to tell of their disorders of the night before; they burst into scandalous laughter. They run and play together in the Palais Royal. At other times they quarrel, hit each other, and call each other Wh[ore]." A tailor spoke of seeing "disgusting battles" between these women, where they would pull each other's hair and hit each other with "their feather dusters."[25] This witness's emphasis on "disgust" rather than fear or contempt when discussing the behavior of the merchants reflects a growing tendency to conceptualize urban issues in terms of public health. Already evident in the eighteenth century, the concern with public health became particularly acute following the cholera outbreak of 1832. Cholera hit the poor especially hard and was associated in the minds of contemporaries with revolution and popular unrest.[26] Eugène Roch wrote his two-volume *Paris malade* (published in 1832) with the goal of explaining how the cholera outbreak had given rise to "popular movements." His pessimistic ending linked the problem of public health with that of public order: "Ah! Paris! at last cured of the cholera, but on the brink of civil war: you are still very ill!"[27] Public health concerns were also used to condemn the presence of working women in public areas of the city. Thus the stories and information shared among women who congregated around female merchants was described as a sort of moral contagion. Similarly, contemporaries also believed that insubordination was easily spread from woman to woman. Many shared the belief, recorded by the author of an 1830 study of legislation concerning prostitution, that "the sensibility proper to [women] and their assembly in the same place bring forth excesses that outrage modesty and nature."[28]

Assumptions that gatherings of women in public tended to foster disease, disorder, and moral corruption were powerful incentives to controlling the presence of female merchants. A merchant's presumed ability to undermine the authority of the bourgeoisie by making her private knowledge public provided further incentive. Contemporaries repeatedly stated that gossip exchanged in gatherings of women included information concerning residents of the neighborhood. Domestic servants recounted the goings-on of their households at early morning get-togethers around the milk merchant and thereby exposed to public view the private lives of the neighborhood's wealthy and powerful. At the hub of networks of sociability and information, the milk merchant, like the laundress or female porter, was able to pass judgment on her social superiors by her access to their private behavior. Contemporaries believed that judgments made by neighborhood women could damage one's reputation, and by extension, one's public credit. In an article published in May 1870, writer Elie Frebault warned readers of this danger: "Unfortunate tenants, late paying your rent, tremble when you see your *concierge* and the woman who delivers bread talking on the steps . . . . Between the two of them, they have better knowledge than your banker, your notary, and your confessor of the budget of your income, your virtues, and your hardships; they'll tell you . . . within fifty *centimes* the amount of credit you could obtain."[29] Contemporaries argued that the propensity of merchant women to reveal their knowledge through comments to passersby regarding their appearance or reputation was threatening and immoral.

Such behavior helped condemn the merchants of the Palais Royal. A guardian testified that one of the Rousseau sisters called out to men walking by, "Say there, you, English, I like *goddems* [goddamns] a lot because they have money." A dealer in chessboards recounted the following anecdote: "One of these merchants, in my presence, bet her neighbor that she would call a *gentleman* of a respectable age and appearance, who was passing by at that moment, a *cuckold*, and effectively, she attacked [*apostropha*] this *gentleman* with these words: *You're a cuckold!* He shrugged his shoulders and walked on." The same witness stated that he had seen "ladies turn their head at the sight of this disgusting spectacle, and move rapidly away from this part of the Palais Royal as if from a site of infection."[30] Female merchants were described as spreading "private" information in the same way that they spread disease. Such accounts served to convince readers and authorities that female merchants acted out of self-interest; their supposed "commerce" consisted of a traffic in reputations and sex. Rather than contribute to the wealth and good of the whole, female merchants were believed to act as conduits for the disruptive aspects of market culture.

Authors of popular literature illustrated the power of a female merchant to attack the bourgeoisie in accounts of her frequent outbursts against the *flâneur*. These accounts linked the ability of women to damage the reputation of the *flâneur* to their aggressive quest for profits. Thus writers warned that potential clients who refused the merchant's asking price risked being assaulted by a stream of vulgar and degrading insults. Merchants at the Temple market for used clothes, for example, would reputedly reveal that the *flâneur*'s wardrobe consisted entirely of used clothes and that he didn't have a *sou* to his name if he refused their commercial advances. The fishwife of the *halles* had an especially bad reputation, shouting out insults to uncooperative clients in, according to an 1834 article, "an idiom that would make our teeth rattle if they were hit by these words of iron."[31] In these accounts, the dormant aggressiveness of female merchants became manifest with the initiation of an economic transaction, as the haggling over prices threatened to erupt into insubordination and rebellion. The uncertain value of the object in question, fixed only through a process of negotiation, symbolized in these anecdotes the instability of the social order.

Female merchants in these accounts typified the unruly effects of self-interest, as unregulated commerce was shown to pose a danger to the bourgeois consumer, threatening his economic power by cheating him or attacking his reputation, and thus his credit. The belief that consumer desire was dangerous, expressed by both middle- and working-class journalists, came through in accounts of the interaction between merchant and client in popular literature. Police authorities also feared this encounter, and the bargaining process that was still integral to the majority of commercial transactions at this time.[32] Prefect of police Delessert warned in his circulars of the potential disorder that commercial transactions could bring about. The problem, according to the prefect, was that the transaction was usually accompanied by a "more or less prolonged" argument between two people. He stated that it was the presence of buyer and seller engaged in debate, "in the midst of a public thoroughfare" that was the source of trouble, and he directed his agents to oppose this long-standing custom with "a constant vigilance."[33]

The bargaining process was considered dangerous when engaged in by women in part because it posed the potential of female aggressiveness. Authorities also worried that in the process of completing a commercial transaction, the object being negotiated might become the female merchant herself. At a time when money rather than land was increasingly considered the most important form of wealth, how money circulated, and through whose hands, became an issue of concern. By labeling female merchants prostitutes, authorities were able to justify regulations aimed at limiting their commerce and removing them from public view.

The case of the oyster merchant, or *écaillère*, provides a good example of this process. Oyster merchants were only one of a number of merchants that police authorities felt posed an undue obstacle to public circulation, yet they alone were targeted for removal from public areas. In 1825, prefect of police Delavaux decreed that oyster merchants would henceforth be permitted to ply their trade only inside the establishment of a *marchand de vin*. No such restrictions were issued concerning chestnut merchants or merchants of fried foods, whom police also identified as creating a public nuisance.

The particular targeting of oyster merchants was due to the long-standing link between these women and prostitution. In addition to being considered an aphrodisiac, oysters were a luxury product that was commonly associated with prostitution. Oysters and champagne were de rigueur at dinner parties with lorettes. Furthermore, since oysters were a luxury product, oyster merchants came into contact with a different type of clientele than did, for example, chestnut merchants. The oyster merchant, a stock character of popular literature, was commonly described in terms that highlighted her beauty and sexual availability. Edmond Texier, for example, wrote nostalgically in 1852 of the oyster merchant of the Restoration, exclaiming, "How many flaming passions and incandescent punches have been lit in her honor! But then she was young, pretty, and seductive: all of Paris hastened to see the *belle écaillère* of the Bastille."[34]

The transaction between the female oyster merchant and male bourgeois client was therefore dangerous because it presented an opportunity for prostitution. Delavaux may have been motivated by this fear when he decided to remove oyster merchants from public spaces. The prefect cited the wealth of oyster merchants as the reason for his decision, stating, "I am convinced that their commerce is lucrative enough to allow them to procure a boutique or any other type of situation, off the public thoroughfare, to continue. They are not indigent." But oyster merchants protested that they could not afford a boutique. Like most street merchants, they probably possessed very little capital. Delavaux's insistence on their supposed elevated revenues may have been based on the assumption that they had other sources of income, such as prostitution.[35]

This was certainly the assumption behind the investigation of the Palais Royal merchants since the moment of transaction between female merchants selling men's toiletries and bourgeois men also created an opportunity for prostitution. According to an inspector at the Palais Royal, these women who "call and pull to their counters men who pass by" were interested in selling not merchandise, but themselves. Another inspector said that the process of bargaining over items was no more than a "pretext" for setting price and rendezvous.[36] And, as with oyster merchants, authorities used unexplained revenues to help prove that these women were prostitutes. In his report of July 1841, the officer of the peace wrote, "the counter girls are not paid; they only come there to turn tricks [*faire des hommes*], but it is very difficult to catch them because they often change mistresses, and, when they get what they call a good client, they are not seen for a week."[37] As these examples reveal, fear of prostitution among female merchants was another manifestation of unease concerning unregulated economic transactions, as authorities wondered what it was that merchants were really selling, their wares or themselves. The growing tendency in popular literature to portray women as economically dependent and unable to earn a living wage raised further doubts about the merchant's commerce. Fear of female prostitution was thus closely related to the question of women's economic power.

Female merchants possessed an exceptional economic status that was based in law. By virtue of article 220 of the French Civil Code, female merchants had powers that no other married women in France possessed. "The wife, if she is a public trader, may, without the authority of her husband, bind herself for that which concerns her trade; and in the said case she binds also her husband, if there be a community between them."[38] Article 220 gave female merchants the right to buy and sell goods and to enter into contracts, rights denied to all other married women. In addition, their actions bound not only themselves, but their husbands as well. In almost all other cases concerning the relationship between husband and wife, the wife was subsumed under the husband's authority and identity. Female merchants thus occupied, by law, a status that granted them control of property and recognized them as individuals.

Mid-nineteenth-century contemporaries were not unaware of the exceptional situation of female merchants, as their frequent references to article 220 reveal. In their *Lettres sur Paris*, the Saint-Simonians Doin and Charton argued that "our commercial code seems to have given the signal for female emancipation."[39] In her short-lived *La Gazette des femmes,* Mme Poutret de Mauchamps argued that the special status of women in commerce justified their recognition as citizens. Arguing that "in commerce, women are useful, necessary, almost indispensable" and that women carried out their commercial tasks with "as much honesty, energy, order and economy" as anyone else, *La Gazette des femmes* demanded that women be recognized on the same basis as men in all legal and political documents.[40]

In celebrating the link between merchant women's exceptional legal status and women's possible recognition as citizens, these authors were in the minority. For most, the economic power of women was considered unusual at best, and dangerous at worst. A growing interest in women who were economically independent is evident in popular literature beginning in the 1840s. The popular stereotype of the lorette, a courtesan who will be discussed in chapter 4, symbolized for many the economic prowess of which women were capable. A whiz at managing money, the lorette of the 1840s supported her entire family. Like the prostitute of the streets with whom she was associated, the lorette's economic power made her, rather than her male lover, the primary breadwinner. At a time when the idea of female economic dependency was gaining in acceptance, the lorette's financial independence was increasingly used to symbolize her immorality and lack of respect for the social hierarchy.

During the 1850s, it became more common for authors of popular literature to identify the economic independence of female merchants as a source of danger. In the 1854 *Paris anecdote,* for example, Alexandre Privat d'Anglemont, journalist for the *Siècle,* argued that families of merchants and other female breadwinners were organized along a reversal of middle-class gendered lines: "Most men married to merchants or to steady workers do nothing, or almost nothing. They barely help their wives in her tasks; they spend their days in the bar."[41] This statement was meant as an indictment of working-class men, challenging their claims to responsibility and respectability.

D'Anglemont also targeted, through ridicule, the pretensions of women who claimed to be the sole supporters of their families. For this attack he chose a merchant of the *halles,* "Mother Brichard," who, at forty-five, was "fat, round, short, a sort of laboring cow, a workhorse. She is active, turbulent, always moving; she comes, goes, cries, denies, speaks, sings, works, all at once." Remarking that his readers might be "astonished that a woman alone could earn a living," d'Anglemont clearly, by his description of Mother Brichard, indicated that a truly "feminine" woman could not earn a living, at least not honestly.[42] The subtext of this passage was reinforced by d'Anglemont's choice to end with a description of prostitution around the *halles.* This time, he located disorder not in working-class men who shirked their rightful responsibilities but in the women who did not fit the norms of bourgeois respectability: "The honest worker on his way to work greets her [the prostitute] with jokes when passing by. The men are ashamed of these remarks; they are vaguely horrified by what they have done. But the women, on the contrary, seem proud of their abjection; they face scorn with head held high, and return joke for joke. The instinct for morality is completely destroyed in them. Of all beings in creation, woman is always the worst when she isn't the best."[43] The economic independence of female merchants, associated with immorality and disorder, was troubling to observers and authorities alike. In conflating women's economic independence with prostitution, authorities and observers were able to justify regulations that limited women's ability to earn a living.

The spatial independence of the female merchant—her ability to come and go as she pleased and to move about the city—was often portrayed in police reports as well as in fictional accounts as a counterpart to her economic independence, and both were used to "prove" that prostitution was her "true" profession. In the case of the merchants of the Palais Royal, the women were said to leave their counters regularly during the day; some, according to a hairdresser, left their post as many as "fifteen times a day." According to a guard, these types of actions were enough to suspect them of prostitution: "according to their comings and goings with the first passerby and their provocations, . . . they act, with few exceptions, like public women [*filles publiques*]."[44]

Despite testimonials given by most of the *concierges* where these women lived that they were not seen coming back to their lodgings at odd hours, either with men or alone, the police decided on 21 July that these women were prostitutes. As a result of this decision, a delegation was sent to arrest fourteen merchants at 4:30 A.M. on the fifth of August. After noting with whom they were found sleeping, the police brought the women to the dispensary to have them examined for venereal disease. Although none of them was infected, one was registered as a prostitute, another sent to St. Lazare, the women's prison, and three others put in a holding cell. The other women, despite the fact that no charges could be brought against them, were asked to "no longer appear at the counters of the galérie d'Orléans."[45]

The question of whether or not these women were acting as prostitutes is difficult to answer; probably some were and some were not. The prefect wrote that all the women concerned admitted that the men who came to their stalls were interested less in buying "necessary objects than in talking libertinage with them."[46] For some, like Marie-Florence Langlois, this talk led to action, as she stated when she asked to be registered as a prostitute in November 1842.[47] Others, however, even if registered, were no longer necessarily active. Jeanne Jacquin, one of the participants of the "scandalous scene" investigated by the police, petitioned the prefect following his decision. In her letter she expressed her desire to be taken off the registers (which seems to have been done) and explained, "in the hope of creating an honorable position she has used all she had and all her savings to buy merchandise, so as to be able to raise her family . . . the petitioner . . . is no longer young, is the mother of a family and would be the victim of the most false appearances."[48]

Jacquin was apparently given permission to remain at her counter, since she appeared for a second time in a police report dated 8 September 1845, again for fighting with another merchant. This time also arrests were made, but in addition the prefect recommended that the practice of renting out these stalls to women be stopped. A representative of the monarchy complained that they could not help but rent to "immoral" women, since "women who respect themselves would not wish to put themselves in evidence at the counters" and that the revenues lost by suppressing the counters altogether would amount to between ten and twelve thousand francs. Police officials replied, "It is not necessary to remove the counters, but to rent them exclusively to men." Women, the police concluded, should not be allowed to rent stalls that not only put them "in evidence in the midst of a continuous concourse of people" but also left them "free with their time and their person."[49]

As the case of the Palais Royal merchants illustrates, removing women from public view was the goal of many of these regulations. Charges of immorality, and especially prostitution, were used to do this. But removing all female merchants from public view was a utopian notion; by the very nature of their profession, merchants came into contact with the public. Furthermore, street merchants were a necessary component of the city's network of provisioning. Authorities could not completely eliminate street merchants in a city that did not contain enough markets to provision its expanding population.[50] In addition, the profession of street merchant seems to have been for many a source of temporary or supplemental income, especially during times of crisis, when the number of "casual" or unregulated street merchants tended to increase.[51] As Caussidière stated in 1848, Parisians, both men and women, seemed to consider it a right to sell on the streets to earn extra income.[52] The popular classes apparently wished to preserve their ability to participate in the marketplace on their own terms.

Given the impossibility of ridding the streets of merchants altogether, authorities and observers sought to control them by making them appear less threatening. This was done in part by associating the profession of merchant with mendicity. To this end, police authorities specified that permissions should be granted to only the old or infirm. For example, in the ordinance of 19 June 1830, it was specified that only those "whose age or infirmities have deprived them of all other means of providing for themselves" should be granted permission to sell on the street. In 1851, authorization was further restricted to the "deserving" poor; in a circular accompanying the October ordinance of that year, prefect F. Carlier stated that in the inevitable case of overdemand, preference should be given to those whose morality and "unhappy position" made them of special interest. Those who possessed "a notably turbulent character or with intemperate habits" were to be denied permission, as were "individuals professing demagogic principles."[53]

In emphasizing the charitable nature of public commerce, authorities implied that merchants were not active and successful participants in the marketplace; they were not producers of wealth, nor did they serve as nodes of economic exchange. Rather, they were passive recipients of bourgeois charity, economically dependent on the goodwill of others. The redefinition of merchants in public as a manifestation of municipal charity made them appear less threatening. This tendency occurred in the popular literature as well, as images of female merchants in the 1850s and 1860s emphasized their powerlessness and misery. In contrast to female merchants represented in the 1830s and 1840s, these women were not described talking to or looking at passersby; rather they were portrayed as looking down without speaking, some were even described as veiled. The brochure *Paris gagne-petit,* published in 1854, provides several examples of this trend. In one passage the author states, "Previously on the boulevards one saw . . . the pretty flower vendor; she lasted only a short while longer than the beautiful oyster vendor, whom the beautiful drink vendor had already preceded into the common grave of the forgotten. Flowers today are no longer anything more than a means of mendicity."[54]

Examining the actions of police authorities regarding street merchants within the context of a larger literature on female merchants indicates some of the fears and concerns felt by the bourgeoisie regarding popular commerce, fears that were expressed and resolved by emphasizing the gendered aspect of this commerce. The way in which these fears and concerns shaped the course of urban renovation can be seen in the case of the redesigning of the city's two largest popular markets, the *halles* and the Temple.

The Taming of the *Poissarde*

Le Ventre de Paris is Emile Zola's moral tale of the skinny versus the fat, set in the central food market, the *halles*. It was written in 1873. In the novel, the painter Claude introduces the protagonist, Florent, to the market space. As the two stroll through the market in the early morning, the market takes on shape and atmosphere for both Florent and the reader.

> They walked side by side, two comrades, stepping over baskets and vegetables. At the square on the rue Rambuteau were gigantic mounds of cauliflower, arranged in piles like musket balls, with a surprising regularity. The white and tender flesh of the cauliflower burst through the midst of great green leaves, like enormous roses, and the mounds resembled a series of bridal bouquets, lined up in a colossal garden. Claude stopped, uttering small cries of admiration.[55]

As this quote illustrates, it is a space of ordered abundance, where mounds of vegetables are carefully arranged and contained within neat rows. It is also a space of color and sensuality, identified with female nature as yet unsullied, although prominently displayed. It is a space through which the two men stroll (*flânent*), free from fear of contamination, dirt, or insult. The *halles* have been tamed, all is orderly; the merchants, like paintings, are there for the visual enjoyment of the male spectator.[56] Nature has been rendered harmless, serviceable, and attractive. As Claude, "in ecstasy," comments at the end of this first tour of the market, "It's famously beautiful all the same."[57]

Zola's *halles,* while still depicted as the pre-renovation market, did not exist in Paris of the July Monarchy. For the middle class, the *halles* of the 1830s, 1840s, and even 1850s was a space of fear, disorder, and unregulated female sexuality. Police authorities, urban planners, and middle-class journalists joined in creating both a renovated market (the material space) and a renovated merchant (as portrayed in popular literature) during this period. Driven by similar fears as those regarding street merchants and the merchants of the Palais Royal, these men created an image of the market as a space in which commerce was carefully controlled, and in which female merchants no longer posed a threat.

The *halles* had long been considered in need of renovation.[58] In 1811, Napoleon had expressed his desire to build a larger and more impressive central market. Continued population growth during the first half of the century, the popular insurrections of the early 1830s, and the first bout of cholera in 1832 lent urgency to the project of renovation. By the early 1830s, the market was identified as both a center of popular revolt and a breeding ground for disease. By 1840 the project was a top priority. According to a member of the municipal council, "the *halles* quarter, . . . unhealthy, badly built and crowded, is of a repulsive appearance . . . . No other point of Paris requires improvement with such urgency, under the triple goal of improving public health, beautification, and public security."[59]

In 1842 the municipal council established a committee to study the question of renovation. For nearly twelve years, members of the committee argued over various approaches to renovation, studying numerous plans and even commissioning a study of markets in other European countries. Their debates reveal disagreement over the role of popular commerce in the capital. Some members of the commission expressed concern that the continued presence of the popular classes in the center of the capital would encourage the movement of luxury commerce to the fashionable and growing western part of the city. The area around the *halles* would as a consequence be transformed into a homogeneously poor and working-class neighborhood, similar to that of the Arcis quarter, "with its obstacles to circulation that pose a danger to public safety."[60] Others argued that moving the market to the outskirts of the capital would cause undue hardship for the working men and women who depended on the *halles* for their provisions and could consequently give rise to popular unrest.

Eventually, most agreed that the problem was not so much the location of the *halles* as its appearance. In an 1842 report, the inspector-general of public weights and municipal taxes, Daniel, recommended that the market remain in the center of Paris, but that it be covered and enclosed.[61] The principle of an enclosed market, reproduced in all subsequent plans, was deemed "indispensable" in 1850.[62] After much deliberation, the prefect of the Seine, in conjunction with the *commission des halles* and the prefect of police, decided to leave the market in the center of Paris, but to enclose and renovate it. They hoped that in this way they could stop the flow of luxury commerce out of the area without causing undue hardship for the popular classes that resided in the center of the capital.[63] Expropriations of property around the old market began in 1848 and construction of the definitive new market commenced in 1854.[64] With six pavilions completed by 1867, the *halles* designed by Baltard became the prototype for covered markets throughout France.[65] In Paris, the market for used clothing and household goods, the Temple, was renovated along the lines of the *halles* in 1863 and much resembled it in appearance.[66]

Authorities discussed the practical motivations for renovation in terms of public order and the protection of commerce. Police officials invoked the dangers posed to shoppers and merchants alike by a food market that spilled into the city streets due to insufficient structures. Commercial practices in the *halles* were also said to be disorderly. Standards for weights and measures were unclear and not enforced, market spaces were shared by wholesale and retail merchants, and there existed few regulations concerning hygienic practices used to prepare and display perishable foods. Police authorities discussing these matters portrayed the *halles* as a chaotic and unhealthy space. When authorities turned their attention to the Temple market in the 1850s, similar complaints were made: the market was badly laid out; merchants moved between stalls located in the market space and shops on its periphery, rendering the boundaries of the market unclear; the market was dirty; the merchants were dishonest.

With their many complaints, police officials depicted the *halles* and Temple markets as sites of danger: physical danger (one risked being run over by carriages, poisoned by rotten fish, or made ill by old clothes) and also economic and moral danger. Fear of dishonesty among merchants revealed a mistrust of unregulated commerce and a worry that merchants, through unethical commercial practices, were sapping the bourgeoisie of its wealth.[67] In discussions of renovation, concern regarding the moral dangers posed by the market, indicated by references to prostitution and female aggressiveness, overlay all other concerns. The use of images of women to symbolize the physical, economic, and moral imperatives behind the projects justified the massive expense, considerable expropriation of property, and reconfiguration of the social and economic landscape of central Paris involved in renovating the markets.

Despite the fact that there were male merchants in the *halles*—largely, although not exclusively, in fresh meats and baked goods—as well as male workers (the burly *forts de la halle*, who carried heavy loads of merchandise), the *halles* was identified by contemporaries as a female space. Cadastral records indicate that the majority of merchants in the *halles* were women, but this identification of the market as "female" was also due to the influence of traditional depictions of popular commerce as primarily a female domain. Thus in popular literature from this time, the most frequent and colorful types used to represent popular commerce (including not only the *halles* but the Temple market for used clothing and street merchants as well) were female. The bold and opinionated fishwife, the alluring young flower seller, the mischievous merchant of fruits and vegetables, the shrewd merchant of used women's clothing—these were the stereotypes that peopled popular literature and popular consciousness. Moreover, the *halles*, due to the political importance of the *dames de la halle* under the Old Regime, was identified as a site of female power. The perception that merchants were opinionated, meddling, and troublesome women was continually reinforced during renovation, as it was overwhelmingly the female merchants who made their complaints and requests known to the police and departmental authorities, and even to the emperor himself.[68]

The language and images used to evoke the need for renovation of the *halles* relied heavily on overlapping references to nature, femininity, primitivism, and disease. Whereas bourgeois commerce was often touted as an agent of civilization and peace, popular commerce in the *halles* was portrayed as barbaric and aggressive. In his reports of the early 1830s, for example, Inspector-General Lenoir portrayed the *halles* as an unruly and primitive space, in which natural forces were out of control: "[A]s population growth increased the arrival [of provisions], the invasion of the streets extends in all directions—large vegetables that could formerly be contained in the rue de la Féronnerie, are at present occupying the rue Saint-Denis, . . . the rue Saint-Honoré is invaded as far as the rue du Roule . . . peas . . . can no longer be contained at the pointe Sainte Eustache . . . ; they are penetrating the rues Montmartre and Montorgueil."

Portraying the neighborhood of the *halles* as one under siege by vegetables, Lenoir employed the metaphor of invasion so often used to apply to street merchants. Nature also made its presence felt by the unrelenting effect of the elements: "Everywhere merchandise and provisions are without shelter and exposed to the inclemency of a climate where it rains 180 days of the year and where winters are often rigorous." Lenoir continued, linking the image of merchandise exposed to the cold and rain with one of unprotected women in public: "miserable women spend in this way seven or eight hours of the night, crouched in baskets next to their merchandise, huddled with cold or soaked to the bone; . . . there is always something better to do than to give them a shelter."[69]

The threatening force of nature, as embodied by invading vegetables or inclement weather, also manifested itself in the female merchants, whom Lenoir portrayed as having reverted to a state of primitivism. He thus described the women as "crouched" in their baskets, a verb that connoted a state closer to that of an animal than a human being. In addition, by placing the merchants within their baskets rather than next to the merchandise, Lenoir blurred the distinction between the woman and the goods she sold. Thus when we consider Lenoir's opening description of central Paris invaded by vegetables, the reader is implicitly led to imagine city streets "invaded" by hordes of primitive females. Lenoir significantly closed by asking for a structure to contain these women. Such a "shelter," he argued, would add both dignity and order to the capital.

In his report, Lenoir employed several images of merchant women that were common in the popular literature of the period. Journalists often portrayed these women as frightening and uncivilized beings. In his 1834 article, L. A. Berthaud talked about the "brutality" and "barbarism" of fish merchants, among whom, he wrote, "instinct exaggerates all movements, . . . their gestures are brusque, irregular, rugged like those of grimacing apes." For Berthaud, as for so many of his contemporaries, the central market was a "sewer," a site of disease and disorder where "women in rags . . . move through the sheds like worms through a cadaver."[70]

Journalists' descriptions of merchants focused most often on their language and behavior. Increasingly, the outspoken *poissarde* (fish merchant) was portrayed in these accounts as threatening, and the traditional role of merchant women as public and political actors was problematized. Under the Old Regime, the *dames de la halle*, a contingent of female merchants, had acted as the representatives of the people of Paris to the monarch and the aristocracy.[71] These women had played an important role during the Revolution as well, most noticeably in the October 1789 March on Versailles that brought the royal family back to Paris. In an 1825 work, the writer and journalist Montigny invoked the revolutionary heritage of the merchant women and complained that all efforts to get them to play a nonrevolutionary role had failed.[72] In 1840, another writer described the present merchants as descendants of those "historic viragos, known by the derisive name of the *dames de la halle.*" He continued, stating that the present-day merchant was "an abominable parody of the [female] sex. Every word she pronounces, every gesture she makes, offends. . . . If she's not as cynical as the unhappy creature of the street [the prostitute], she surpasses her perhaps in the rudeness of her manners."[73]

Authors focused on the supposed "debauchery" of the merchant's language and on her lack of respect for passersby. Thus the authors of these accounts reproduced scenes in which the protagonist was subjected to the insults of merchant women. In one such account, the author likened the insults of women to a successful artillery barrage, calling it a "machine-gunning [*mitraillade*] of filthy remarks, of obscene jokes, of cheers and curses that would make even soldiers run as fast as their legs could carry them."[74] According to Edmond Texier, when wandering through the Temple market if one refused the "enticements of these commercial sirens," one risked being followed by unflattering, even damaging remarks concerning one's appearance and fortune.[75] With their insults, the merchant women subjected the middle-class observer to ridicule, thereby attacking his reputation, and by extension, his creditworthiness. They also challenged his ability to wander uncontested through the public areas of the city. Insubordinate, disease ridden, and debauched, merchant women as portrayed in popular literature clearly demanded control.

Demands for the renovation of the market space increased in urgency following the 1848 revolution. In 1850, Antoine Senard, a Parisian lawyer who had been minister of the interior under Cavaignac, drafted a report concerning the need to renovate the market. In this text, moral arguments were given predominance, and the entire market area was targeted as a site of danger and disease: "There, . . . one finds in one place vileness and vice in their most disgusting forms; and in the days of trouble and public calamity, sedition is sure to find there formidable reinforcements."[76] In making such an argument, Senard was drawing on a wealth of literature describing the population of the area produced by journalists. For example, in his 1842 work, *La Grande ville,* the writer Paul de Kock gave an overview of some of the bars found in the area of the market, the most popular of which was patronized by "male and female thieves, stool pigeons, prostitutes and ex-offenders."[77] He emphasized that women were admitted in all these establishments and that they were common recruiting grounds for prostitution. The development of a discourse linking the market to female vice and prostitution made the apparent invasion of women in central Paris not only more explicit but also more threatening. At the same time, linking the female population of the market area to prostitution gave reformers a moral and hygienic justification for "cleaning up" the area. By targeting prostitution and disease, authorities were able to sidestep issues of social control through urban planning.

Similar concerns regarding the Temple began to appear in the 1840s, despite the fact that the market had been hailed as a model of cleanliness and order when it was opened in 1811. While police documents invoked fire danger and fear of popular insurrection as the reason for renovation, journalists portrayed the market and its mostly female merchants in terms similar to those used to describe the *halles*. Described as "four large sheds, somber, hideous, open to the winds," the market was a site of fear and disgust for bourgeois observers.[78] The Temple market was considered, in the words of one author, an "impure and repulsive bazaar, hideous receptacle of all pretentious and lying rags . . . warehouse of profound ruins and ephemeral splendors! in truth one needs courage to venture into its shadowy detours, at the angle of boutiques where harpies of small-scale commerce and sirens of secondhand are waiting."[79]

Renovation prompted debate over the proper venue for popular commerce. Whereas most argued that enclosure of the market spaces would help to control the dangers of the market, a few dissented. Architect and former inspector of public works Storez, for example, wrote in 1853 that the market should not be completely surrounded by walls since "in general, commerce requires public display."[80] Merchants echoed the concern expressed by Storez regarding the effect enclosure might have on sales. One of the several petitions sent to authorities by merchant women, in this case signed by eleven poultry merchants, asked explicitly that the market not be entirely hidden from public view: "Permit us, sir, to address one more prayer to you! Our desire would be that grills replace the walls surrounding each pavilion. Our commerce is all *Temptation,* please allow us this expression. One has no intention to buy, one passes by the market, notices such and such object for which one bargains and finishes by buying it. We do not want to lose this advantage that would disappear with the surrounding wall."[81]

Merchants of the Temple market, who also asked in an 1866 petition that the proposed wall of brick be replaced by a grill with frequent openings, invoked as well the importance of impulse buying on the part of passersby. According to these merchants, the success of their commerce depended upon being seen: "It is the unforeseen sale, the accidental, the fantasy of the passerby whose eye is caught by merchandise that he had no original intention to buy. . . . It is *chance*, that adds to *opportunity[;]* today, this type of sale is impossible."[82] Enclosing the market would harm the commercial interests of these merchants, just as relegating street merchants to less frequented areas hurt their business. In each case, however, authorities saw the demands of "order" taking precedence over the principle of freedom of commerce. The "temptation" the women of the *halles* spoke about was seen as dangerous when in an open and popular space. Authorities therefore aimed at reducing the perceived power of merchant women through mechanisms of enclosure, achieved through the actual structure of the markets and through isolation within the market itself.

Inside the markets, authorities focused on changing the layout of the stalls. In the Temple market, each stall was to be erected on fixed bases that would separate one stall from another, thus transforming it into a miniature "boutique." Such changes sought to render the traditional jumble of merchandise, merchants, and clients that characterized popular markets into a reproduction of a bourgeois shopping district, characterized by a series of separate shops. Although the principle of free competition seems to have been less important to most of the capital's merchants than that of mutual aid, bourgeois observers saw in this "confusion" another manifestation of their anxiety regarding the potential of laissez-faire ideology to confuse boundaries and categories. The compartmentalization and separation of stalls within the market thus became one of the guiding principles of renovation. When the company that contracted to construct the market, the Compagnie Fereire, proposed suppressing these partitions to cut costs, the prefect of police wrote that of all the proposed changes, this was the only one that was unacceptable, arguing, "the absence of [such structures] would singularly detract from the appearance, the cleanliness, and the uniformity of the market's galleries." He continued, linking order and regularity with the decreased visibility of the merchants and their merchandise, "It would, in effect, be impossible to maintain the merchants in the regularity of alignment that the bases oblige, each one would want . . . to place his merchandise the most in evidence so as to attract from afar the client's eye." This lack of regularity, he concluded, would result in "the most shocking disparities."[83]

Despite such measures, merchants at the Temple market were determined to retain control over their placement within the market so as to make themselves as visible as possible. Mignot, the inspector of the market, wrote to the prefect in May 1858 that merchants were refusing to occupy stalls on the second floor and that those on the ground floor with the greatest exposure to passersby were not numerous enough to contain all the merchants. Merchants preferred to retire rather than move to the second floor, where they believed the lack of visibility would ruin their commerce and "exhaust the few resources they have."[84]

In the *halles,* the use of fixed stall and counter space made divisions between the stalls less necessary; only in the poultry market were stalls separated by metal grates, at the request of the merchants themselves. Yet a general fear of enclosure and isolation seems to have led other merchants to believe that grates would be erected between their stalls. Repeatedly, merchants petitioned the police to remove the "proposed" separations. Despite assurances that they were not in the plans, a delegation of merchant women went to the Tuileries to present in person a petition to the emperor "against the supposed installation arrangements injurious to their commerce."[85]

Although grates were not used to separate the majority of the stalls in the renovated *halles,* assigned places were separated by "steps in iron and marble" that some merchants found to be too restrictive. In October 1857, a group of forty-six greenery merchants sent a petition to the prefect, asking that they be allowed control over the disposition of their places: "*Madames* [sic] the greenery merchants solicit from your benevolent bounty the favor to be able to arrange their places according to the needs of their commerce, as for many of them the steps in iron and marble . . . are more detrimental and constricting than useful."[86] The conflict over how the places were to be arranged and by what means they were to be separated was so disruptive that work was stopped on the market altogether in June 1856 by order of the prefect of the Seine.[87] Work was resumed shortly thereafter, yet merchant women continued to protest dispositions they saw as harmful to their livelihood.

Authorities thus attempted to replace the traditional disposition of stalls with one that more resembled the orderly and compartmentalized nature of bourgeois commerce. In this way, the perceived "confusion" of market life was replaced by an easily supervised layout of stalls and merchants. The new design for the market space addressed the fear of women in groups felt by so many bourgeois observers. By separating the stalls, market authorities also separated the merchants, making it more difficult for them to share information or to band together against a client. This new layout also addressed more generalized fears regarding the ability of laissez-faire principles to erase distinctions within society. Just as middle-class observers emphasized the "confusion" of working-class families to criticize the new economic principles, so too market authorities referred to the "confusion" of market life to justify measures that merchants clearly believed impinged upon their ability to compete for clients and sales.

The need to reinstate distinctions and boundaries within the market space also manifested itself in the redefinition of relationships between merchants and their assistants. While evidence suggests that merchants considered their assistants to be apprentices whose presence was necessary for the merchant's commercial success, market authorities interpreted the economic relationship between the two women, in the context of a public and popular commerce, as a sign of prostitution. Regulations attempted to limit the use of assistants and encourage their replacement with children, thus replacing the economic bond between the two women with one of love and kinship. Not surprisingly, these new regulations appeared within a context of a growing emphasis on female economic dependency.

In 1854, a regulation was issued for the Temple market that forbad merchants from allowing hired assistants to watch over their stalls in their absence.[88] In 1868, this regulation was extended to all public markets in Paris, including the *halles*. The decision was designed to prevent a practice that the police believed to be widespread: the subletting of stalls to people who did not have permission. Police authorities believed that merchants let their stalls while engaging in other forms of commerce elsewhere, and they stressed that the stall was not a business opportunity but was strictly personal. In addition, the practice of hiring workers was strongly discouraged. In the case of the Temple market, authorities opposed the hiring of young women assistants by implying that their real source of income was prostitution.

For authorities, the relationship between the older merchant and the younger assistant appeared dangerously similar to that between procuress and *fille publique*. This fear appears in written reports beginning in the 1840s and is part of a growing trend to associate all forms of female commerce with prostitution. Thus, for example, in an 1842 note to the prefect of police, the adjunct inspector-general of the Temple market wrote that agents of disorder in the market were "not the merchants themselves . . . but rather the salesgirls who are paid according to their greater or lesser degree of prettiness, of . . . shamelessness."[89] Fear of prostitution among assistants manifested itself as concern regarding the sales technique of *racolage*, literally "solicitation." Solicitation consisted of merchants calling out to or approaching passersby with flattering comments in order to attract customers. Repeated regulations, from the 1840s on, forbad the use of solicitation. The younger and, in the eyes of observers, more seductive assistants employed by merchants were those believed most likely to engage in solicitation and therefore most worrisome and in need of policing.

By targeting hired assistants, market authorities struck a blow at both the traditional system of apprenticeship and at merchant networks. That merchants considered their assistants apprentices is evident in an earlier petition from stallholders at the Temple market, which stated, "In our commerce, either to help us sell, or to act as guardians . . . over merchandise continually exposed for sale in a market that is not closed, we employ young people for wages, who are fed by us; and who will become later on *Marchandes* themselves; who will sell one day for themselves in the Market."[90] The use of hired assistants was part of a practice of mutual aid that governed market relations, described most eloquently by merchants in the Temple market who argued that they had "all and at every instant need for each other in their commerce."[91]

The eventual entry of assistants into the market as independent stallholders was made more difficult by an 1868 regulation that privileged the relationship between mothers and daughters in matters of succession. Prior to this date, merchants possessed by law the right to designate a niece or daughter to take over their commerce when they retired.[92] By custom, merchants often granted their stalls to members of an extended family, which could include assistants as well as blood relatives. In 1868, Prefect of the Seine Haussmann restricted succession to a merchant's daughter, who was required to have worked at the stall with her mother for two years prior to occupying it herself to be eligible.[93]

The progovernment newspaper, *Le Moniteur universel*, depicted the 1868 regulation as an agent of progress and modernization, identifying merchant control over the process of succession with the corrupt practices of privilege, monopoly, and female rule that for many characterized the Old Regime. The traditional practices, the newspaper argued, led to an "infeudation of places . . . for the profit of certain families, to the exclusion of all others, with rights of transmission from woman to woman, not only in the direct line, but also in collateral lines."[94] By modernization, however, *Le Moniteur* clearly did not mean the creation of a market compatible with the principles of a merit-based, free-market society. Rather, by reinforcing the daughter's right to succession, the administration sought to recreate the market as a "familial" rather than "commercial" space.

The desire to valorize family relationships in determining succession attests to the force of cultural assumptions concerning women's roles. By the 1850s, assumptions regarding women's economic dependency made it difficult for them to be considered as individuals competing in a free-market, merit-based society. Extended family networks, targeted as archaic remnants of the Old Regime, were thus replaced by the bourgeois nuclear family. Indeed, according to *Le Moniteur,* reinforcing nuclear family ties was one of the primary goals of the 1868 regulation. It argued that the regulation actually restored the right of daughters to succeed their mothers, a right that it falsely claimed had been lost under the earlier decree.[95]

Under the new regulations, merchants' assistants would henceforth be required to apply, like any outsider to the market, for permission to run a stall. In the meantime, the 1868 regulation required that merchants give market authorities the *livret,* a sort of passport necessary for employment in which notes about misconduct or money owed could be made of all hired assistants; the authorities thus rendered assistants employees, rather than apprentices, and brought them under their direct control. In addition the 1868 regulation made it clear that merchants could not sublet their stalls nor employ substitutes since these stalls were not personal property but were provisionally granted in order to provide a means of support. By extension, merchants were not independent entrepreneurs; they were recipients of charity.

As granting a stall came to be considered an act of charity, stallholders were redefined as weak and needy. While authorities rejected requests for stalls in the market based on extended or created family relationships after 1868, they were more receptive to petitioners who framed their demands in terms of charity. In her 1869 request, a sixty-one-year-old widow emphasized her physical weakness, "affected by weakened vision and neurological pains in the lower part of the body," and her economic dependency, "without resources and able to depend only on the help of her twenty-five-year-old daughter." Invoking herself the equation of market activity with charity—"she dares to hope that she will find favor in your eyes and that, always good and charitable, you will deign, Monsieur le Préfet, to grant her the only means of existence"—this widow was convened by market authorities and told to make a formal request for a stall in one of the pavilions.[96]

By separating the stalls in the *halles* and Temple markets and by targeting practices of succession and the use of assistants, police and market authorities attempted to isolate merchants from one another while at the same time emphasizing the importance of nuclear family ties. By redefining the work that women did in the city's markets as charity, authorities sought to redefine merchant women as economically dependent and strengthen their relationship to market authorities. Both approaches attempted to weaken or eradicate the strong bonds that united merchants and their assistants, and that made these markets tightly knit communities of work, family, and friendship. Fear of women in groups underlay much of this project of renovation and regulation, as did fear of women's independence and mobility.

In 1843, for example, the inspector of the Temple market argued that female merchants should not be able to look after each other's stalls, since when women got together "the purpose of their meeting is more often to recount their misconduct, than to meet business needs."[97] Reports noted the fights between women who looked after each other's stalls, and said that the mobility of the women who had others looking after their stalls was problematic since it was impossible to control them while not in the market space. In general, fear of the disruptive nature of popular commerce, especially when engaged in by women, shaped authorities' understanding of market life and influenced their strategies for policing and control.

Merchants protested these attempts to control their mobility and independence. A petition sent to the prefect in 1843 argued that being able to come and go and to interact with other merchants was a necessary part of the commerce of used clothes, which required "the ability to buy from others and then buy and sell among themselves."[98] As with merchants' defense of the use of replacements, the petition emphasized the importance of community and mutual aid for these merchants. Like the merchants of the Palais Royal, however, the combination of female mobility and independence was troubling to the police.

In the *halles* also, regulations were designed to decrease the mobility of merchants within the market space. In the plans for enclosing the open-air fruit and vegetable market, for example, merchants were no longer to be allowed to move about the market, but were assigned a fixed area of one meter squared in which they were to remain throughout the day.[99] In general, merchants were not to leave their stalls during the day for any reason whatsoever. These types of regulations were designed both to decrease the sociability of merchant women and to allow for more complete surveillance of their activities.

The general attempt to control the behavior of merchants was summed up in an 1865 police ordinance concerning public markets. This ordinance served to bring together in one piece of legislation many of the tendencies of regulations since the early part of the nineteenth century. The behavior of merchants was of great concern in this ordinance; it explicitly stated that the market space was to be a "moralized" space, where "any offense to good morals or public decency will be rigorously prosecuted before the competent authorities." In particular, it targeted what were often depicted in police reports as "female" modes of behavior: "It is strictly prohibited to trouble the order of the market . . . by brawls, quarrels, rows, cries, songs or games of any sort." Article 59 prohibited merchants from standing or sitting in passages, from calling clients to their stalls, or from announcing by cries the nature and price of merchandise. Relations between merchant and client were to be restricted to the moment of the commercial transaction alone; no longer were merchants able to call out to passersby with comments on behavior or appearance.[100] The market was henceforth to be an orderly place of business, where merchants stood ready to serve an equally "civilized" clientele of middle-class women.

Implementing these types of controls depended on silencing the merchant women. As the numerous petitions demonstrate, these women felt they had a right and a duty to inform police, municipal, and governmental authorities of their wishes and desires. By the 1850s, however, merchant women's claims to authority had lost much of their resonance. Growing acceptance of women's economic dependency—and certitude that controlling the market meant controlling women's relationship to commerce, exchange, and money—led police and other authorities to treat these women's complaints differently than they might have earlier. The physical and regulatory controls manifested in the actual market space were echoed in popular literature that, from the 1850s on, denied merchant women the power to shock or frighten. In 1856, Paul de Musset remarked upon a notable improvement in the language of the merchants: "She no longer speaks the *poissarde*'s catechism, and dirty words no longer leave her mouth at every turn."[101] Because of this, he added, bourgeois women no longer approached the market with terror, fearing insult. The domestication of the *poissarde* was linked in such accounts to a regulation of commerce that was meant to increase the safety and enjoyment of the consumer. No longer fearing fraud or attack, the consumer was free to stroll the market, to make or reject purchases according to his or her desires without fear of reprisal or injury.

Just as the renovated market was considered to have contained and controlled popular commerce, so too it was believed to have lost its potential for insurrection. At the same time that renovation began, writers started to deemphasize the importance of the merchant women's political role. A good example of this is the 1852 play, *La Dame de la halle,* in which the heroine, Françoise, renounces her traditional place in delegations of merchant women to noble or royal households. When a countess tries to buy her honor to separate Françoise from her son, Françoise, although angry, does not insult her in the traditional *poissarde* manner. Indeed, she tells the audience, "It's not my anger that I feared letting loose, but my pain . . . I didn't want to cry in front of her."[102] In refusing both her public role as representative of the people and the monetary advances of the countess, Françoise demonstrated that economic disinterest, feminine "sensibility," and withdrawal from the public sphere went hand in hand.

Perhaps the most telling example of the power of "masculine" expertise to control the economic transaction with the merchant, and thus the merchant herself, can be seen in the anecdote related by Edmond Texier in his 1852 *Tableau de Paris.* A young student of the Polytechnic school is wandering through the market one day when he comes upon a fish merchant. He argues with her over the price of a carp, and when he offers considerably less than she was asking, she begins insulting him. As she stops to catch her breath, the student jumps in with insults of his own that silence her forever: "Will you shut up, awful potassium hydrocyanide! Detestable chlorasotic acid! hideous logarithmic progression, terrifying hygrometer of Saussure, detestable hypotenuse squared, abominable parallelepiped!"[103] Faced with this barrage of scientific babble, the merchant is silenced, and openmouthed with shock, hands him the carp for free. In Texier's account, as in that of the men responsible for renovating the market, science triumphs over nature, and the merchants, as well as popular commerce, are brought under bourgeois control. Texier described this episode as the disappearance of the last *poissarde;* with her passing, Zola's market had arrived.

As renovation proceeded, contemporaries agreed that the "civilizing mission" undertaken by the city in regards to the *halles* was turning out to be a success.[104] For observers and commentators, there was no doubt that renovation had brought about a change in the character and population of this neighborhood, giving it a much more "bourgeois" tone. Louis Lazare, editor of *La Revue municipale,* wrote in 1858 that the opening of the newly renovated pavilions of the *halles* had been accompanied by a shift in the neighborhood's population, from primarily working class to "commercial and well-off."[105] And even critics of the empire, such as Emile Zola, henceforth identified the market as a "bourgeois" rather than popular space; in *Le Ventre de Paris,* the market was meant to symbolize not popular insurrection and disease but rather "the fattening of the bourgeois who humbled himself before the coup d'état and who amply profited."[106] And while complaints that the market was already too small, that merchandise and merchants had begun once again to block circulation by occupying the surrounding streets, began to reappear during the early Third Republic and would continue until the market was finally moved outside the city in 1969, the image of the merchants held by contemporaries seems to have been definitively altered. Observers seem to have unanimously agreed that, in renovating the market, "the *dames de la halle* themselves have been transformed into calm retailers, serious shopkeepers."[107]

Authorities and observers alike used a double-edged discourse concerning women and money to redefine the status of female merchants in the capital. Whether by portraying merchants as weak and dependent recipients of charity or as economically independent prostitutes, this discourse denied the viability of a virtuous female breadwinner. Women who claimed to support their families through hard work were depicted as either immoral or dishonest. While such conflicting representations make it extremely difficult, if not impossible, to determine the actual economic situation of the merchant women of Paris, they do reveal the intense anxiety felt by middle-class observers faced with evidence that women could support themselves and their families by working at a trade. This anxiety influenced the content of regulations concerning the newly renovated market, where every effort was made to render market life compatible with the norms of domestic ideology.

Underlying much of the fear of merchant women was a widespread mistrust of commerce, especially commerce engaged in by women and carried out in public. This fear became more pronounced as the image of the economically dependent woman gained acceptance in French culture. Images of women of the popular classes were used in a variety of contexts to explore the balance between private interest and public good, and to understand the workings of the market society that in its various manifestations—commercialization, industrialization, the growth of consumerism—was contributing to the political and social changes that were transforming French society. The problematic relationships between women, money, and public space exemplified by the regulation of merchant women also influenced contemporary attitudes toward an institution that was increasingly believed to define and dominate modern France: the stock market.

"The Prostitute." With head held high and arm akimbo, this prostitute openly circulates through Parisian urban space. The prostitute's freedom in public became a troubling topic in the mid-nineteenth century. Source: M. and Francis Girault, Les Abus de Paris *(1844). Photo courtesy of the Bibliothèque Nationale de France.*

In the 1840s, images of the grisette usually reflected her identity as a worker. This grisette, a delivery girl in the fashion trades, occupies public space, but her downcast eyes signify her "virtue." Source: Les Français peints par eux-memes (1841). Photo courtesy of the Bibliothèque Nationale de France.

"He Studies Law." By the early 1850s, the grisette was almost exclusively associated with the student. In this illustration, the student and the grisette appear in the window of an attic room in the Latin Quarter. Source: Bibliothèque Nationale, Cabinet d'Estampes. Photo courtesy of the Bibliothèque Nationale de France.

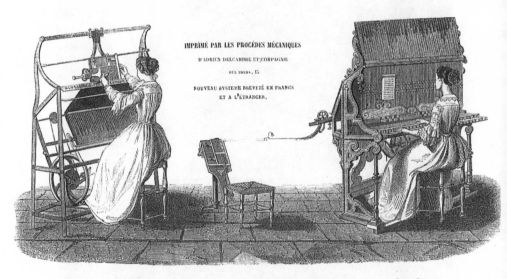

These typesetting machines designed especially for women "naturalized" women's work by associating it with stereotypically feminine activities. The use and promotion of such machines also made male workers more aware of the importance of gendered distinctions. Source: Frontispiece of Paris chez soi (1854). Photo courtesy of the Bibliothèque Nationale de France.

"Enough and for too long men have forced us to do nothing . . . it's becoming tiring!" This illustration, part of the "Women in Revolution" series published by the satirical periodical Le Charivari *following the 1848 revolution, mocks women's demands to be included as active workers and citizens by portraying their position as illogical: how could doing nothing become tiring? Photo courtesy of the Association pour la conservation et la reproduction photographique de la presse.*

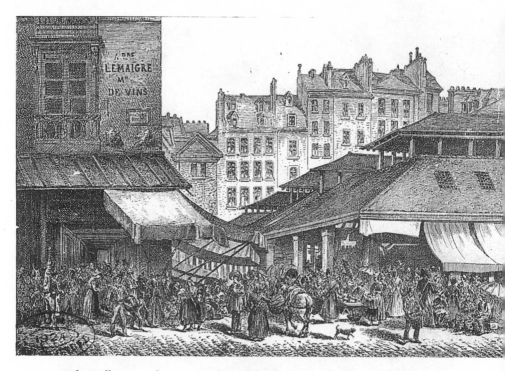

"The Halles centrales *in Paris during the Restoration." The crowded, busy central food market in the early nineteenth century, before renovation. Source: Bibliothèque Nationale, Cabinet d'Estampes. Photo courtesy of the Bibliothèque Nationale de France.*

The halles *after renovation, interior view. The new market resembles an orderly shopping district. Source: Bibliothèque Nationale, Cabinet d'Estampes. Photo courtesy of the Bibliothèque Nationale de France.*

This 1869 depiction of a street merchant is typical of the sorts of illustrations that portrayed street commerce as a form of mendicity. Source: L'Héritier, Les Mystères de la vie du monde, du demi-monde et du quart du monde. Vol. 2, Les Grisettes et les grisons (1869). Photo courtesy of the Bibliothèque Nationale de France.

"Female Gamblers in a Smoking Parlor." These fashionably dressed lorettes doubly invade male space: by gambling and by being present in a smoking parlor, a masculine space par excellence in the nineteenth century. *Source:* Physionomies Parisiennes: Les Joueuses (*1868*). *Photo courtesy of the Bibliothèque Nationale de France.*

"Interior View of the Stock Exchange." Before 1848, women were allowed in the second-floor galleries. Source: Bibliothèque Nationale, Cabinet d'Estampes. Photo Courtesy of the Bibliothèque Nationale de France.

"Braving the Remarks of Others." Female speculators outside the stock ex-change are unconcerned that others might unfavorably remark upon their "un-feminine" behavior. Source: Bibliothèque Nationale, Cabinet d'Estampes. Photo courtesy of the Bibliothèque Nationale de France.

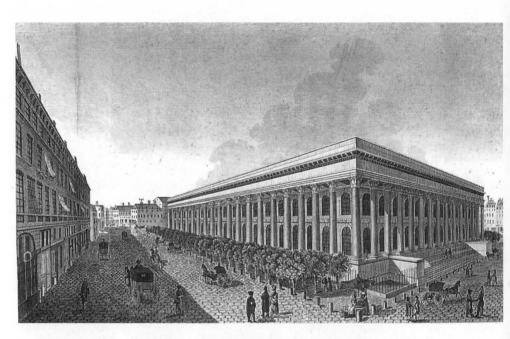

"View of the New Stock Exchange." This pre-1830 image of the stock exchange shows the tree-lined walkways on the two sides of the building. These walkways were fenced in during the Second Empire to prevent female speculators from illegally playing the market. Source: Bibliothèque Nationale, Cabinet d'Estampes. Photo courtesy of the Bibliothèque Nationale de France.

FOUR

The Lorette

SPECULATION AND THE
SOCIAL ORDER

Throughout the nineteenth century, critics of laissez-faire doctrines used images of women to discuss how to limit aspects of the market that they believed weakened social bonds. Self-interest, competition, a lack of regularity, and the blurring of distinctions and boundaries were all believed to be the result of the unfettered adoption of laissez-faire principles. The debate over whether the market could be rendered virtuous was especially heated when discussing the stock exchange.

Journalists had a lot to say on this matter because by the Second Empire the newspaper had become a lucrative investment vehicle. During this period, newspaper owners were involved with growing frequency in the world of high finance, looking to the stock market to increase the fortunes they made from the popular press. Many writers expressed concern that the intermingling of publishing and the stock market damaged publishing's integrity. As during the July Monarchy, however, journalists and writers were not concerned solely with their own professional status. The impact of the so-called democratization of the stock market, caused by an influx of modest investors, concerned them as well. Once again, images of women, and in particular that of an enormously popular female type, the lorette, were used to debate whether such an expanded and powerful market could also be virtuous.

The lorette, a courtesan, was created to discuss the impact of big capital and finance on French society. The lorette first appeared in the pages of the literature on Paris and the Parisians in 1841 and was from the beginning associated with credit and speculation. During the July Monarchy, the lorette was a transitional figure, used to discuss the shift from older networks of credit and investment (in which women could participate) to newer, more formalized (and exclusively masculine) institutions. During the Second Empire, when these new institutions had gained in acceptance, the lorette was used to discuss their impact on French society.

Writers and journalists during the Second Empire opposed the lorette to the grisette in order to comment upon the growing influence of big capital on their profession. While these writers often lamented the grisette's supposed disappearance at the hands of the lorette, their texts also reveal an acceptance of market forces that was not evident during the July Monarchy. These writers tended to associate the lorette with their exclusion from positions of power within the press, which they depicted as controlled by the wealthy and privileged few.

On the other hand, the lorette was also used to indicate fears regarding the "democratization of credit" during the Second Empire. Thus while some used the lorette to discuss the creation of new hierarchies within journalism, others used her image to discuss the supposed breakdown of social hierarchies brought about by the growth of the stock market and the passion for speculation that it was said to have inspired. Images of the lorette, like those of the common prostitute, were used to impose limitations on access to the stock market and the wealth that was created there. These limitations were established through regulations governing access to the stock exchange, the supervision and management of urban space in the neighborhood of the stock exchange, and the reinforcement of beliefs concerning the inappropriateness of women's participation in the marketplace. Tracing the multiple and changing images of the lorette during the mid-nineteenth century provides insight into the varied, and sometimes conflicting, views of what was rapidly becoming one of the defining institutions of Parisian life.

Speculating on One's Charms: Women and Credit in Popular Culture

During the July Monarchy, one of the transformations of French society that appeared most significant to contemporaries was the growing importance of the Paris stock market. The stock market was first established in 1724 as a means to control and prevent the unregulated speculation that had occurred under the financial system of John Law.[1] At its origin, the Paris stock market was devoted to the sale of *rentes,* or loans and annuities issued by the government; trading was carried out by *agents de change,* brokers who bought their office from the monarchy. Trading outside the hours of the market and speculation on the value of *rentes* was formally and repeatedly forbidden by law. For most of the eighteenth century, the stock market remained an institution of limited size. Moved

from site to site, it was not until 1825 that the exchange found its definitive home in the Palais Brongniart.

In the 1820s, the extension of the canal system and the development
of new residential neighborhoods in northwestern Paris resulted in speculative booms. However, it was the construction of the railroad system
during the July Monarchy that radically changed the nature and scope
of the Paris stock market. To finance their construction, the government
issued stock in the railroads that was available for sale on the Paris stock
exchange. With the announcement of the Paris–Saint-Germain line in
1835, investors flocked to the stock exchange, where shares of railroad
stock, along with those of numerous "chimerical" companies trying to
profit from the speculative fever, were available in denominations as low
as twenty francs.[2] Although illegal, speculation on the value of this stock
soon became rampant, and for the first time in over a century, people
began making considerable sums of money on the stock market. Speculative fever had not yet reached the majority of the French, but among
a certain segment of the middle class, the stock market was changing people's lives by allowing them to increase their fortunes rapidly. The possibility of becoming rich enough to move up the social ladder, to improve
one's standard of living, and to obtain the vote was attractive to those
members of the middle class increasingly drawn to this ever more powerful institution.

The new power of the stock market in French society was manifested
by the appearance in the literature on Paris and the Parisians of the figure of the speculator. Daumier's Robert Macaire and Monnier's Joseph
Prudhomme, both "quintessential con-[men]," were at different times
each identified as speculators.[3] However, the most consistent image of the
speculator during the mid-nineteenth century was a female image, that of
the lorette. In fact, the lorette was the most frequent stereotype associated with the stock market during the 1840s, 1850s, and 1860s. Associated with modernization, masculinity, and speculation, the lorette seemed
to embody, for good or for bad, the new mores and attitudes of a society
in search of easy money.

In 1841, the journalist Nestor Roqueplan coined a name for a female
figure that had been recently appearing in the popular literature on Paris
under diverse monikers. Roqueplan gave the title of "lorette" to the young
single woman who abandoned her working-class origins and attempted to
acquire wealth and position through her affairs with wealthy men. He
drew the name lorette from the neighborhood where he believed this type
of woman could be most easily found: the area around the church Notre-
Dame-de-Lorette. Roqueplan's choice of name immediately caught on,

and the lorette became a stock character in a variety of writings concerning Parisian life and institutions.

In many ways, the lorette seemed to embody the "new" Paris. The term "lorette" caught on as rapidly as it did in part due to Roqueplan's evocation, with this name, of a neighborhood associated with upward social and economic mobility, with speculation, and with modernization, all characteristics that were also associated with the lorette. While the grisette had prior to 1840 been placed primarily in the area from the Palais Royal to the rue Saint-Denis, traditional centers of the luxury trades, the lorette was said to have come into existence on the tails of a flurry of real-estate speculation. Writers thus placed her in the new residential sections in the northwestern area of the city, notably, as Roqueplan indicated, the neighborhoods of Notre-Dame-de-Lorette, Saint-George, and Breda, areas that had undergone a tremendous speculative boom in the 1820s. The lorette was thus identified with the shift in the center of luxury commerce and high finance from the center of Paris to the northwestern corner of the city that began in the final years of the Restoration and accelerated during the July Monarchy.

Popular legend had it that the first lorettes were the mistresses of landlords who, having overestimated the demand for new housing, had been unable to find tenants for their recently constructed apartment buildings. They thus allowed their mistresses to move in rent free until paying tenants could be found. According to Roqueplan, "chased from more serious neighborhoods, the more or less young women who devote themselves to ruining sons of [good] families flow toward these fantastical constructions . . . that form a kind of new city, from the end of the rue Lafitte to the rue Blanche, including rues Neuves-Saint-Georges, La Bruyère, Breda, and Navarin, and taking its name from the main street of *Notre-Dame-de-Lorette.*"[4] By the 1840s, this section of the city was the territory of the new financial elites of the July Monarchy, and it was from their ranks that the lorette was said to take her lovers. The lorette, whose lovers were, according to one description, "normally a stockholder, a moneylender, an old bachelor living on the debris of a fortune devoured by gambling," was from the outset identified with finance and speculation.[5]

The lorette was, by all indications, an unusual and independent character. Possessing little respect for the niceties of social intercourse or for the ranks of status and wealth that structured the social hierarchy, the lorette did exactly as she pleased. The lorette possessed freedoms shared by virtually no other woman; her unusual liberty was indicated by her penchant for masculine dress and masculine behavior.[6] According to Maurice Alhoy's 1841 *Physiologie,* the lorette "changes her sex, one would believe that she had worn a hat all her life, that she was born with boots. She twirls her cane, stops passersby who are smoking and lights her cigarette from theirs. At the theater, she invades the place of those who have gone out and puts in her pocket the glove they left to signal their return."[7] Perhaps drawing their inspiration from George Sand, another independent woman who used masculine dress as a means to enter into areas otherwise off-limits to women, July Monarchy writers frequently commented on the lorette's many masculine habits. Although no one would consider Sand a lorette, both she and the lorette captured the popular imagination for the apparent ease with which they crossed the boundaries between masculine and feminine behavior at a time when those boundaries were not as tightly drawn as they would be during the Second Empire.

Despite frequent identifications with masculine dress and behavior, the lorette also retained a fundamental femininity. Authors mocked her attempts to disguise herself with masculine dress, and illustrations of the lorette reveal a feminine body under masculine attire. If anything, the lorette's masculine dress tended to emphasize her femininity. In this sense, the lorette was unlike the *garçonne* of the 1920s, whose body was depicted as devoid of the female curves that the lorette retained.[8] The lorette's masculine disguise was immediately transparent; yet for all its transparency, it succeeded in allowing her access to male privilege. The stereotypical lorette had thus not abandoned her femininity, but rather had brought her female nature with her into masculine spheres of activity. A true "hermaphrodite," the lorette's gender bending signaled a blending of categories that retained their fluidity.[9]

The lorette's class identity was also unstable. The lorette was a girl of the popular classes who had abandoned work for the dream of becoming a lady of wealth and leisure. The lorette was thoroughly modern in part because she had successfully moved up the social hierarchy, with nothing but her own beauty and skill to help her. The lorette was thus the ultimate symbol of successful social mobility; she was also an *arriviste*, whose achievements could not obscure her origins. The lorette thus embodied the potential for social disruption that speculation posed, as it allowed people to increase their wealth, and thus alter their status, with great rapidity. The popularity of the lorette lay in her ability to translate, through her shifting class and gender identity, the tensions inherent in a shifting social order. Contemporaries thus both praised her success and condemned her usurpation of wealth and position.

The blending of female and male, popular and elite, within the image of the lorette also symbolized the continuity between traditional, popular, female power and what was becoming identified as modern, middle-class,

masculine power. In this sense the stereotype of the lorette, with its blurring of gender and class distinctions, can be seen as a figure meant to signify transition. In particular, the lorette of the July Monarchy was a hybrid
character, one appropriate to a society in which old and new forms of
credit and old and new attitudes toward speculation were juxtaposed.
The stereotype of the lorette functioned to make the new role of the stock
market comprehensible by framing the figure of the speculator within the
context of female credit networks.

In Old Regime France, before the existence of banks, extensive credit
networks ranging across the social scale facilitated the borrowing and
lending of money.[10] The creditors of an aristocratic couple might include
not only other nobles, high officeholders, and wealthy merchants but also
artisans. Among those creditors might be more than one single woman
who considered her loan a form of investment that, when repaid with
interest, would increase the value of her fortune. In early modern Europe
in general, women, and especially widows, were important sources of
capital for those seeking to borrow. Women were unable to buy offices
and had less access to land ownership; they thus sought outlets for their
capital, of which the dowry was the most important source, in less traditional forms of wealth, notably commerce and money lending.[11]

Money lending was therefore a form of financial investment for women;
it was also an investment in their future. Credit networks often doubled
as social networks, especially at the lower rungs of society. Whereas the
wealthy and powerful would often employ a notary as an intermediary
in organizing networks of credit, those of lower social standing would
arrange loans through social and neighborhood networks. By building a
reputation as one who was willing to lend to others when they needed
funds, women might be able to expect the same sort of help if they met
with hard times. As William Jordan put it, "Long-term credit sales and
mortgages to those needing them helped large numbers of women create
dependable clients for those times when circumstances might otherwise
tell against them. Like pawn-broking and small-scale money lending among
women far less wealthy, these financial networks were potentially useful
social networks."[12]

Networks of information that could facilitate the borrowing and lending of money tended among the popular classes to be dominated by
women.[13] Philip Hoffman and his colleagues have argued that potential
lenders who turned to notaries to help them find borrowers did so because notaries "knew all the intimate details of the borrower's financial
dealings, for borrowers and their families typically remained with the
same notary for years."[14] Lower down on the social scale, we can assume

that lenders would turn to intermediaries with the same type of informa-tion regarding a borrower's creditworthiness: the women who dominated neighborhood networks.

Although the *Banque de France* had been established in 1800, projects to found banks that would facilitate credit and investment for a significant segment of the population did not really get off the ground until the Second Empire.[15] For the first half of the nineteenth century, then, pri-vate credit networks continued to function. The ins and outs of borrow-ing and lending money was one of the topics treated in the literature on Paris and the Parisians, in works such as *Physiologie de l'argent* and Tax-ile Delord and colleagues' *Paris-boursier*. While these works naturally discussed male moneylenders, they also recognized the important role played by women in private credit networks. Women who were believed to have privileged access to information concerning the neighborhood's inhabitants were often depicted as possessing the power to destroy one's reputation for creditworthiness through their public insults. Since "an eighteenth-century person's very reputation was bound up with his abil-ity to obtain loans," the power of women to comment upon the financial resources of others in the neighborhood constituted an important theme of this literature.[16]

The female moneylender was thus a frequent character in the litera-ture on Paris. This type was immortalized in Balzac's *Splendeurs et misères des courtisanes* in the person of Mme la Ressource. Mme la Ressource was a *marchande à la toilette,* a dealer in secondhand women's clothes. The *marchande à la toilette* operated within a largely female network of credit and exchange. She bought used clothes from wealthy women, which she then sold (through a shop or a stall at the Temple market) to women lower down on the social scale. At both ends of her commerce, the *marchande à la toilette* doubled as a moneylender. In her most sinis-ter incarnations, such as in Emile Zola's *La Curée,* the *marchande à la toi-lette* doubled as a procuress, taking advantage of the financial distress of her wealthy clients to sell them into prostitution.[17]

In the popular literature on Paris, the *marchande à la toilette* facilitated the circulation of women, old clothes, and money. Her access to women's homes gave her access to their secrets. Despite her claim to maintain the most "absolute discretion," she could destroy reputations by publicizing these secrets.[18] This was significant because during an era in which money was increasingly believed to be the constituent element of identity access to credit was strongly linked to one's public reputation. An 1844 text argued that in a society in which privilege had been abolished, only wealth could bring happiness: "the new regime favors no one, and each . . . is free to lay claim to all the happiness possible, certain to obtain only as much as he can buy!"[19] Within this context, the reputed ability of the *marchande à la toilette* to establish the value of people and objects took on even greater significance. This explains the frequent description of the Temple market as a sort of unofficial stock exchange.[20] For one observer, who likened its workings to those of the illegal stock exchange, the *coulisse,* "the speculation is just as murderous and ferocious [at the Temple] as in the Passage de l'Opéra or the Place de la Bourse. On can buy on account and upon delivery on the stock of trousers and overripe clothes exactly like [one does with] stock in the government, the north [a railroad line], gas or spirits." Similarly, just as private credit networks crossed social and economic boundaries, so too the Temple market was depicted as an institution that mixed, if not members of the various social classes and both sexes, at least the clothes used to signify their rank, position, and gender. The Temple was thus a "congress of clothing where the rags of the poor and the lace mantilla that veiled the shoulders of a duchess meet and fraternize. There . . . lying on the same table [are] the satin slipper and the wooden clog, . . . the ball dress and the coal man's jacket."[21]

Through such descriptions of the Temple market and its merchants, the link between women of the popular classes and networks of credit and investment was kept alive in the popular imagination. Even as the stock exchange, and the banks associated with its growth, took on greater importance as intermediaries between lenders and borrowers, making credit available to those who needed it and offering new outlets for investment, female imagery did not disappear. In fact, although writers attempted to develop a social type associated with these new institutions, the speculator, this character never caught on the way his female counterpart, the lorette, did. Although the two shared many traits, the attractiveness of the lorette as a type to explain new forms of credit and investment lay in her similarity with other female types such as the *marchande à la toilette.* This similarity established a link between a tradition of private credit networks and new institutions. Clearly associated with modernization, the lorette also echoed tradition. The lorette thus offered a means of seeing in these new institutions a continuity with the past, making their growing importance appear less jarring and less revolutionary.

The image of the lorette was therefore used to describe the very new social type of speculator. The lorette made her living by having several lovers at once, using her intelligence to keep their identities secret (from each other at least), and extracting as much money as she possibly could from each one. The lorette exploited male vulnerability to her sexuality in order to increase her income. The lorette possessed a financial savvy that allowed her to become increasingly wealthy and influential at the cost of her lovers, whose affairs with the lorette most often left them financially ruined. Her heart was not that of a sentimental woman, but of the consummate businessman. As one author wrote, "As for love, don't ask it of her . . . she doesn't have the time to devote herself to it. She is also immune from sentimental declarations . . . she is straightforward."[22]

The lorette lived on credit, extracting money from her lovers on the promise to pay with sexual favors at the same time as her food, furniture, and clothing were all bought on credit made available to her because of her association with wealthy men. The lorette was portrayed as a prime example of the way in which easy access to credit could boost the luxury trades of an entire neighborhood. And although the lorette suffered an occasional reversal of fortunes, in texts from the July Monarchy at least, she bounced back with astounding rapidity. Such accounts reveal a sense of optimism concerning the prospects of capitalist development and the expansion of the market at the same time as they parodied the lorette's materialism and social climbing.

During the July Monarchy, then, writers displayed an ambiguous attitude toward the lorette; although they criticized what they characterized as her heartless materialism, they couldn't help admiring and envying the wealth she created. This ambiguous attitude reveals a measure of uncertainty concerning new forms of wealth and exchange in general. While writers criticized the growing materialism of their era, they also began to speak of themselves and their work in language that evoked the world of finance and exchange. According to Alain Plessis, new approaches to monetary policy and investment during the Second Empire constituted a genuine revolution; poised at the edge of this revolution, writers of the 1840s were uncertain whether the lorette was to be emulated or eliminated.[23]

In contrast to these earlier authors, writers of the Second Empire revealed a greater acceptance of wealth as an indicator of social and political success. The growing familiarity with and sense of control over mechanisms of credit and speculation is reflected in changing images of the lorette, whom writers depicted as an object of exchange among men, an "amorous commodity that has its highs and its lows—like common railroad stocks!"[24] Significantly, lorettes in these later writings lost much of their power over men as writers stressed the lorette's economic dependence on her lovers. Accounts in the 1850s and 1860s depicted men as cynical and knowledgeable concerning the ways of the world and the marketplace. In an 1855 review of Gavarni's series on the lorette, for example, the writer Félix Mornand emphasized the naïveté of the men of the 1840s

regarding the lorette, writing, "a certain polish covered these strange customs . . . . The first lorettes of Gavarni, in the clutches of their decrepit
and imbecilic protectors, offered us the eternally pleasant spectacle of
feigned innocence struggling against senile conceit." In contrast, he ob-
served, the men of 1855 were cynical and knowledgeable, and could no
longer be taken in by the lorette. In an anecdote, Mornand made clear
the power this new knowledge gave men; when a lorette threatened to
withhold her affections if she was not given what she wanted, her lover
calmly replied, "No longer love me! . . . but, Paméla, that would be a
luxury that you can't afford!"[25] Like the grisette, the ouvrière, and the
female merchant, the lorette of the Second Empire was increasingly portrayed as financially dependent on men and therefore unable to act independently. Indeed, the most common way of describing the relationship
between the lorette and her lovers in Second Empire writings was to
characterize it as "love by limited partnership." Increasingly, accounts of
lorettes from the Second Empire focused on her future prospects, which
were depicted with an unrelenting grimness. Marriage to a worker or the
owner of a small shop if she was lucky, the hospital or the street if she
(more commonly) was not: these were the futures writers imagined for
the lorette. If descriptions of the lorette from the 1840s invoked the image
of a financial wizard managing a large and important portfolio, those from
the Second Empire implied that the lorette had become an investment
shared by a group of men whose value would inevitably depreciate.

Such accounts reveal a certain cynicism regarding the market that was
absent during the July Monarchy. They also manifest an increasing desire to differentiate between masculine and feminine approaches to the
market. Ironically, assurances of male dominance over the lorette and cer-
tainty regarding her eventual failure allowed some to express greater
appreciation for her skills. In an 1861 account, Gabriel Pélin insisted that
the lorette deserved more respect, arguing that a successful lorette needed
intelligence, even genius, to better her position. He thus described her as,
"the little girl who, lacking a dowry, in order to position herself in society,
allows herself to be traded, and once her value is established, uses all her
skill to raise . . . the rate of exchange." The skill and creativity needed by
the lorette, he continued, would make her an artist if she didn't need to
be so heartless to succeed. Pélin argued that men who played the stock
market should in particular sympathize with the lorette, since "if you could
sell your soul, you would without waiting . . . if your body could . . . My
God! you would do as the lorette."[26]

Whereas in earlier accounts the lorette was used to symbolize the qualities that were believed to characterize the speculator in general, Pélin's

text distinguished between speculators and lorettes, who, in this text as in others dating from the Second Empire, lost their "masculine" attributes. Thus, while the lorette was for Pélin "the counterpart of the stockbroker, licensed or unlicensed," she operated in a completely feminine sphere, "speculat[ing] on the feminine style she possesses and issu[ing] currency on her feminine intuition."[27] The feminization of the lorette invalidated her presence in the masculine sphere of the market and accounted for her eventual failure and fall into poverty. In accounts from the July Monarchy, the lorette was used as a symbol for speculation in general that situated the emergence of new modes of investment within the context of traditional credit networks. As these new modes of investment gained in acceptance and familiarity, the image of the lorette changed. In writings of the Second Empire, the lorette served to signify the irreversible impact of market forces in general and of the stock market in particular. Within this context, images of the lorette were used to differentiate between approaches to the market that maintained virtue and those that destroyed it.

Lamenting the Grisette: High Finance and the World of Letters

The image of the lorette reiterated many of the traits associated—for good or for bad—with the prostitute. A model of social mobility, the lorette was also a metaphor for the impact of market forces on French society. Whereas the grisette, as the prostitute transformed by love, had been used to indicate the possibility, however difficult, of resisting market forces, the lorette unabashedly embraced the market and all it represented. Writers thus frequently opposed the grisette and the lorette, lamenting the former's supposed disappearance as a means to indicate the inroads market ideas had made on French society.

By the Second Empire, the grisette, associated with the "old" heart of Paris, came increasingly to be considered a symbol of an earlier era. Writing in 1865, Henry de Kock (son of Paul de Kock, famous for his novels dedicated to describing the lives of grisettes) lamented that grisettes had "disappeared, never to return, from Parisian soil, as all those simple and comic types of the streets and the shops have [also] disappeared."[28] Authors such as de Kock likened the grisette's demise to changes in the city's physical and commercial landscape in a nostalgic lament for the "old" Paris. In Jules Noriac's tragicomic account, the grisette asphyxiated herself because she could not compete with the lorette and was found many years later "completely mummified in her *mansarde* [attic room]" when demolition began in the Latin Quarter.[29] By the late 1850s, as new social and economic forces took hold within a rapidly changing urban environment, some writers expressed doubt that the grisette had ever existed. Most believed that she had existed in the past; nonetheless, by the 1860s all agreed that the virtuous grisette of old had been replaced by the thoroughly modern lorette. However, although during the Second Empire women were less likely to work in public than before, young working girls who would have been referred to as grisettes were still evident in Paris. Laments concerning their "disappearance" thus must be taken less as literal reflections of changes in the Parisian population than as nostalgic metaphors for an era perceived as lost.

Complaints regarding the grisette's decline began to appear as early as the 1840s and were in fact simultaneous with the development of the image of the "virtuous" grisette described in chapter 1. Thus even as writers and journalists lauded the grisette's ability to resist the lure of temptation in the midst of poverty, they questioned how long such resolve could last. Anxiety regarding the grisette's disappearance served in the 1840s to emphasize writers' critique of materialism; they thus portrayed the grisette as an endangered species in a society driven by the search for wealth. Writing in 1848, Alfred Delvau complained, "The grisette, the true grisette—is dead, dead and gone—in this era of bankers and charlatans, of secondhand clothes dealers and of crooks,—in this time of positivism, mercantilism, and illegal speculation—when men's minds are buried by the needs of their bodies."[30] In the words of another writer, the grisette fell victim to a "minting century, in which everything is materialized and respect is based on piles of gold."[31] In a society in which, these authors complained, money had become the be-all and end-all of existence, the poor grisette finally succumbed.

Thus at the same time that writers were developing the image of the virtuous grisette, they also began to signal her disappearance. These laments continued through the Second Empire, but their tone and meaning changed. During the July Monarchy the disappearance of the grisette was portrayed as an immediate danger or recent event, but one that could be stopped or reversed. By the 1850s and 1860s, on the other hand, the intense nostalgia or knowing cynicism that pervades comments regarding her disappearance place her in the irretrievable past. By the Second Empire, then, market forces appear to have triumphed; it is the dream of escaping their pull, a dream symbolized by the grisette, that has truly disappeared.

Changes in journalism no doubt contributed to this change in attitude. The September Laws of 1835 increased the amount of caution money required by the government to start a newspaper. Louis-Napoleon's government raised the amount once again in its 1852 law regulating the press. The success of new publishing tactics designed to gain a wider audience, techniques pioneered by Emile de Girardin, attracted investors to journalism who were driven less by idealistic visions of the public role of the press than by the desire to make a profit. As a result of these developments, during the Second Empire newspapers became expensive properties that often changed hands. Many of those investing in the newspaper business were also associated with the world of high finance; according to Arnould Frémy, whose 1866 *La Révolution du journalisme* chronicled the changes affecting this profession, most men who founded newspapers during the Second Empire were either bankers or speculators.[32]

The high financial stakes involved in publishing a large paper served to restrict entry to the major papers to all but the best-known or best-connected writers. In Texier's 1868 study on journalism, he wrote of the problem of overcrowding amongst aspiring journalists and estimated that out of a thousand who tried, only one might succeed.[33] Whereas during the July Monarchy writers who faced stiff competition seemed to believe that success was a possibility, writers of the Second Empire portrayed the world of journalism as a two-tiered system in which movement between the upper and lower ranks was virtually impossible. J. F. Vaudin, in his 1863 *Gazettes et gazettiers,* wrote that underneath the elite of journalists was a group of miserable writers willing to take up any cause to make a living.[34] Some, such as Léon Rossignol, wanted to make this second-tier group of writers, what he called the "petits journalists," respected and respectable, but even he feared that the precarious economic situation of many writers combined with a loss of opportunities for advancement made them more susceptible to "selling themselves," to editors as well as to the general public.[35] These conditions led Frémy to complain that the French press in 1866 was "up for sale."[36]

Awareness of the importance of capital in founding and sustaining a newspaper combined with a perception of limited professional opportunities to shape journalists' views of their profession during the Second Empire. The comparison of journalists and prostitutes was common in July Monarchy texts, yet by the Second Empire, the alternative to the prostitute, the grisette, was widely believed to have disappeared. Many writers thus seemed to indicate, in their texts, a feeling of being trapped in a system that was corrupt and imperfect, without real alternatives. For several authors, expressions regarding the grisette's disappearance were thus often linked to nostalgia for an earlier era, one in which, it was assumed, idealism and equal opportunity conveyed a sense of dignity of purpose that several Second Empire writers argued was lacking in their day. Thus Henry de Kock linked the disappearance of the grisette with his own inability to follow his father's path to success: "Alas! A hundred times alas! weep, unfortunate sons of too fortunate fathers! There are no more grisettes; they have disappeared."[37] Likewise, Gabriel Pélin identified the grisette with his life as a journalist during the July Monarchy in a nostalgic lament for the past that is worth quoting at length:

> We danced [with grisettes] at the Chaumière [a popular ball], and that evening we came back yelling and singing . . . M. Prunier Quatremère placed us in a holding cell for a few hours . . . those were the days.
>
> Bohain was at *Le Figaro*. There was a newspaper called *Le True Mayeux* . . . the incomparable Lequeux philosophized . . . we fought duels and lived [in rooms costing] sixteen francs a month (with Louisette), Grès Street, Cambray Place, or Mathurins Street.
>
> But, alas! . . . there are no more grisettes in Paris, no more students! O Latin Quarter, what has become of you?[38]

Added to personal and professional nostalgia was a sense of political nostalgia. In his *Souvenirs du quartier latin,* Antonio Watripon associated the disappearance of the grisette with a turn away from the youthful republican idealism of the early July Monarchy, asking, "where is the grisette of old, this delicious creation that is forever lost, this Parisian type that gave way when faced with big money? . . . Where are the students of the good old days, . . . the brothers of 1832 who lay down for eternity on the flagstones of Saint-Méry [*sic*]?" The grisette, typified by Watripon as the character Carmagnole, was a republican, "the proud citizeness of the Latin Quarter that placed liberty higher than the crown"; her passing was a symbol of a general turn away from the republican idealism of the early 1830s.[39]

Several writers joined Watripon in identifying the agent of the grisette's disappearance as the students themselves, who took advantage of her good nature without caring for her or left her to chase after the more glamorous lorette. These authors manifested a guilt concerning the fate of the grisette, who came back in these texts to haunt both authors and readers, reappearing as a destitute woman begging on a street corner, a cynical prostitute walking up and down the boulevards, or in the most chilling accounts, a cadaver on a dissecting table. In such accounts, the authors' sense of remorse concerning the grisette can be understood as an indication of regret for the principles with which she was associated—virtue, talent, concern for the public good—and which were later perceived as having disappeared from writers' political and professional lives.

In the years following the 1848 revolution, when republican idealism was replaced with disillusionment or fear of revolution, grisettes were increasingly assimilated to prostitutes who circulated disease and vice throughout the ranks of society. For the authors of an 1858 work, the grisette had become part of the world of clandestine prostitution, which was itself associated with the revolutionary tradition. The authors of this text argued that the government set a precedent in 1791, which it repeated in 1830 and 1848 when it "opened the doors of the prisons holding prostitutes and female thieves. All the previous regulations concerning them were abolished at the beginning of the first revolution in the name of *individual liberty*. Once freed from any restraint by the Constituent Assembly, nothing could stop the *filles publiques* [public women], who abandoned themselves to the most scandalous licentiousness."[40] The grisette, a symbol of liberty and republicanism for some, became, in a passage that echoed the fears of Parent-Duchâtelet, a manifestation of an excess of freedom that threatened the social hierarchy. These writers often contrasted the grisette as prostitute with the ouvrière, who was identified as dependent upon a male provider, as weak, defenseless, and, perhaps most importantly for these authors, limited by her class boundaries. Thus whereas the virtuous grisette of the 1840s crossed class lines in her association with the student (a metaphor for the alliance between middle-class republicans and "the people" during the July Monarchy), the working woman in texts from the Second Empire either married a working-class man or became a prostitute. The middle ground represented by the virtuous grisette had disappeared from the Parisian popular imagination.

Disappeared, abandoned, or debauched, the virtuous yet fun-loving, loyal yet independent, selfless yet sexual grisette of the 1830s and 1840s was no more than a memory in the pages of Second Empire popular literature. Writers took a variety of positions concerning their own role in her disappearance, and their opinions concerning the positive or negative aspects of the grisette's demise varied as well. Yet whatever their political position, and whatever their view of the changes in their profession, all authors agreed that the grisette's disappearance was one more indication of the extent to which market forces had changed French society. Accounts that contrasted the grisette and the lorette tended to condemn the impact of the stock market on French society. In literature devoted specifically to the stock market, however, the lorette served a different function. In this context, writers used the image of the lorette to distinguish between moral and immoral approaches to the stock market. Creating a virtuous marketplace was the primary concern for these writers, many of whom were involved, as brokers or investors, in the market.

The Passions of the Stock Market

Writers and journalists argued that the growing impact of the stock market had forever altered the world of letters. They used the image of the lorette, which they opposed to the virtuous grisette of the past, to discuss this impact on their profession. During the Second Empire, the image of the lorette took on a wider resonance as well. Representations of the lorette from this period reflect new fears and concerns regarding the influence of credit and exchange in general, and of the stock market in particular, on all aspects of society. They also reflect a distrust of the growing political force of the people.

The reign of Napoleon III inaugurated an era that contemporaries described as a "democratization of credit."[41] Whereas access to the stock market had been limited during the July Monarchy, more and more people were investing their money in stocks and bonds during the Second Empire. There were several reasons for this change. First, and most importantly, the government actively encouraged small investors to buy shares in government loans issued to continue work on the railroads, to carry out the renovation of the capital, and to finance its many military expeditions. The imperial government preferred raising capital through public borrowing to raising taxes; supporters of this policy believed that the increased revenues that would result from the modernization of France would be more than sufficient to pay back the state debt, which rose significantly during this period. Linking participation in the market with citizenship, government backers promoted the successful subscription of a public loan as a manifestation of public support for the regime, a "universal suffrage of capital," as it was frequently called.[42]

Napoleon III had been influenced by Saint-Simonian economic doctrines and believed that the key to ending class conflict was to encourage the general enrichment of society by making credit more readily available. The imperial government thus encouraged the establishment of cooperative credit societies that had been the subject of worker demands in the 1840s. Their rise was especially dramatic in the late 1860s, when credit was restricted following a downturn in the business cycle. In the capital, the number of credit societies nearly trebled between 1866 and 1870 from a base of 120.[43] To ensure that workers could manage their credit, the government, along with private institutions, founded schools to teach workers economics. Designed in part to combat the spread of socialist ideas by teaching the supposed benefits of liberal capitalism, these schools recognized workers' claims to inclusion in the marketplace at the same time as they dictated a certain vision of that marketplace.[44]

The emperor's belief that workers could viably participate in the market influenced his support for institutions and measures designed to encourage investment. He supported, for example, the establishment of the Crédit Mobilier by the Péreire brothers, a bank that departed from the techniques of the "old bank," dominated by the Rothschilds, in its willingness to tap into the resources of small investors, its aggressive pursuit of domestic and international projects to finance, and its commitment to paying high dividends to investors regardless of the actual rate of returns (a policy that eventually proved to be its downfall). Legislation passed during the Second Empire also encouraged private companies to issue stock in order to finance and expand their operations by limiting personal liability. The practice of offering reduced shares made investing on the stock market much more accessible to even those of modest means.

As a result of all these changes, the Paris stock market became an institution of major importance. The number of stocks listed on the Paris exchange nearly tripled during the Second Empire, growing from 118 in 1851 to 307 in 1869. The value of the exchange also tripled during this period, increasing from 11 to 33 billion francs. Capital was so abundant that investors sought foreign outlets, and by the late 1860s, one-third of the stocks listed on the market were in foreign investments.[45] The Paris stock market thus became a powerful international finance market during this period, where shares in projects such as the construction of railroads in Russia or the building of the Suez Canal were bought and sold with much energy and excitement.[46] As the stock market grew in importance, specialized newspapers were founded to track its movements and tendencies. One didn't have to be a specialist, however, to follow the market; all newspapers followed its ups and downs, and wins and losses on the stock market became a frequent and convenient plot device in plays and novels.

Some praised banks such as the Crédit Mobilier, which had allowed those with limited financial resources to invest in the market. Charles Duvivier, for example, in his 1854 pamphlet, *La Bourse*, argued that the issuance of bonds in small denominations, as well as the success of the first municipal loan, changed the nature of the stock market for the better: "the market became more democratic; it seemed before to be a monopoly profiting the financial aristocracy, today it encompasses every sphere of human activity and extends even to the people."[47] Likewise, the anonymous author of an 1856 pamphlet argued that the stock market was "the most catholic monument in the world, . . . whose faithful included a mixture of all the ages, all the sexes, all the races, all the religions." Because of its inclusive nature, the author concluded, the stock market served as "the metronome . . . of social harmony."[48]

Others, however, worried that greater access to the stock market would lead to an erasure of social distinctions. The wild swings of the stock market during this period, the slowdown in economic growth after 1857, and some fabulous financial disasters, such as the crash of the Crédit Mobilier in 1867, raised fears concerning the capacity of the stock market to undermine the stability of French society. The growing "democratization of capital" lauded by the imperial government also worried many, who felt that the working classes were being corrupted by an increasing desire for material gain. Debates concerning these practices became especially heated during times of economic crisis; the fall in stock prices in 1857, which signaled a period of significantly slower growth, perceived as a stagnation or decline following the boom period of the early 1850s, resulted in a flurry of books, pamphlets, and articles devoted to discussing the effects of the stock market on French society.

While most accounts referred to the problem as one of "materialism" spreading throughout society, some authors used humor to reveal an underlying fear that the popular classes might use gains from the stock market to threaten the authority and position of the elite. This is one of the themes of Cham's *La Bourse illustrée;* in one anecdote, a porter responds to a bourgeois in robe and slippers, who complains that the front steps of the building haven't yet been swept, by menacing, "I'm going to play the market . . . . I'll perhaps buy your house this evening," thus both refusing to follow his orders and threatening to usurp his position.[49] Such fears were particularly evident among those who opposed the Crédit Mobilier, and they increased in frequency following its crash. The Crédit Mobilier was strongly supported by the emperor and was thus associated with both the municipal borrowing program undertaken by the Baron Haussmann and the policy of universal manhood suffrage, restored by Louis-Napoleon upon his 1851 coup d'état. Some authors equated universal suffrage with the spread of speculation, noting that speculators could now be found from every class. According to Oscar de Vallée, this "spirit of equality has become the great dissolvent of all social bonds." As those from the popular classes followed the example of their social superiors, they too were overwhelmed by "passions" that "attack each barrier destined to contain individual pride and maintain a bit of order among men."[50] In a more violent and anti-Semitic attack on speculation, Eugène de Mirecourt argued that Jewish rogues encouraged the small investor to play the market, taking advantage of their ignorance to cheat them, and then using their gains to keep mistresses. While Mirecourt argued that sober investment increased the public good, "[speculation], the daughter [of investment], . . . intriguing, greedy, without shame, is nothing more than abuse, corruption, prostitution, a plague that we must fight and cause to fade away."[51]

As Mirecourt's gendered imagery indicates, concerns regarding the dissemination of materialism throughout society were frequently expressed in popular literature through images of female investors, especially those from the popular classes, and the lorette. The lorette became a symbol for the potential disorder that the growth of speculation threatened to bring about. Depictions of the lorette reveal that the stock market served as a metaphor for French society as a whole; fear concerning the effects of speculation thus translated into concerns regarding the reorganization of French society in the mid-nineteenth century. The prevalence of the lorette and of other female types in literature on the stock market reveals the importance of gender to the construction of a stable social hierarchy.

Discussions of the lorette, and of the stock market in general during this period, attempted to distinguish between "good" and "bad" approaches to playing the market. The "good" approach, which we might characterize as investment, was seen as that which produced wealth for the country as a whole; the "bad" approach, making money by anticipating the rise and fall in the value of stocks and bonds, served only to enrich the individual playing the market. Pierre-Joseph Proudhon, for example, in his *Manuel du spéculateur à la bourse,* distinguished investment from *agiotage,* or speculation. Proudhon defined investment as "that which invents, which innovates, which provides, which solves, which, like the infinite Spirit, *creates from nothing,* everything," and characterized it as that which was "most unconquerable by power, . . . the most free."[52] *Agiotage,* on the other hand, resulted in "eccentricities of luxury, sumptuous debauchery, gilded vice, orgies of *five hundred thousand francs worth of stock,* prostitution under cover of gold and silk."[53] In short, while investment served to enrich the nation and promote the public good, speculation was driven by private interest and served to enrich and promote the lorette.

In literature from the Second Empire, the lorette became a common symbol for speculation. The brochure, *Boursicotiérisme et lorettisme,* published in 1858, identified the lorette with "the sensual and systematic speculation of vice, selling easy favors for ready cash; (the lorette) is always debauched, continually selling and reselling her feminine honor with as much indifference as an *agioteur* trades his masculine and financial honor in (shady) speculations."[54] Concern with one's reputation was believed to function as a break to one's self-interest; the lorette, who disregarded the force of public opinion in her quest for greater wealth, thus came to symbolize the dangers the stock market could pose to society as a whole. The potential of the stock market for undermining a healthy balance between the public good and private interests was expressed through the use of feminine imagery. Thus an 1855 work warned: "one can compare the stock exchange to the sirens of antiquity: gifted with the most attractive charms . . . they draw you into perilous reefs."[55]

Speculation, which appealed to the passions rather than to a sentiment of public good, was particularly identified with women. Women were believed to be especially avid traders, who during the July Monarchy took advantage of opportunities to play the market. Although women had never been allowed on the floor of the stock exchange, before 1848 they were allowed to watch the action from the second-floor galleries, giving them the opportunity to communicate with traders on the floor. They also sought out alternate venues. In the late 1830s, for example, women of high society seeking to speculate on the railroads were said to have sought out invitations to Madame Rothschild's salon.[56] These opportunities would diminish during the Second Empire, when women's participation in the market was seen in more negative terms and after they had been barred from the stock exchange altogether.

The move to exclude women from the stock exchange in 1848 paralleled that of women's political exclusion. Participation in the stock market had, in fact, long been linked to citizenship. Thus, although in the first half of the nineteenth century women were not formally forbidden entry to the exchange, a decree issued in the year IX (1801) limited access to the floor of the stock exchange to those "in possession of their political rights."[57] This association between political and economic rights led the humorous newspaper *Le Charivari* to imagine the question of equal political rights for women during the 1848 revolution as one of equal access to the stock exchange: "For the last five months the prefect of police has not had sufficient force at his disposal to prevent women from invading the stock exchange. . . . Unfortunately, these *boursicotières* play with such raw violence and indulge in such loud discussions that they drown out the voice of the traders. . . . Obviously, things cannot go on like this, [however,] the *boursicotières* have sworn to not give in except if faced by bayonets!"[58] Although *Le Charivari* linked access to the stock exchange and political rights to parody women's claims to inclusion in the new republic, it was a question that was taken seriously by many. In the conservative mood following the 1848 revolution, women's access to the stock exchange, like her access to the political arena, was severely curtailed when a law that novelist Henry de Kock described as "not very gallant, perhaps, but most wise and prudent" forbad entrance of the stock exchange to women.[59]

Second Empire writers seeking to justify women's exclusion from the stock exchange after 1848 described their former presence in the galleries as a source of grave disorder: they were loud and boisterous spectators, most of whom were playing the market, either through the intermediary of a lover or husband or by directly calling out to traders on the floor. When they lost, and it was axiomatic in texts from the 1850s and 1860s that women lost frequently, they produced "scandalous, or at the very least, ridiculous scenes" that distracted the presumably more sober male traders.[60] Furthermore, women's disorderly conduct was said to pose a physical threat to men: "Some of the most hardy and desperate women waited for the important capitalists at the door . . . and accused them, not without reason, of having produced the downward movement of stocks of which they had been victims, and threatened to tear out their eyes."[61] The behavior of female speculators, motivated by passion and the desire for gain, typified the excesses the stock market was thought capable of producing.

The exclusion of women from the stock exchange, although considered by most a step in the right direction, did not solve the problem of female speculators. Once women were excluded from the second-floor galleries, the authors of popular literature tell us, they took up position outside the building. There one could see groups of women of the popular classes stationed outside the fence surrounding the stock exchange, speculating on the day's events: "Look over there under the trees, you will see a group of animated beings that are called women because they wear . . . a skirt. These so-called women are trying to get close to the fence that surrounds the stock exchange."[62] This group was composed uniquely of women of the popular classes—including *marchandes à la toilette*. As the class origin of these female speculators indicates, women's participation in the market was often conflated with that of the popular classes as a whole. As with the merchants of the *halles*, writers emphasized the "unnatural" and "distasteful" spectacle posed by women of the popular classes engaged in financial transactions in public. Writers repeatedly argued, for example, that playing the market caused women to lose their femininity; rather than devoting themselves to their families, they discussed politics and stock prices: "there is no spouse, father, nor public; they worry only about the stock market. [They will frustrate] the wandering *flâneur* looking over these enervated flowers with his insolent and inquisitive eyeglass in the hope of finding a preference upon which to fix his irregular love, [because] the *joueuse* [gambler] has no sex."[63]

Another venue for these problematic speculators was the *coulisse*, a roaming stock exchange that met in the back alleyways and out-of-the-way spaces of the neighborhood surrounding the stock exchange. The *coulisse,* which operated outside of the control of the official stock exchange, allowed those who would not otherwise have access—especially, it was believed, women—to play the market. It also encouraged speculation on stocks, which was officially illegal (although widely accepted). The illicit nature of this exchange was highlighted by the name it was given— the term *"coulisse,"* literally, the back stage, traditionally referred to the backstage of the Paris Opéra, a meeting ground for wealthy spectators and attractive dancers. Its reputed location in areas known to be favored by prostitutes, the passage de l'Opéra and around the café Tortoni, further reinforced the link between illicit speculation and female vice. And like clandestine prostitution, the *coulissiers,* as they were known, "carried out [their trade] all along the sidewalk, rain or shine, snow or wind."[64]

Such descriptions of illicit speculation engaged in by women encouraged police authorities to increase their surveillance of the public areas in the neighborhood of the stock exchange. The police attempted to close the *coulisse* several times during the Second Empire; each time they were unsuccessful.[65] Police authorities also attempted to control women's access to the stock market by regulating their use of public space. In September 1851, for example, the public prosecutor of the republic wrote to the prefect of police concerning the problem of women playing the stock market illicitly. "It is [a topic] of public notoriety," he wrote, "that despite orders given that women be excluded from the stock exchange and rendered unable to indulge in [a form of] gambling that is more perilous to them than to anyone else, every day during the time the stock market is open a group of women form along the outside grill to the left of the peristyles who, by means of hired intermediaries, are able to communicate with the brokers." The public prosecutor asked the prefect to stop this abuse so as to "save from an almost certain ruin honorable but uninformed mothers of families, or even only poor old women whose hopes to increase their feeble resources often reduce them to [trust in] awful swindlers."[66] As with the city's street merchants, this argument invoked female weakness, dependency, and poverty to call for the policing of women in public.

After verifying that there were "in fact a significant number of women" gathered outside the stock exchange during its hours of operation, the head of the division of the police in charge of the stock exchange recommended that the same methods used against the *coulisse*—namely, constant surveillance by police agents, who would break up the groups of speculators—be adopted in regards to these women as well.[67] The prefect of police ordered that his agents take the recommended action, reporting back to the public prosecutor that the problem had been taken care of.[68] A little over a year later, the prefect repeated the injunction against women congregating outside the stock exchange, ordering his agents to ticket any woman suspected of playing the market as well as her intermediaries. He further ordered the investigation of women's use of semiprivate spaces in the neighborhood surrounding the stock exchange, following reports that an unlicensed trader had been seen entering and leaving the home of a certain Dame Boutard, who provided meals for paying guests at the corner of the place de la Bourse and rue Notre Dame des Victoires.[69]

In his report dated December 13, the investigating agent reported that he had infiltrated the Dame Boutard's home and that she had confessed that "the ladies who had been chased from the public way had asked that she receive them in her dining room from 1 to 3 P.M. [and] paid her a monthly indemnity of twenty-five francs."[70] The women, all between fifty and sixty-seven years of age, included one professional caretaker of the sick; the rest were identified only as *"rentières."* While it is difficult to ascertain with precision the social status of these women, the use of the title *"Femme"* rather than *"Madame"* in listing their names indicates that they belonged to the popular classes. Despite the prefect's orders to ticket women caught speculating, the agent, perhaps softened by the presence of several elderly women in the group, let them go after taking their names and making them promise to stop meeting at the home of the Dame Boutard.

Although in the early 1850s the government had encouraged the growth of credit and investment, on the eve of the 1857 recession, as the stock exchange was ending its "golden age," the government began to express concern regarding the perhaps unanticipated widespread participation in the market. Numerous books and pamphlets that condemned both the democratization of the stock market and the participation of women in the market may have influenced the emperor because in 1857 he praised two of the most damning works on this topic.[71] In an effort to put a brake on speculation, the imperial government decreed a moratorium in March 1856 on the creation of new joint-stock companies. In December of that same year, the emperor authorized the city of Paris to collect a one-franc fee for entrance to the stock exchange. Perhaps to facilitate collection, turnstiles were also installed at the entrance. With this measure, which was designed to limit access to the stock exchange, the question of popular participation in the market, and its links to the participation of women, was addressed more explicitly than ever before.

Before the turnstiles were installed, the stock exchange had been, in the words of one observer, "crowded with people of every condition; it

offered an unbelievable jumble [*pêle-mêle*] of professions. The doors of
the temple opened to a population whose *tenue* [deportment] was not
always irreproachable. One had to line up at the entrance just like at
a boulevard theater." Their installation, however, "brought about a true
reform. The crowd is always just as large, but it is better dressed, more
serious, and better company."[72] Writing in *Le Constitutionnel* in 1861, Auguste Vitu argued that the imposition of a one-franc fee, an idea proposed
by several newspapers, was designed to limit access to the stock exchange
to the wealthy, and thereby "stop the development of speculation [since]
the small speculators, those recruited even among the laboring classes,
would recoil from this barrier."[73]

While the intention of this decree was thus to limit access to the stock
exchange, Vitu remarked that it was later discovered that entry to the
building itself was not what attracted these small speculators, it was
rather the ability to buy and sell stocks and bonds that were being issued
in increasingly smaller denominations.[74] If such investors could not play
inside the exchange, they could still play outside, a fact attested to by the
prefect of the Seine, who wrote to the prefect of police in March of 1857
that "since the establishment of a fee at the entry to the *Bourse,* a fairly
considerable number of people have taken to gathering in the two walkways planted with trees that line the sides of the monument, and that are
at this time outside of the area circumscribed by fences." These groups,
which the prefect estimated at twelve to fifteen hundred people, were
from "the lowest classes," in other words, those targeted by the entrance
fee.[75] Furthermore, he continued, women could be seen in considerable
numbers among these groups.

The prefect of police was already aware of the continued problem of
female speculators; in May 1856 he had issued yet another order, for
agents to ticket women who were gathering outside the bourse.[76] This
new situation, however, demanded more far-reaching methods, and the
prefect of the Seine recommended that these wooded walkways be enclosed by fences and made off-limits to those not having paid the one-
franc fee during the day. In his report on this matter, the superintendent
of police for the section des Italiens argued that the enclosure of the area
surrounding the bourse would not solve the problem of illicit speculation
since these people would simply move elsewhere.[77] He further stated
that such a recommendation did not take into account the multiple uses
to which this public space was put. Inhabitants of the neighborhood sent
their children, accompanied by their maids, to this area to play, teachers
who gave courses nearby took students there for recreation, and travelers
waited for the omnibus, sitting on benches in the shade provided by the

trees. As with the central food market, however, authorities tended to discount the varied and complex use of public space by the population of Paris in the name of order. Thus, in a meeting attended by a representative of the prefecture of the Seine, the architect of the stock exchange, and several entrepreneurs, it was decided that the fence surrounding the building would be extended so as to enclose "all the space that today serves as a public walkway."[78] A sidewalk would be built outside the fence, allowing individuals to circulate, but not to linger.

The case of the turnstiles sheds light on the relationship between the control of the stock market, the control of public space, and the definition of citizenship. In theory the imposition of a one-franc entrance fee contradicted the legislation that allowed entry to all those in possession of their political rights. Casting speculators of modest means outside the market made policing them easier, since speculation was clearly illegal outside the confines of the stock exchange. Furthermore, once outside the exchange, speculators from the popular classes became conflated with female speculators, against whom measures could be more easily taken in the name of public morality and the protection of the weak. The combination of limited access to the exchange and enhanced policing outside the exchange was meant to restrict participation in the stock market to men of a certain economic level. In this way, authorities made a statement about the nature of political participation, revealing their strong conviction that under no circumstances should women be allowed political recognition, but also indicating their suspicion of universal manhood suffrage. As with the case of the central food market, public space served as a metaphor for political and social space. The control and enclosure of public institutions was meant in both cases to send a message about who had access to public power and who did not.

The enclosure of the stock exchange was not the only measure taken to limit the ability of those of modest means to invest; Auguste Vitu of *Le Constitutionnel* wrote that a change in the law that fixed the minimum value of stock issuable by joint-stock companies at 500 francs effectively prevented members of the popular classes from playing the market.[79] He argued that this change allowed the emperor to rescind the decree authorizing the imposition of an entrance fee in November 1861.[80] The disappearance of the turnstiles was met, as noted elsewhere in *Le Constitutionnel,* with cries of "Vive l'Empereur!"[81] Yet while *Le Constitutionnel, Le Siècle,* and *Le Journal des débats* all saw this change as a move toward greater "liberty of exchange," the other measures taken to control the popular presence at the stock exchange were maintained.[82]

The enclosure of the stock market can be seen as part of a trend toward the growing privatization of bourgeois space during the Second Empire.[83] As in the case of the *halles,* the enclosure of the stock exchange was a response to anxiety regarding the ability of women and the popular classes in general to participate in the market. Proponents of these changes justified the measures taken by arguing that women in particular, and the popular classes in general, could not be trusted to exercise the same sort of self-control as middle-class men. Whereas the enclosure of the *halles* was imposed from without and was protested by the merchants who used the market, the enclosure of the stock exchange was brought about with the willing support of its most vocal and influential denizens. Despite this difference, however, in each case the transformation of the space occupied by and surrounding the institution was meant to coincide with a change in behavior. Just as the merchants of the renovated *halles* were supposed to exercise restraint when dealing with customers, so too participants in the stock market were encouraged to exercise self-control.

The desire to restrict access to the stock exchange was the result of both fear of the popular classes and a need to create new methods of policing behavior in the exchange. The importance of the stock market in creating wealth made elites particularly anxious to restrict entry to this institution to those whom they believed deserved access. Access to the stock market signified the possession of a recognized public position. In Balzac's novel concerning the risks of commerce and the dangers of bankruptcy, *César Birotteau,* the ambitious Birotteau's bankruptcy signified his nonexistence in the public realm. His eventual rehabilitation and reentry into society was marked by his reappearance at the stock exchange, where he was met by "an ovation à la stock exchange, . . . the most flattering compliments, [and] handshakes."[84] Likewise, Auguste Vitu, writing in 1861, compared the stock exchange to a club where the wealthy went to "see the faces of one's acquaintances, hear the news, and keep up with the impressions of the day."[85] This club lost its value and function, Vitu argued, if entry were unrestricted.

The desire to create and maintain a clublike atmosphere in the stock exchange may have been a response to the increasingly impersonal nature of credit networks. During the early modern period, credit was extended based on knowledge concerning one's finances and character that was gleaned through personal acquaintance. Both notaries and women of the popular classes matched borrowers and lenders based on personal knowledge of each party's situation. The "public perception of the self in relation to a communicated set of both personal and household virtues [loyalty, thrift, sobriety, dependability]" became the most important factor in both allowing people to obtain credit and ensuring that they did not subsequently default on their loans.[86] During the Second Empire, the increase in both number and scope of credit-providing institutions tended to dilute the communal quality of credit networks at the same time as it made those traditionally concerned with enforcing communal norms, namely women, less important. In the stock exchange, the ability to judge another person's ability and willingness to pay his debts was of crucial importance, in particular because so many people during this period were buying on margin and trading in options.[87] According to the author of an anonymous 1859 pamphlet, the fast pace of trading on the exchange meant that brokers were forced to trust that each person playing the market had the funds to cover any possible losses and the integrity to pay: "these brokers who contract an engagement while on the run, if you will, with barely the time to pencil a note to themselves, consider it sacred, although it sometimes entails the loss of very considerable sums."[88] With large numbers of people of all social classes playing the market, judging a participant's integrity became a difficult task.

Attempts to create communal regulations of the stock exchange were manifested primarily through the promotion of one of the defining characteristics of middle-class masculine identity: honor.[89] Worthy and honorable members of the stock market were required to put their own desire for gain second to considerations regarding the functioning of the market as a whole (which broke down if people did not fulfill their obligations), as well as the interests of other players. Honor differed from reputation in that it was not dependent upon external signs that could be read by others; rather, honor was understood as part of an internalized code of ethics that proscribed certain types of behavior that could harm others. Significantly, discussions of honor in the stock exchange focused less on what individuals did than on what they did not do. Honor was most often defined through implication, as accounts focused on examples of dishonorable actions taken by those who attracted the attention of others. Indeed, one of the defining characteristics of honor as it was understood in relation to the stock exchange was its lack of visibility, a quality associated with the absence of self-interest and a dedication to the well-being of others. The definition of honor in the stock exchange thus reveals tendencies toward the internalization and individuation of policing mechanisms that is characteristic of modern society as well as a concern with the preservation of the public good. Honor was a trait to which all men could aspire, but which not all men possessed. The distinction between honorable and dishonorable approaches to the market, which tended to be built upon the difference between investment and speculation, was used to argue that universal male access to the stock market was a chimera since not all men could be trusted to act honorably. Furthermore, these accounts made it very clear that women never possessed honor. Dishonorable actions were regularly associated with the presence or influence of women, whose participation in the marketplace rendered the maintenance of virtue impossible.

Many authors believed that those who engaged in *agiotage*, or speculation, were the least honorable because they were the least likely to pay their debts. At the end of a play by Alexandre Dumas, fils, *La Question d'argent*, Jean, a parvenu who has made a fortune on the stock market, is exposed as one who "disappeared more than once from the stock exchange without paying" and branded as "one of those who dishonor [the exchange]."[90] Observers worried that people did not always feel a compunction to pay debts incurred as the result of what many considered to be a "fictional operation," that of speculating on the values of stocks and bonds that one did not necessarily possess.[91] Such observers argued that speculation led to a devaluation of hard work or prudent investing. For the author of the pamphlet *Boursicotiérisme et lorettisme*, the speculator and the lorette were one and the same; both were drawn by the lure of easy money and a dislike for work: "*Boursicotiérisme* and *lorettisme* are . . . two synonymous words for theft, vice and laziness." The speculator's lack of respect for the effort involved in making money resulted in a lack of respect for the fortunes of others. He thus sought to "cleverly intercept the property of others by a variety of means unanticipated by the law or outside the reach of justice."[92] In this way, the speculator threatened the fortunes of those who made their money through inheritance or hard work, both of which were believed to be more legitimate avenues to wealth.

The term *"agioteur"* dates to the 1740s, when it was first used to describe someone who engaged in immoral speculation.[93] In the late eighteenth century, the defining characteristics of the *agioteur* were his lack of honor and, inextricably linked to the first, his common birth. The *agioteur* inherited the negative qualities regularly imparted to financiers in general as early as the seventeenth century, who were seen as an "emanation of the mob," typifying all that was base, servile, and lacking in virtue.[94] While this association between the speculator and the lower classes also appeared in Second Empire texts, its usage and meaning shifted somewhat. Sensitive, perhaps, to the more "democratic" political climate of the Second Empire and less likely to emanate from the aristocracy, commentators rarely denounced the speculator as one of low birth (although this was often implied). Rather, the speculator was deemed dangerous because he was unable to exercise the self-control necessary to render his interaction with the market virtuous. The speculator neither respected the fortunes of others nor invested for the good of others. Instead, he was driven by an unfettered self-interest. His actions threatened to rend the social fabric by unleashing forces of materialism and selfish ambition.

The speculator's lack of honor was manifested by his absence of loyalty to either family or nation. As early as 1841, the vicomte d'Arlincourt argued in *Les Français peints par eux-mêmes* that the speculator valued his family only to the extent that it could benefit him, writing, "the speculator has a family: nephews, cousins, brothers. This is not however required ... [, but] if it should prove to be so, what matters is to get something out of it."[95] Later authors picked up on this theme, arguing that the speculator only valued the family insofar as it could be of financial use to him. In *La Question d'argent*, Jean reveals his true colors when he offers to give his fiancé a dowry of a million francs, provided she keep it separate under the terms of the marriage contract. Since she has nothing but her name, Jean does this not to protect her fortune, as would normally be the case when such an agreement was made, but to protect his own fortune from creditors who could not pursue money kept in his wife's name. Elisa, his fiancé, is horrified and tells him that since her father ruined himself to pay his own creditors (thus manifesting his honor), people would think he stole the money for her "dowry" from his employer. Doubts expressed throughout the play regarding Elisa's virginity, however, suggest another interpretation since Jean's attempt to combine a romantic and financial transaction would essentially render his future wife a prostitute. By eventually refusing her intended, Elisa asserts her rightful place outside of market relations. Jean's lack of honor and respect for his future wife are made evident when Elisa tears up the marriage contract.[96]

By the 1850s, the private world of love and marriage was increasingly identified as a realm outside of market relations and marked by an evident absence of self-interest. By mixing this private world with the public world of the stock market, the speculator introduced market forces into areas in which they did not belong, thus endangering the stability and reputation of families. In Henry de Kock's 1858 collection of stories concerning the stock market, he tells of a man whose desire for easy money leads him to court both a mother and her daughter. The mother, outraged by his behavior, accuses him of "having trampled upon any concern for what people might say, in making a daughter the rival of her mother ... the mother a rival of her daughter."[97] The untrammeled force of self-interest, represented in this example by the speculator, was considered to pose a danger to personal relationships by perverting hierarchies within the family.

The speculator's disregard for his own reputation was mirrored not only by his lack of respect for the reputation of others but also by his disregard for the good of the nation as a whole. In Ernest Feydeau's play *Un Coup de bourse*, the speculator Silberstein "profits from the unhappiness of his country, benefits from its ruin" in speculating on the Crimean War.[98] The journalist E. Pellisson believed that speculation encouraged betrayal to the nation by promoting a desire for wealth at all costs: "thirst for gold! thirst for gold! it produces a madness for luxury, a fever for pleasure! It is the principle of egoism, one of the most active causes of the decadence of nations."[99] The virtue of the nation, as the family writ large, could only be safeguarded by maintaining the stock market within strict limits. Female members of this family (and nation) had to be protected from the influence of market forces. To do so, male members had to muster all the self-control and honor they possessed to resist these same forces, while channeling them into productive outlets. Many thus expressed the belief that, if controlled, the stock market could serve to advance the cause of civilization. Unrestrained, however, the stock market threatened the individual, the family, and the nation. In emphasizing the honor and restraint of some men, and in comparing the behavior of such men to that of unscrupulous speculators and impassioned women, contemporaries sought to promote a positive masculine identity in relation to the marketplace. Much like male workers during the 1840s, these authors argued that participation in the marketplace was not only possible for men, it was laudable, if done for the right reasons. And, like the male workers of the 1840s, writers used a patriotic discourse to make these distinctions.

As part of an attempt to emphasize the national character of masculine honor in relation to the stock exchange, by the late Second Empire, the character of the speculator was increasingly vilified using an anti-Semitic discourse. Eugène de Mirecourt's works on the stock market, for example, contain a violent anti-Semitism that linked speculation with an international Jewish conspiracy. Mirecourt believed that only by eliminating passion and self-interest from the stock market could one combat "the network of Jewish power that spreads throughout the entire world [and] is centered in our country [*chez nous*]."[100] Attacks in the press against the power of "Jewish finance" were particularly virulent during moments of crisis, although during the 1860s they became more constant, if less violent in tone.[101]

Although during the Second Empire the Jewish community in France was mostly poor, a few very wealthy individuals were highly visible in connection with the new forms of credit, banking, and speculation.[102] Many of those who supported these new institutions had been strongly influenced by the Saint-Simonian movement. Although always a minority in the movement, several Jewish men who rose to prominence in French society—the Péreire brothers, Olinde Rodrigues, Léon Halévy, and Baron Gustave d'Eichtal—were influenced by and associated with its ideas. Indeed, the rival Fourierists considered Saint-Simonism to be a primarily "Jewish" movement that sought to further the interests of "commerce" and sought to discredit it on these grounds.[103]

During the Second Empire, the Péreire brothers, founders of the Crédit Mobilier, were in particular highly visible. The projects of the Péreire brothers were strongly supported by the government, who saw them as furthering its goal of democratizing credit. An earlier unrealized project for a new type of bank was described by the brothers as designed "to increase the salaries of workers and diminish the *revenues of the lazy*."[104] This idea that a better redistribution of income could come about through facilitating credit, a key Saint-Simonian concept, was central to the early success of the Crédit Mobilier, which was supported from the outset by small property owners.[105]

Jules Mirès and Moïse Millaud, also Jewish, were also associated with the world of high finance, as well as with the world of journalism. Mirès, who made his name in journalism in 1848, owned at various times during the Second Empire *Le Constitutionnel, La Presse,* and *Le Pays,* all newspapers with significant readership. Mirès also founded the *Caisse des actions réunies* in 1850, a fund dedicated to the buying and selling of stock, and participated in 1854 in founding another new bank, the Crédit Foncier de France. Mirès, according to *Le Figaro,* "was in the habit of saying, 'I represent the *democratization* of credit.'"[106] Like the Péreire brothers, he was associated with the introduction of new methods of banking and finance that not only made it possible for more people to invest in stocks but also encouraged widespread investment as a means to produce wealth that would benefit the society as a whole.

Critics, however, represented this democratization as a "democratization of material appetites."[107] By arguing that Jewish financiers and speculators did not belong to the French nation, critics attempted to undermine the claims of Mirès or the Péreire brothers that they were acting to increase public wealth and to promote industrial advancement. This criticism was all the more prominent as it was shared by conservatives, who feared what they considered to be unrestricted access to financial markets, and by socialists, who targeted these new institutions as a means to criticize the government of Napoleon III, a strong supporter of the Péreires. Thus critics from both sides of the political spectrum argued that "Jewish" finance was destroying the nation.

Critics of "Jewish" finance frequently linked female vice with the speculative practices that they believed individuals like the Péreires or Mirès encouraged. Georges Duchêne's 1867 *La Spéculation devant les tribunaux* argued, "The *Jews* have become once again *the kings of our era* . . . . Public morality has suffered the backlash of economic upheaval." As signs of this crisis, he cited, "the extravagance [in the clothing] of women, the shamelessness of prostitution, the literature of the alcove."[108] Many writers argued that their associations with women could explain the excesses of male speculators in general. Thus for example, Ernest Feydeau, a novelist, playwright, and trader on the *coulisse* wrote in his memoirs that if a man didn't pay what he owed on the stock market, "100 times out of 100 . . . one can be certain that it is his wife, or some woman, who prevents him [from doing so]."[109] Likewise, both Jean, who did not respect the sacred bonds of marriage, and Silberstein, who betrayed his country to make money on the stock market, had lorettes as mistresses. Lorettes, who as a type were far more prevalent in popular literature than the speculator, served to define all that was believed to be dishonorable about speculation.

The lorette, and female speculators in general, were particularly identified with investments in foreign countries. As early as 1836, Frédéric Soulié wrote that women preferred to invest in foreign government bonds and argued that this was perhaps because such investments, whose "variations [in value] were serious, capricious, and almost always without any foreseeable cause," fulfilled women's needs for "strong, rapid and profound emotions."[110] This equation of female speculation and foreign investment took on greater significance during the Second Empire, when the growing internationalization of the French capital market had begun to make some observers uneasy. The author of a journal devoted to describing the trends and movements of the stock market warned that investment in Russian railroads was potentially dangerous since one day the railroads could be used against France.[111] Another author wondered whether the French hadn't invested too much money in Egypt, asking, "have we no longer anything to undertake in France that would be useful, that would be necessary?"[112] Many authors joined this chorus, arguing that the French should only invest in other countries "on one condition, that above all our own enterprises don't suffer."[113] Others argued that any investment at all in foreign countries was dangerous. Alexandre Durant, for example, denounced "this unheard of, profound sentiment that pushes so many who play the market to desire, for feeble gains, a diminishing of our power, and sometimes even national disasters."[114] Women's supposed proclivity to invest in foreign countries thus marked them as driven by self-interest rather than a concern for the good of the nation. Ernest Feydeau depicted the treachery of female speculators in his play set during the Crimean War: "one hears [the women playing the market] laugh at times at tales of public disaster that make the entire nation shudder . . . sometimes also they stand there, pale and stupefied, while all the citizens of the country congratulate each other on a victory that should hasten the conclusion of peace."[115]

As this quote illustrates, by playing against the national interest in order to increase their own gains on the market, women manifested their unsuitability to be included in the category of "citizen." By the Second Empire, the preservation of both female virtue and national interest demanded that women distance themselves from the affairs of the market in general. Women were redefined over the course of the nineteenth century as beings who had no concern for money, who were unable to earn a living wage, and who could not be considered independent entrepreneurs. Likewise, the assertion that women did not pay their debts served to reinforce the sentiment that female virtue entailed an inability to act in the public good, and thus justified women's exclusion from both the stock market and from citizenship.

In the 1841 *Physiologie de l'argent*, the author asserted that the lorette rarely paid her debts.[116] He continued, however, with anecdotes that illustrated that the lorette did pay her debts, either with sex or with money. By the Second Empire, however, authors largely agreed that women who played the stock market did not pay their debts. Popular literature from the 1850s and 1860s is full of stories of women who cheat brokers who have given them credit, sometimes refusing outright to pay on the basis that legally women were not able to enter into contractual agreements and thus could not be held liable (what one author called "theft à la civil code").[117] Women's lack of honor in upholding their financial obligations made them unworthy participants on the stock exchange and disqualified them for consideration as citizens.

While women were believed to possess virtue, a quality that made them exceptional guardians of the private sphere; they did not possess honor, a characteristic necessary for the proper functioning of the public sphere. In fact, several authors argued that women's virtue in the private sphere necessarily precluded their possession of honor in the public sphere. Thus Ernest Feydeau argued that women were unsuited for the stock market because the only virtue they were taught was chastity: "What does the society mean by an *honest woman*? Is it a woman who is polite? Or a woman who is scrupulous in matters of money? Not in the least. It is a woman who doesn't cheat on her husband."[118] Such comments were not, however, calls to educate women in other virtues but rather were meant to reinforce the distinction between female (private) virtue and male (public) honor.

Whether male or female, the self-regulation of one's conduct was necessary because the social transformations caused by new economic and political structures made it increasingly difficult to identify the class position and moral character of others. Unless he gave himself away by his conduct, a parvenu who yesterday had nothing could be mistaken for a man from a well-established family. This fear that the spread of speculation through society allowed people to present a false appearance was once again concentrated on the lorette.

The ability of the lorette to change her class position had been expressed during the July Monarchy through her adoption of masculine dress. By the Second Empire, the lorette's upward mobility was much more discreet. Consonant with her loss of independent financial power, she was no longer portrayed as wearing masculine clothing. The lorette of the 1850s and 1860s was a model of femininity, at least in appearance. Riding in her carriage or in the midst of her "salon," it would be impossible, writers noted, to distinguish her from her wealthy bourgeois counterpart. The lorette was a trendsetter; she set the style that bourgeois women then strove to imitate: "she is barely stripped of the rags of her first position, (when) she sets the style, she invents, she creates the fashion and all its coquettish and provocative trifles."[119]

This inability to distinguish between respectable women and the lorette was what writers found most troubling since the lorette differed from honest women in that she was essentially a prostitute. One writer lamented that although debauched women had always existed, "never has the woman who sells her body dared to take on, as we see in our own day, the dress and the habits of virtue, and underneath these false coverings, display everywhere her shameless speculation."[120] The lorette, still associated with the stock market, threatened the social order by blurring, through an appearance that was the envy of middle-class women, the boundaries between vice and virtue, between the elite and the popular classes.

Writers therefore feared that the influence of the lorette would both undermine the difference between the classes and encourage the growth of speculation among the general population. Writers believed that if "honest" women adopted the fashions pioneered by the lorette, they would also adopt her mores. The popular novel by Ernest Feydeau, *La Comtesse de Chalis ou les moeurs du jour*, gave what must have been for many readers a most horrifying example of this blurring of boundaries between the lorette and the respectable woman; in this novel, the countess, who recognized in the lorette a similarity to herself, enters into a bisexual love triangle with her and a speculator.[121] The lorette of the Second Empire was thus used to signify a general moral decay spurred by the desire for material gain that was also depicted as a dissolution of the social hierarchy. The lorette evoked fears associated with the Second Empire's democratization of capital, fears that superficially seemed to be concerned with the issue of female virtue, but that, in their evocation of the dissolution of boundaries brought about by equal access to the stock market, touched on more fundamental questions of access to power.

The seriousness of these fears can be seen in the responses designed to allay them. In 1865, Attorney General Dupin introduced in the Senate a project that sought to prevent women from displaying their wealth through the wearing of expensive clothing. In his speech to the Senate, Dupin associated the spread of materialism with both democracy and the lorette. Justifying his project as an attempt to put an end to clandestine prostitution, Dupin argued that one of the primary causes of prostitution was "*the exaggeration of luxury, the excesses of fashion* [which] throws everyone off of their track. [Even those] in the most favorable situations are appalled [by this excess], and with each winter, with each season, the revelation [of such excess] manifests itself over the clothing bills that the most considerable fortunes will barely suffice to liquidate and which sometimes fall into delayed payments or settlement. This descends to the inferior classes by imitation, by the spirit of *equality*. Each woman wants to have the same outfit as the others." The model for these fashions, Dupin stated, was the lorette, "the courtesans who display themselves in public places. . . . [High society] sees them, takes them as a model, and it is these young ladies who set the fashion even for women of society." To pay for these fashions, Dupin argued, women of every class had to resort to credit: "one's dignity takes over, one loathes to ask one's husband [for money], the conjugal cash-box is empty; one [therefore] dresses oneself on credit, one signs promissory notes, letters of change, for which one seeks backers and whose due date is always fatal to one's virtue." While Dupin implicitly recognized the problem of women's economic dependency, he did not endorse their greater financial independence. Rather he recommended that "mothers of families" establish "temperance societies" designed to discourage the "superfluous" in fashion. As women of the popular classes followed this new example, he argued, women would no longer be tempted by speculation and (therefore) driven to prostitution.[122]

Dupin's project inspired a flurry of pamphlets. Both those who supported and those who opposed the project criticized the growing materialism of French society that they believed was manifested in female dress. Despite this consensus, however, the project was ultimately defeated on the grounds that the restriction of luxury in clothing would unduly hurt the Parisian economy. The serious pamphlets emphasized the importance of the luxury trades and defended female virtue. Ernest Feydeau, for example, argued that luxury was not only useful "since it returned to the poor, in the form of a salary, the necessary due to them; . . . it is moreover the exterior manifestation of civilization and the most direct agent of the socialization of peoples."[123] Such responses argued that aside from the lorette, who took everything to excess, most women stayed well within the bounds of good taste and common sense in choosing their wardrobe. Other authors, and especially the authors of pamphlets meant to parody the debate, addressed under the cover of humor the underlying issue of female access to wealth and credit, and the larger problem of political equality that it evoked. In making comments such as, "Just as all Frenchmen [Français] are equal before the law, all French women [Françaises] believe themselves to be equal before fashion," these parodic pamphlets highlighted the political stakes involved in this debate and raised the issue of control over the generation of wealth under the guise of consumption.[124]

Feminists also understood Dupin's proposal to limit women's choices as consumers as an attack on their freedom in general. Since the 1830s, feminists had repeatedly demanded women's access to the stock exchange and the commodities market. In the first issue of La Gazette des femmes, which appeared in 1836, Madame Poutret de Mauchamps argued that since women had paid taxes that were used to construct and maintain the Stock Exchange they should be allowed entry.[125] Her repeated calls for women's access to the stock exchange were echoed by Second Empire feminists such as Julie Daubié, who maintained that access to the stock exchange, like education or employment opportunities, were necessary to prevent female poverty and thus ensure public virtue.[126]

In making such arguments, feminists such as Daubié provided an alternative model of the virtuous marketplace. While most of the authors we have discussed argued that the maintenance of virtue within market society demanded the exclusion of women from the marketplace, feminists argued that a virtuous marketplace demanded women's inclusion. One place in which this argument was developed was in the pages of Le Droit des femmes, which began publication in 1869. Certain contributors to this newspaper presented the market not as the agent of women's downfall but rather as a source of their freedom. In particular, they revalorized the image of the lorette by once again associating her with the carefree and ambitious prostitute. Although they condemned prostitution as immoral, they also used the image of the prostitute to demonstrate the importance of choice and freedom for women.

An article by Amélie Bosquet provides a good example of this process of redefinition. In this article, Bosquet employed the story of the grisette and the lorette to discuss women's economic dependency. Significantly, Bosquet shifted the focus of her tale away from the woman's "fall" by entitling her article, "Types Masculins. Don Juan." Bosquet began her article with familiar imagery: "During the Restoration and the reign of Louis-Philippe, Don Juan [was] a simple student of the Latin Quarter, keeping house with the grisette." The grisette, according to Bosquet, was aware that "her inferior position" dictated that she would eventually be abandoned by the student, but "she was too loving and too reasonable" to prevent it. One day, however, the grisette decided that she could spare herself the pain of heartache by hardening her heart and "preoccupying herself less with the future of her lover and more with her own." Although Bosquet did not praise the grisette's choice, her rendition of the story was unusual in that it conferred upon the grisette the ability to think and act rationally. Bosquet emphasized the power of female agency; rather than the object of forces over which she had no control, the grisette acted to take a decision that affected all those around her. In remaking herself into the lorette, Bosquet argued, the grisette killed Don Juan, the student, transforming him into a simple "buyer." Bosquet's tale becomes one not concerned, after all, with the demise of the grisette at the hands of men and the forces of modernization but one of the demise of Don Juan at the hands of women. Evoking the distinction between giving and selling love that runs throughout stories of the grisette in her assertion that in women it is either "the head or the heart that governs," Bosquet made a powerful argument for the dangers of women's economic dependency. Although she condemned the "impious and evil victory" of the lorette, she used this tale not to argue for women's exclusion from the public sphere but rather to prove that women needed to have an independent source of income, one that would allow them to make the decision to love with their heart rather than their head, to reject self-interest in favor of the public good. "There is only one path to salvation open to a civilization in danger," she concluded, "it is that of work, true love, and justice, where women should march first in giving an example."[127]

Like the Saint-Simonian feminists, Bosquet contrasted work and prostitution. Unlike these earlier authors, however, she emphasized female agency. Like Parent-Duchâtelet, Bosquet implied that women chose prostitution as a means of obtaining a better income. However, whereas

Parent-Duchâtelet depicted prostitution as a false choice since the prostitute could not escape her economic dependency, Bosquet presented prostitution as the only opportunity for women to be truly independent.

Another contributor to the paper, Maria Deraismes, took a similar approach. In an article entitled "L'Hétaérisme," Deraismes used the stereotype of the lorette to argue that women required an outlet for their ambitions and greater control over their finances. Deraismes played with critics' attempts to associate *Le Droit des femmes* with free love by exposing the double meaning of the term "free woman."[128] Arguing that "only the courtesan has been a free woman," Deraismes maintained that the possibility of upward social mobility was denied to all other women. Whereas any young man with talent, intelligence, and the will to succeed could make his way in the world, Deraismes argued, a poor woman, "despite her talents, . . . is definitively poor for the rest of her days, because she will never occupy any but the lowest rungs on the ladder of work; the superior rungs being forbidden to her. Her resource is a husband. If she lacks a husband, it is necessary to fall back on the lover." Concluding that certain women simply found it easier to start with the lover, Deraismes argued that the only way to put an end to the reign of courtesans was to "emancipate women with dignity by the exercise of their talents, by their introduction to the liberal professions, by the restitution of their individuality in marriage."[129] Unlike the Saint-Simonians, Deraismes used the image of the prostitute to argue that women wanted to be able to participate in the market on equal terms with men. The difference between her approach and that of the earlier writers indicates the extent to which participation in the marketplace had become identified with citizenship by the late 1860s.

Despite the various measures taken to limit access to the stock exchange and control the spread of materialism through French society, a number of factors encouraged both modest investors and women to continue to seek access to the market. A greater familiarity with and acceptance of the market, the knowledge that others were making money on the market, and the existence of institutions, like the Crédit Mobilier, that depended on modest investors for their existence, all dictated against the ability of middle-class men to preserve their exclusive club. Popular and female participation in the stock market thus continued to be an issue throughout the Second Empire, and even beyond. In the 1880s and 1890s, for example, contemporaries worried about the extension of the stock market into the French countryside, while newspaper articles concerning the *coulisse* regularly included photographs of female participants.[130]

As the spread of the stock market's influence came to be seen as inevitable, contemporaries focused even greater attention on rendering the market virtuous. For feminists such as Deraismes and Bosquet, virtue could only be retained if women were allowed equal access to the marketplace. This position was, however, a minority position, even within the pages of *La Droit des femmes*. Most French men and women seemed to believe by the late 1860s that the creation and maintenance of a virtuous marketplace required women to be economically dependent. Just as women workers were increasingly believed to be unsuccessful wage earners and as merchants in the city's markets were defined as recipients of charity rather than businesswomen, so too were women who hoped to take charge of their finances by investing in stocks and bonds portrayed as unsuccessful or unscrupulous. Similarly, men were required to exercise restraint, a central characteristic of bourgeois honor, and to act out of the desire to help others. Demure selflessness on the part of women and discreet self-control on the part of men were opposed to self-interest and were to become the new characteristics that defined both the virtuous marketplace and the French nation.

Conclusion

At the dawning of the nineteenth century, the political economist Jean-Baptiste Say wrote, "It is said that virtue should be made lovable. I would dare to add that it should be made profitable. Vice is ugly; let us also make it ruinous."[1] Say's interest in the relationship between virtue and profit was shared by many of his contemporaries throughout the nineteenth century, who strove to control what were perceived to be the damaging effects of market forces without rejecting the market altogether. They did this with the goal of creating a virtuous marketplace. Central to the creation of this virtuous marketplace was the elaboration of new definitions of masculinity and femininity, definitions that implied a differential relationship of the sexes to money and the marketplace.

In differentiating between two approaches to the market that were believed to be complementary and indispensable, mid-nineteenth-century French men and women were using money to create meaningful distinctions. In her fascinating study of the social meaning of money in the late-nineteenth- and early-twentieth-century United States, Viviana Zelizer demonstrates how people differentiate between different types of money that they earmark for different purposes; for example, money from an inheritance might be used differently than that earned from one's trade or profession. Drawing on the work of anthropologists who have studied the meaning of money in diverse societies throughout the world, Zelizer argues that the practice of earmarking is especially prevalent when attempting to control others or to establish or maintain hierarchies. Money, she concludes, is not an impersonal or universal entity; it is rather a vehicle used to create, express, and maintain social and family relationships and to establish distinctions between moral and immoral, masculine and feminine, self and community.[2]

Zelizer's insights into the social meaning of money can be usefully applied to the discussion of different approaches to the market. Just as in many societies different gendered currencies are used to express the different status of men and women, in nineteenth-century France different gendered understandings of the relationship between an individual and the marketplace were established.[3] The idea that men and women approached the market differently, in realms as diverse as consumption, production, commerce, investment, and speculation, was developed as a response to changes in French economic structures and the conflicts between the public good and private interest that these changes were believed to have initiated. The notion of differential approaches to the market, approaches that were gendered masculine and feminine, helped contemporaries understand and accept the economic, social, and even political changes they were experiencing. This belief in different approaches to the market also allowed contemporaries to shape and regulate economic structures and institutions, justifying, for example, the exclusion of women workers from well-paying trades, the enclosure of the capital's central food market, the *halles*, and the restriction of the stock exchange. As mastery of the marketplace became linked to definitions of what it meant to be a citizen, the difference between "masculine" and "feminine" approaches to the marketplace could be used to decide who would be excluded and who included in the polity. And as the question of self-control in relation to the marketplace became a central component of middle-class masculine identity, charges of its absence could be used against the less powerful and influential to limit their access to wealth and power.

By the 1860s, the idea of different approaches to the marketplace based on gender was being used to define and celebrate French national identity. In particular, the French celebrated the relationship of French women to the marketplace as a characteristic that distinguished them from others, including their chief economic rival, England. French and English women did, in fact, experience the market differently. English women were granted control over their wages as early as 1857; French women had to wait until 1907. Married women in France kept nominal control over their property if they wed under the regime of *séparation des biens* (a contractual arrangement that allowed each spouse to retain individual ownership of property held before the marriage). Husbands, however, had the right to "manage" this property, a right that left women with little recourse against unscrupulous or inept spouses. By contrast, married women in England gained complete control over their property by 1882. Likewise, in England "no legal or even social barriers prevented [women] from playing an important economic role by putting up risk capital and by playing the stock exchange."[4] The difference that attracted by far the most attention of contemporaries was, however, prostitution. While English women successfully fought an attempted imposition of the regulatory system for prostitutes developed in France in the name of preserving women's modesty and freedom, French men celebrated the greater control of prostitutes in France as a sign of their country's moral superiority.[5] J. Jeannel's 1868 study on prostitution, for example, argued that France's system of surveillance and medical examinations proved her superiority over England because it revealed the country's awareness that "moderation is necessary in all things." He depicted England's lack of regulatory system, on the other hand, as a manifestation of a commitment to unfettered laissez-faire. "Respect for the law and the love of liberty," Jeannel wrote, "are the most marvelous agents of public power and prosperity. English society offers the most striking example of this. One must nonetheless concede that [in England] respect for the law sometimes becomes the sole fetish for progress, and the love of liberty is taken to limits that are incompatible with the dignity and morality of the nation." The French, Jeannel stated, more willing to bend the law, less attached to liberty for its own sake, were better able to safeguard morality and virtue. Jeannel argued that although "[o]ne can object in vain that each [individual] has the right to dispose of her person, and that one cannot restrain, reprimand, or regulate prostitution without attacking the liberty of woman," prostitutes, because they compromised public health and public safety, fell outside the boundaries of law.[6]

Like Parent-Duchâtelet and so many after him, Jeannel argued that women's state of economic dependency justified her subordination to the force of [masculine] law. Women's special relationship to the market thus both determined her special legal status and became a source of French moral superiority in the global economy. The authors of the Chamber of Commerce's 1860 survey of Parisian industry took a very similar approach. Whereas the 1848 survey had been designed largely to reassure Parisians of the essential stability of industry in the capital following the revolution, the 1860 survey was a celebration of the recently concluded free-trade treaty with England. This survey placed women's work, so vital in the fashion trades and in the fabrication of *articles de Paris*, at the center of France's industrial success. Whereas the 1848 survey had attempted to hide women's work, the 1860 survey glorified it. As the authors wrote in their introduction to the study, the "intervention of women in [the world of] work is, as one can see, essentially varied and very diverse; it gives Parisian industry its own special physiognomy and creates in several branches of production a source of important foreign commerce."[7]

While the survey thus placed women's work at the center of France's international economic success, it also defined the participation of women in the economy as one of influence rather than manufacture. In women's clothing, for example, the authors stated that "in general the best women workers are those who create [the designs], while their husbands execute them."[8] Women's ability to create objects of beauty was depicted as arising not from a learned skill but from an innate biological ability. The female worker in the fashion trades thus "invents, modifies, improves [her designs] by trying them on herself."[9] The ability of the woman worker in women's fashion, one of the most lucrative sectors of the export trade, was tied to qualities believed to be innately feminine, in particular her desire for nice clothes. Women workers were thus valued not for skills or abilities associated with production but rather for qualities that made them natural consumers. No mention was made of skill or the need to earn a living. Indeed, in comparison to the 1848 survey, this study gives much less information concerning salaries and virtually no information regarding women's wages.

Consummate consumers themselves, women workers were able to draw upon their own wishes and desires to create new fashions and luxury items that would appeal to consumers both at home and abroad. While women's abilities to produce, exchange, and manage wealth had been largely discounted by the 1860s, women were increasingly identified with consumption. In the case of the 1860 Chamber of Commerce survey, women's special relationship to the market, a relationship defined as one of consumption even if it was actually one of production, was celebrated as the source of French economic superiority.

On the other hand, areas in which French industry was suffering damaging international competition were associated with female prostitution. Thus despite their attempt to paint a rosy picture of the Parisian economy, authors of the 1860 survey also revealed their anxiety regarding the French ability to compete, repeatedly citing the lower prices of goods produced in the German states, Switzerland, and England. In sectors of the economy where France was suffering, such as in the production of elasticized cloth, authors noted that "women workers employed in the workshops possess, like the men, habits of laziness and dissipation."[10] While those trades that were prospering were said to owe their success to women's innate love of luxury and beauty, poverty among workers in the sectors most affected by international competition was explained by reference to their immoral conduct. Like Jeannel's study of prostitution, the 1860 survey thus used women's relationship to the marketplace—as either consumers or prostitutes—to explain the relationship of France to her economic competitors.

Despite the especially strong presence of women workers in the luxury trades that were the backbone of France's international economy, authors of the 1860 Chamber of Commerce survey were unable to imagine women's contribution to the economy in terms of production. By the 1860s, the widespread acceptance of the idea that women could not produce wealth made it difficult to imagine virtuous women as producers of wealth. This was true even for some feminists. A play written by Ernest Legouvé, a contributor to the feminist newspaper *Le Droit des femmes,* illustrates how even a feminist who supported greater work opportunities for women expressed the belief that women should not retain control over their finances. Legouvé wrote the play entitled *Les Doigts de fée* in collaboration with the prolific playwright Eugène Scribe.[11] The title, "fairy fingers," was a term commonly used by the 1860s to refer to women's supposedly "magical" abilities to create objects of beauty. The increasingly common use of this term reveals a growing conviction that women's participation in the economy was due to an innate and irrational talent that constituted an extension of her "natural" feminine attributes rather than an incursion into the world of the marketplace. Legouvé and Scribe drew on this belief to create a story about the dangers of the marketplace. In the play, Hélène, an orphaned noblewoman who becomes a seamstress when her protectors throw her out, rises to fame and fortune due to her ability to translate into cloth the sartorial desires of the aristocracy and wealthy bourgeoisie. Her uncle risks the property of her cousin, Tristan, by engaging in a shady speculative deal. He is only saved from utter ruin by Hélène, who gives her cousin Tristan sixty thousand francs from her own savings to rescue the family's property and honor. Hélène's reward is to marry Tristan and withdraw from the world of work.

Les Doigts de fée echoed contemporary beliefs that mastery of the marketplace and the maintenance of virtue depended upon one's ability to resist the temptations for luxury and pleasure that wealth could bring about. The authors' message was a feminist one, in that it implied women could resist consumer desires and save money. However, although it was Hélène's years of hard work that produced the wealth necessary to save the family, Legouvé and Scribe emphasized not her talent with money but rather her selflessness and willingness to give up her fortune to save those she loved. Instead, Tristan, who wished to renounce the aristocratic culture of leisure that was his birthright in order to embrace the bourgeois ethic of hard work, would be the agent to carry on the family's new motto: "Erased by time, regilded by industry and work."[12]

Although Legouvé attempted to portray women's work in a positive light, he found himself falling back on the belief that women should not really participate in the marketplace. Most, however, did not even try to imagine women's involvement in the market in positive terms. Critics of *Le Droit des femmes*, to which Legouvé contributed, criticized the paper's demands for women's equality by arguing that if women became the equals of men, they would let loose the disruptive forces of the market-place on French society. *Le Charivari*, for example, condemned women's emancipation by arguing that if they were not kept under control, women would deplete men's fortunes and undermine their honor. "Legitimate wives and mistresses," *Le Charivari* insisted, "have rivaled to corrupt men. The first in trying to seize from them all the higher preoccupations in order to inject them with the sole love of lucre, of lucre all the same, of lucre to the death; the others, the *farceuses,* have driven them crazy with pleasure and have destroyed the few scruples of integrity or honor that could still stop them."[13] Even male contributors to *Le Droit des femmes* had trouble ridding themselves of the association between women's freedom and destructive market forces. Thus Léon Richer, the paper's editor, replied to *Le Charivari* by stating, "you justify our painful and difficult campaign! The *bourgeoise* [middle-class woman] herself has a great need, I agree with you, to be uprooted from her rapacious interests."[14]

Despite attempts such as that by the authors of the Chamber of Commerce survey or male feminists to valorize women's work as a source of stability and a civilizing influence, contemporaries continued to assume that exposure to the marketplace posed a threat to women's morality, and thus to the nation as a whole. One reason French men may have had such difficulty in accepting the possibility of women as agents within the market economy was that the inability of women to engage successfully in the economy was a mainstay not just of feminine identity but of masculine identity as well. The definition of masculine honor that developed in the mid-nineteenth century was built in part around the notion that women required men's protection. This protection was defined in economic terms, since women's vulnerability in regards to the market was believed to require men's economic support. In order to protect women, men were required to exercise the self-control that was necessary for a successful negotiation of market forces. To argue that women could also negotiate the market was thus to undermine one of the central tenets of masculinity in the mid-nineteenth century. This helps to explain the violent opposition many expressed to women's economic emancipation. In 1869, for example, a writer for *L'Union savoisienne* responded to an article by Legouvé on reforming the civil code by stating, "If woman wants to be the equal of man . . . she *ceases to be a woman;* she becomes a man; her tastes take on a masculine tone. She *dresses like us, smokes cigars,* drives a carriage."[15] If women became men, then what would men become? Arguing for women's economic emancipation threatened the stability of masculine identity as well as that of the society as a whole.

As women lost opportunities to produce and manage wealth, their identity as consumers received increasing emphasis. As the 1860 Chamber of Commerce survey indicated, consumption could be seen as the natural counterpart of production; the one, gendered female, worked together with the other, gendered male, to create wealth for the nation as a whole, just as husband and wife cooperated in raising a family. Indeed, both male and female writers in mid-nineteenth-century France "believed that women had a natural inclination toward tastefulness, simply by virtue of being female—and French."[16] The "natural" good taste of the Parisienne in particular was said to be a source of international envy and the justification for the spread of French "civilization" throughout the world. At the same time, however, the belief that consumer desires held dangers for women, and to a lesser extent men, was widespread throughout the nineteenth century. From Parent-Duchâtelet to the Baron Dupin, the belief that the temptation of material goods lured young women into prostitution was a common theme in mid-nineteenth-century writings. As women's economic identity became increasingly restricted to that of consumers, women as consumers became the locus of increased anxiety. This anxiety was related both to a perceived commercialization of French life and to a shift toward a more democratic political and social system.

Concern regarding female consumers surfaced in the last two decades of the nineteenth century. The choices a woman made as a consumer "could reveal her personality, [yet] so too could [they] betray her weaknesses and deviations from the norm."[17] Consumption provided women an outlet for their individuality; in so doing, it threatened the identity, reputation, and thus stability of the family. Fear of female consumers also led to concerns regarding women's conduct within department stores. By the end of the century, contemporaries worried that the abundance and luxury of consumer goods within department stores caused women to lose control and steal items they did not really need and that they could easily afford. Market forces overwhelmed female shoplifters, causing them to lose their restraint and reason and endanger the reputation of their families.[18] As the example of shoplifters demonstrates, women as consumers, like women as workers, merchants, and speculators, were believed to be simultaneously vulnerable and powerful; vulnerable to market forces, they also possessed the power to unleash these forces on French society as a whole.[19]

Anxiety regarding female criminality during the fin-de-siècle, including shoplifting, can be seen within the context of concern about the democratization of culture.[20] Many feared that the emergence of a commercialized mass culture in the late nineteenth century was a sign of national decline, while others considered mass culture a potentially useful tool for creating a unified national community.[21] In either case, the debate regarding the positive or negative effects of democratization was expressed in relation to the impact of the marketplace. Given the developments of the mid-nineteenth century, it is not surprising that during a period in which both the working-class and the feminist movements were becoming increasingly well organized and vocal, the debate regarding the impact of market forces—this time focusing on consumerism and the commercialization of culture—should once again take on great prominence.

In this context, those who deplored the democratization of culture as a sign of its cheapening and superficiality sought new ways to relate to the marketplace. Adherents of the French avant-garde, for example, called into question the self-control that was believed to be necessary for men when faced with the temptations of the marketplace. In J.-K. Huysmans's 1884 novel, A Rebours, consumer items become "drugs" whose sole purpose is to induce a sensual pleasure.[22] While some women were taking advantage of new employment opportunities in fields such as teaching to become economically self-sufficient, some men were advocating a more individualist and hedonistic relationship to the marketplace. By the late nineteenth century, then, some women were rejecting the model of female economic dependency inherent in the idea of the virtuous marketplace, while some men began to question the heavy responsibilities conferred upon them as breadwinners for a family.

For most people, however, the idea that the domain of business and the marketplace was that of men while the domain of the family was that of women retained its force long past the Second Empire. To take the stock market as an example, as late as 1933 a female journalist, Odette Pennetier, was expelled from the stock exchange when she attempted to enter the building for a story.[23] In 1967, as the women's movement was picking up steam, feminists protested that although women had once again been permitted to enter the second-floor galleries, they were forbidden access to the ground floor, where the trading took place. In an interview with L'Aurore, a denizen of the stock exchange declared that if women were allowed access to this part of the building it would change the atmosphere so much that one might as well open up a tea shop in the building. Complaining that the stock exchange was the "only place where we can be calm," he pleaded with women to leave men this last bastion of their privilege and identity. "Today," he stated, "you women have the same jobs that we do, the same civil rights, the same salaries, bank accounts in your name. You smoke in the street, you go to the café alone and you wear tuxedos in the evening . . . . So, leave us our temple, if not, we will no longer have anything of our own."[24]

This trader's complaint very much echoed those of his nineteenth-century predecessors, who also believed that the control of money, commerce, and exchange were crucial components of what it meant to be a man. By focusing on the issue of identity, comments such as this obscured questions of access to power and wealth. The development of the idea that women were unfit participants in the marketplace helped contemporaries negotiate the effects of market forces on French society. At the same time, this idea justified measures designed to prevent an equitable distribution of power. The proclamation of the authors of the 1854 *Paris-Boursier*, "if women were allowed access to the stock market they would be the equal of men," was echoed in countless texts dedicated to describing the use and abuse of the stock exchange during the Second Empire.[25] In a variety of texts, the "problem" of women and the marketplace was presented as one of the growing influence of materialism on all social classes and the threat this desire for personal gain posed to the public good. However, the importance of gender difference to the creation and stabilization of the postrevolutionary sociopolitical order rendered this "problem" one of access to power. Whereas opponents to absolutism in the eighteenth century had posited the free market and the pursuit of self-interest as a certain means to ensure liberty and the rights of the individual, many mid-nineteenth-century thinkers, wary of democracy and revolution, preferred to speak not of liberty, but of virtue, not of self-interest, but of self-control. The development of the idea of the virtuous marketplace was thus a response to political, as well as economic transformations.

Notes

Abbreviations

AN   Archives Nationales
APDS   Archives de Paris et du Département de la Seine
APP   Archives de la Préfecture de Police
BN   Bibliothèque Nationale de France

Introduction

1. William M. Reddy, *Money and Liberty in Modern Europe* (Cambridge: Cambridge University Press, 1987), 123.

2. Kristen B. Neuschel, *Word of Honor: Interpreting Noble Culture in Sixteenth-Century France* (Ithaca: Cornell University Press, 1989), 197.

3. Thus, for example, although according to Daniel Dessert the position of "financier" became more acceptable during the reign of Louis XIV, those who occupied this position did so within and by means of traditional networks of familial relationships and often combined this position with military or court offices. Even by the end of the eighteenth century, the growth of speculative practices was closely linked to aristocratic and monarchic institutions, making it part of what George Taylor has identified as "court" rather than "industrial" capitalism. See Daniel Dessert, *Argent, pouvoir et société au grand siècle* (Paris: Fayard, 1984); George V. Taylor, "The Paris Bourse on the Eve of the Revolution, 1781–1789," *American Historical Review* 67:4 (July 1962): 977.

4. Jonathan Dewald, "The Ruling Class in the Marketplace: Nobles and Money in Early-Modern France," in Thomas L. Haskell and Richard F. Teichgraeber III, eds., *The Culture of the Market: Historical Essays* (Cambridge: Cambridge University Press, 1993), 52.

5. Robert Nye, *Masculinity and Male Codes of Honor* (New York: Oxford University Press, 1993), chap. 2.

6. Albert O. Hirschman, *The Passions and the Interests: Political Arguments for Capitalism Before Its Triumph* (Princeton: Princeton University Press, 1977), 58. Emphasis in the original.

7. Adam Ferguson, *Essay on the History of Civil Society*, cited in Hirschman, *The Passions and the Interests*, 120.

8. Jean-Baptiste Say, *Decade philosophique*, cited in R. R. Palmer, *J.-B. Say: An Economist in Troubled Times* (Princeton: Princeton University Press, 1997), 22.

9. Reddy, *Money and Liberty*, 152.

10. Antony Béraud and P. Dufey, *Dictionnaire historique de Paris*, 2d ed. (Paris: Chez J.-N. Barba, 1828), 1:lxxvii.

11. Despite these recommendations, the French government instituted such ideas unevenly. For example, although a free market for labor existed since 1791, with passage of the Le Chapelier laws that abolished the guilds, free trade was not adopted until 1860. On the leading political economists, the dissemination of their thought, and the debates within their ranks, see Yves Breton and Michel Lutfalla, eds., *L'Economie politique en France au XIXe siècle* (Paris: Economica, 1991).

12. Honoré de Balzac, "Ce qui disparait de Paris," in *Le Diable à Paris. Paris et les parisiens. Moeurs et coutumes, caractères et portraits des habitants de Paris, tableau complet de leur vie privée, publique, politique, artistique, littéraire, industrielle, etc., etc.* (Paris: J. Hetzel, 1845–46), 2:18.

13. The most often cited example of the argument regarding French backwardness is David Landes, "French Entrepreneurship and Industrial Growth in the Nineteenth Century," *Journal of Economic History* 9:1 (May 1949): 45–61. Later historiography has argued that although French industrialization may not have resembled that of England in every respect, the French faced different structural conditions to which they were able to successfully adapt by blending tradition and innovation. This revisionist view, now largely accepted, began with Maurice Lévy-Leboyer, "La Croissance économique en France au dix-neuvième siècle," *Annales ESC* 23:4 (July–August 1968): 788–807. In his later work, even Landes modified his pessimistic view of the French economy.

14. On the importance of domestic production in the Parisian economy, see Judith Coffin, *The Politics of Women's Work: The Paris Garment Trades, 1750–1915* (Princeton: Princeton University Press, 1996); Lorraine Coons, *Women Home Workers in the Parisian Garment Trades, 1860–1915* (New York: Garland Publishing, 1987); and Marilyn J. Boxer, "Women in Industrial Homework: The Flowermakers of the Belle Epoque," *French Historical Studies* 12:3 (spring 1982): 401–23. While most of this literature has focused on women's

work, Christopher Johnson has studied the effects of the growing use of domestic labor and the shift to piecework on male tailors in "Economic Change and Artisan Discontent: The Tailor's History, 1800–1848," in Roger Price, ed., *Revolution and Reaction: 1848 and the Second French Republic* (London: Croom Helm, 1975), 87–114. The lasting importance of corporate models for working-class organization has been studied by William H. Sewell Jr. in his *Work and Revolution in France: The Language of Labor from the Old Regime to 1848* (Cambridge: Cambridge University Press, 1980).

15. On paternalism as a model for employer-employee relationships, see Michael B. Miller, *The Bon Marché: Bourgeois Culture and the Department Store, 1869–1920* (Princeton: Princeton University Press, 1981); and Peter N. Stearns, *Paths to Authority: The Middle Class and the Industrial Labor Force in France, 1820–1848* (Urbana: University of Illinois Press, 1978).

16. The Second Empire (1852–70) followed on the heels of the short-lived Second Republic (1848–52), which itself replaced the July Monarchy. The Second Empire was characterized by a combination of progressive reforms, such as the establishment of universal manhood suffrage, and an authoritarian government led by Napoleon III. Examples of the government's strong role in the promotion of industry can be found in Nicholas Papayanis, *Horse-Drawn Cabs and Omnibuses in Paris: The Idea of Circulation and the Business of Public Transit* (Baton Rouge: Louisiana State University Press, 1996); and Lenard R. Berlanstein, *Big Business and Industrial Conflict in Nineteenth-Century France: A Social History of the Parisian Gas Works* (Berkeley: University of California Press, 1991).

17. This is the position taken by William M. Reddy in *The Rise of Market Culture: The Textile Trade and French Society, 1750–1900* (Cambridge: Cambridge University Press, 1984), where he argues that workers rejected market values of self-interest and competition because they were insufficient to describe their experiences and demands. While workers certainly did reject the values Reddy discusses, this did not entail a rejection of a market-based model altogether. Rather, workers, like other groups in society, sought to redefine the market. In other words, specific values are not inherent in a market-based economy but are socially constructed and thus open to revision.

18. Louis Chevalier, *Classes laborieuses et classes dangereuses à Paris pendant la première moitié du dix-neuvième siècle* (Paris: Librairie générale française, 1978).

19. The idea that money, by acting as a medium that indicates the relativity of shared values, is a signifier of relationships both among individuals and between the individual and the community as a whole is discussed at length by Georg Simmel in his 1907 *The Philosophy of Money* (London: Routledge and Kegan Paul, 1978).

20. A similar adoption of a market model occurred earlier in England, where the estates-based model was not as long-lived as in France. See, for example, Craig Muldrew, *The Economy of Obligation: The Culture of Credit and Social Relations in Early Modern England* (New York: St. Martin's Press, 1998); Jean-Christophe Agnew, *Worlds Apart: The Market and the Theater in Anglo-American Thought, 1550–1750* (Cambridge: Cambridge University Press, 1986).

21. Martin J. Wiener, "Market Culture, Reckless Passion, and the Victorian Reconstruction of Punishment," in Haskell and Teichgraeber, *The Culture of the Market,* 137. G. R. Searle reinforces Wiener's observations in his more extensive study of Victorians' attitudes toward the marketplace. G. R. Searle, *Morality and the Market in Victorian Britain* (Oxford: Clarendon Press, 1998).

22. Priscilla Parkhurst Ferguson includes a discussion of the *tableaux,* which she calls "literary guidebooks," in her *Paris as Revolution: Writing the Nineteenth-Century City* (Berkeley: University of California Press, 1994), chap. 2. More attention has been paid to the *physiologies.* See, for example, Ruth Amossy, *Les Idées reçues: Sémiologie du stéréotype* (Paris: Nathan, 1991); Richard Sieburth, "Une Idéologie du lisible: Le Phénomène des physiologies," *Romantisme* 15:47 (1985): 39–60; Andrée Lheritier et al., *Les Physiologies* (Paris: Université de Paris, 1958).

23. Judith Wechsler, *A Human Comedy: Physiognomy and Caricature in Nineteenth-Century Paris* (Chicago: University of Chicago Press, 1982), 33–36.

24. Richard Terdiman, *Discourse/Counter Discourse: The Theory and Practice of Symbolic Resistance in Nineteenth-Century France* (Ithaca: Cornell University Press, 1985), 97.

25. The term "panoramic" is from Walter Benjamin, *Charles Baudelaire: A Lyric Poet in the Era of High Capitalism,* trans. Harry Zohn (London: NLB, 1973), 35.

26. On the *flâneur,* see Keith Tester, ed., *The Flâneur* (London: Routledge, 1994); and Benjamin, *Charles Baudelaire.* On the importance of observation in the construction of new technologies of power in the nineteenth century, see Michel Foucault, *Discipline and Punish: The Birth of the Prison,* trans. Alan Sheridan (New York: Vintage, 1977), especially pp. 170–77 and 195–228.

27. On the use of gendered distinctions and the exclusion of women from politics during the French Revolution, see Lynn Hunt, *The Family Romance of the French Revolution* (Berkeley: University of California Press, 1992); Dorinda Outram, *The Body and the French Revolution: Sex, Class and Political Culture* (New Haven: Yale University Press, 1989); Joan Landes, *Women and the Public Sphere in the Age of the French Revolution* (Ithaca: Cornell University Press, 1988); Dominique Godineau, *Citoyennes tricoteuses: Les Femmes du peuple à Paris pendant la Révolution française* (Paris: Alinea, 1988). On the lasting importance of gender in the postrevolutionary order, see also Thomas

Laqueur, *Making Sex: Body and Gender from the Greeks to Freud* (Cambridge, Mass.: Harvard University Press, 1990); and Geneviève Fraisse, *La Muse de la raison: La Démocratie exclusive et la différence des sexes* (Paris: Editions Alinéa, 1989).

28. The term "popular classes" can be used to refer to a broad stratum of urban society—from street merchants and day laborers to small shopkeepers and master artisans. Because many women worked in commerce and retail, and because many of them owned their businesses, I have preferred to use this term rather than "working classes" in much of this book.

29. Whether due to religious restrictions or to fears concerning the "liminal" nature of economic transactions, commerce and exchange have often been the province of marginal groups. The Jews in medieval Europe, foreigners and women in Vietnam before the French conquest, or resident aliens in ancient Greece are but three examples of this phenomenon. See Agnew, *World's Apart*, 22–24; Neil L. Jamieson, *Understanding Vietnam* (Berkeley: University of California Press, 1993), 34.

30. This phenomenon has been well documented. See: Coffin, *The Politics of Women's Work;* Tessie P. Liu, *The Weaver's Knot: The Contradictions of Class Struggle and Family Solidarity in Western France, 1750–1914* (Ithaca: Cornell University Press, 1994); Elinor Accampo, *Industrialization, Family Life, and Class Relations: Saint Chamond, 1815–1914* (Berkeley: University of California Press, 1989); Gay Gullickson, *Spinners and Weavers of Auffay: Rural Industry and Sexual Division of Labor in a French Village, 1750–1850* (Cambridge: Cambridge University Press, 1986); Bonnie Smith, *Ladies of the Leisure Class: The Bourgeoises of Northern France in the Nineteenth Century* (Princeton: Princeton University Press, 1981). Louise A. Tilly and Joan W. Scott, *Women, Work, and Family* (New York: Holt, Rinehart and Winston, 1978).

31. Joan Scott, "'L'ouvrière! Mot impie, sordide . . . ': Women Workers in the Discourse of French Political Economy, 1840–1860," in *Gender and the Politics of History* (New York: Columbia University Press, 1988), 139–63.

32. Victoria de Grazia, with Ellen Furlough, *The Sex of Things: Gender and Consumption in Historical Perspective* (Berkeley: University of California Press, 1996).

33. Ann-Louise Shapiro, *Breaking the Codes: Female Criminality in Fin-de-Siècle Paris* (Stanford: Stanford University Press, 1996), 6–7.

34. The work of Richard Terdiman, Pierre Bourdieu, and Mikhael Bakhtin have been particularly helpful in this respect. See Terdiman, *Discourse/Counter Discourse;* Pierre Bourdieu, "Le Champs littéraire," *Actes de recherches en sciences sociales* 89 (1991): 3–46; Mikhael Bakhtin, *The Dialogic Imagination,* trans. Carol Emerson and Michael Holquist (Austin: University of Texas Press, 1981).

35. Honoré de Balzac, *La Fille aux yeux d'or* (Paris: Garnier-Flammarion, 1988), 210.

36. Emile Zola, *L'Argent* (Paris: Gallimard, 1993), 490.

ONE The Free Woman

1. Eugène Sue, *Les Mystères de Paris* (Paris: Robert Laffont, 1989), 33, 59.

2. Jann Matlock, *Scenes of Seduction: Prostitution, Hysteria, and Reading Difference in Nineteenth-Century France* (New York: Columbia University Press, 1994), 105.

3. By "libertine" literature I mean works concerned with women's sexual availability that were meant to titillate and entertain, but were not quite pornographic. These usually short and inexpensive pamphlets, sold by the booksellers in the Palais Royal, seem to have become less common over the course of the July Monarchy.

4. On the regulatory system of prostitution in the nineteenth century, see Alain Corbin, *Les Filles de noce: Misère sexuelle et prostitution (dix-neuvième et vingtième siècles)* (Paris: Aubier Montaigne, 1978); Jill Harsin, *Policing Prostitution in Nineteenth-Century Paris* (Princeton: Princeton University Press, 1985). On cultural representations of the prostitute, see Charles Bernheimer, *Figures of Ill Repute: Representing Prostitution in Nineteenth-Century France* (Cambridge, Mass.: Harvard University Press, 1989); Matlock, *Scenes of Seduction.*

5. On the transformation of the Parisian economy, see Philippe Vigier, *Nouvelle histoire de Paris: Paris pendant la monarchie de juillet (1830–1848)* (Paris: Hachette, 1991). On the fashion trades in particular, see Judith G. Coffin, *The Politics of Women's Work: The Paris Garment Trades, 1750–1915* (Princeton: Princeton University Press, 1996); Philippe Perrot, *Les Dessus et les dessous de la bourgeoisie: Une Histoire du vêtement au XIXe siècle* (Paris: Fayard, 1981); and Henriette Vanier, *La Mode et ses métiers: Frivolités et luttes de classe, 1830–1870* (Paris: Armand Colin, 1960).

6. On the plight of poor single women in Paris, see Rachel G. Fuchs, *Poor and Pregnant in Paris: Strategies for Survival in the Nineteenth Century* (New Brunswick, N.J.: Rutgers University Press, 1992).

7. Matlock, *Scenes of Seduction,* 22.

8. A.-J.-B. Parent-Duchâtelet, *De la prostitution dans la ville de Paris, considérée sous le rapport de l'hygiène publique, de la morale, et de l'administration,* 2d ed. (Paris: J.-B. Ballière, 1837), 1:96–97.

9. Ibid., 1:71, 76.

10. Ibid., 1:97.

11. This would remain a frequent complaint throughout the nineteenth cen-

tury among those who opposed the effects of laissez-faire principles on the organization of labor.

12. Parent-Duchâtelet, *De la prostitution*, 1:91.

13. On the grisette, see Joëlle Guillais-Maury, "La Grisette," in A. Farge and C. Klapisch-Zuber, eds., *Madame ou mademoiselle? Itinéraires de la solitude féminine, dix-huitième à vingtième siècle* (Paris: Montalba, 1984), 233–50; and "Une Histoire de grisette" (master's thesis, University of Paris VII, 1980); and the section "Le mariage au XIIIe," in Jean-Claude Caron, *Générations romantiques: Les Etudiants de Paris et le quartier latin* (Paris: Armand Colin, 1991).

14. Louis-Sébastien Mercier, "Grisettes," in *Tableau de Paris*, ed. Gustave Desnoiresterres (Paris: Pagnerre, 1853), 323.

15. *Amours et intrigues des grisettes de Paris, ou Revue des Belles dites de la petite vertu . . . le tout rédigé d'après les renseignemens donnés par une grisette sur le retour; et publié par J.-B. Ambs-Dalès*, 3d ed. (Paris: Roy-Terry, 1830), 92.

16. Louis Huart, *Physiologie de la grisette* (Paris: Aubert, n.d.), 62–63.

17. In later works, including that of Parent-Duchâtelet, women in all trades were increasingly believed to be equally vulnerable to prostitution.

18. *Dictionnaire anecdotique des nymphes du Palais Royal et autres quartiers de Paris, par un homme de bien* (Paris: Chez les marchands de nouveautés, 1826).

19. Parent-Duchâtelet, *De la prostitution*, 1:157, 461, 455.

20. AN F[7] 9305 Aimée Lucas, memo submitted to the minister of the interior, May 1841, 37.

21. APP DA 221 "Procès-verbaux des séances de la Commission Spéciale pour la répression de la prostitution," minutes for the meeting of 7 January 1840.

22. Fears regarding the confusion between shopping and prostitution arose in both France and England in the late eighteenth century. See Jennifer Jones, "*Coquettes* and *Grisettes:* Women Buying and Selling in Ancien-Régime Paris," in Victoria de Grazia, with Ellen Furlough, *The Sex of Things: Gender and Consumption in Historical Perspective* (Berkeley: University of California Press, 1996), 25–53; and Elizabeth Kowaleski-Wallace, *Consuming Subjects: Women, Shopping, and Business in the Eighteenth Century* (New York: Columbia University Press, 1997).

23. APP DA 222 Decree of 14 April 1830.

24. Matlock discusses the political implications of these pamphlets in *Scenes of Seduction*, 70–81. A similar spate of pamphlets linking prostitution, women's economic activity, and freedom appeared in late-seventeenth-century England. James Grantham Turner, "'News from the New Exchange': Commodity, Erotic Fantasy, and the Female Entrepreneur," in Ann Bermingham and John Brewer,

The Consumption of Culture, 1600–1800: Image, Object, Text (London: Routledge, 1995): 419–39.

25. *Le Tocsin de ses demoiselles, ou Mémoire à consulter adressé à tous les barreaux de France, et dénonciation aux cours royales, au sujet d'un arrêté de M. Mangin contre les filles publiques, suivi de plusieurs lettres édifiantes et curieuses* (Paris: Chez Garnier, 1830), 14.

26. *Plaintes et révélations nouvellement adressées par les filles de joie de Paris à la Congrégation, contre l'ordonnance de M. Mangin, qui leur défend de circuler dans les rues pour offrir leurs charmes aux passans; Précis historique concernant les hauts cris des Nymphes du Palais-Royal; La Clameur des Modistes et d'une grande quantité de Demoiselles logées en garni; aussi que le dépit de quelques honnêtes filles de province qui viennent à Paris pour y chercher fortune en pleine vent, et les regrets de quelques honnêtes Femmes à demi-publiques qui aiment à rendre de grands services pour un petit repas* (Paris: Chez Garnier, 1830), 14.

27. *Tocsin*, 9.

28. *Pétition qui doit être adressée à la Chambre de Députés, par 50 MILLE JOLIES FEMMES DE PARIS, demandant la révocation des Ordonnances qui leur font défense de sortir et demandant en outre qu'on en forme des légions armées pour voler à la défense de la patrie* (Paris: Madame de Lacombe, n.d.), 6.

29. *"On n'aime pas à acheter chat en poche," Pétition des filles publiques de Paris à M. Le Prefet de Police, au sujet de l'ordonnance qu'il vient de rendre contre elles, leur interdisant la circulation dans les rues et promenades publiques, et de celle qui précédemment leur a interdit l'entrée du Palais Royal. Rédigée par Mlle Pauline, et apostillée par MM. les Epiciers, Cabaretiers, Limonadiers et Marchands de Comestibles de la Capitale* (Paris: Chez les Libraires du Palais Royal et les Marchands de Nouveautés, 1830), 3–4. It is possible that some of the pamphlets may have been written or commissioned by merchants who feared that the disappearance of prostitution would hurt their business. An 1824 project to expel prostitutes from the Palais Royal was stopped after six weeks for this reason. APP DA/222 letter of prefect of police to minister of the interior, 2 August 1824.

30. *Cinquante mille voleurs de plus à Paris, ou réclamations des anciens marlous de la capitale contre l'ordonnance de M. le Prefet de Police* (Paris: Chez les marchands de nouveautés, 1830), 12.

31. Bernheimer, *Figures of Ill Repute*, 29.

32. Parent-Duchâtelet, *De la prostitution*, 1: 27.

33. F. F. A. Beraud, *Les Filles publiques de Paris et la police qui les régit* (Paris: Desforges, 1839), 2:79.

34. Parent-Duchâtelet, *De la prostitution*, 2:495.

35. Ibid., 2:499.

36. On the Saint-Simonian women, see Michèle Riot-Sarcy, *La Démocratie*

à l'épreuve des femmes: Trois figures critiques du pouvoir (Paris: Albin Michel, 1994), especially part 1; Claire Goldberg Moses and Leslie Wahl Rabine, *Feminism, Socialism, and French Romanticism* (Bloomington: Indiana University Press, 1993); Claire Goldberg Moses, *French Feminism in the Nineteenth Century* (Albany: State University of New York Press, 1984), especially chaps. 3 and 4; Moses, "Saint-Simonian Men/Saint-Simonian Women: The Transformation of Feminist Thought in 1830s France," *Journal of Modern History* 54 (June 1982): 240–67; Laure Adler, *A l'aube de féminisme: Les Premières journalistes (1830–1850)* (Paris: Payot, 1979); Lydia Elhadad, "Femmes prénomées: Les Prolétaires Saint-Simoniennes rédactrices de 'La Femme Libre' 1832–1834," *Les Revoltes logiques* 4 (winter 1976): 62–68; Evelyne Sullerot, *Histoire de la presse féminine en France, des origines à 1848* (Paris: Armand Colin, 1966).

37. In addition to name changes, the paper was erratic in printing dates and issue numbers. I have given this information to the fullest extent possible. For simplicity's sake, and because of the subsequent importance of this name, I refer to the paper as *La Femme libre* throughout the chapter, although I give the particular title of each issue in the footnotes.

38. Other contributors included Claire Démar, Pauline Roland, and Jeanne Deroin.

39. Jacques Rancière, *La Nuit des prolétaires: Archives du rêve ouvrier* (Paris: Fayard, 1981).

40. Barbara Corrado Pope, "The Influence of Rousseau's Ideology of Domesticity," in Marilyn J. Boxer and Jean H. Quataert, *Connecting Spheres: Women in the Western World, 1500 to the Present* (New York: Oxford University Press, 1987), 136–45.

41. Mary Sheriff, "Fragonard's Erotic Mothers and the Politics of Reproduction," in Lynn Hunt, ed., *Eroticism and the Body Politic* (Baltimore: Johns Hopkins University Press, 1991), 14–40.

42. Jean-Jacques Rousseau, *Emile*, trans. Barbara Foxley (London: J. M. Dent, 1993), 419, 444, 489.

43. Joel Schwartz, *The Sexual Politics of Jean-Jacques Rousseau* (Chicago: University of Chicago Press, 1984), 93.

44. Charles Fourier, *The Theory of the Four Movements*, ed. Gareth Stedman Jones and Ian Patterson (Cambridge: Cambridge University Press, 1996), 95.

45. Susan K. Grogan, *French Socialism and Sexual Difference: Women and the New Society, 1803–1844* (New York: St. Martin's Press, 1992), 70.

46. *La Femme libre. Apostolat des femmes*, no. 1, p. 3; no. 9, p. 91.

47. This was of course not the first time such a distinction had been made. For example, the protagonist in an 1804 novel exclaims, "[A]las! I gave myself, and the entire universe will be able to think that I sold myself!" Madame de Genlis, *La Duchesse de la Vallière* (Paris: Librairie Fontaine, 1983), 120. This

sentiment was not, however, made the central component of a social and economic critique, as it was in *La Femme libre.*

48. *La Femme nouvelle. Tribune des femmes,* no. 14, p. 179.

49. *La Femme libre,* no. 1, p. 6.

50. *La Femme libre. Apostolat des femmes,* no. 2, p. 2.

51. *La Femme nouvelle. Apostolat des femmes,* no. 10, p. 113.

52. *La Tribune des femmes,* vol. 2 (no issue number) 1834, p. 155.

53. *La Femme nouvelle. Tribune des femmes,* no. 14, p. 179.

54. Ibid.

55. *La Femme nouvelle. Apostolat des femmes,* no. 9, pp. 92–93.

56. Ibid., p. 94.

57. *La Femme nouvelle. Apostolat des femmes,* 8 October 1832, no. 5, p. 38.

58. Leslie Wahl Rabine, "Feminine Text and Feminine Subjects," in Moses and Rabine, *Feminism, Socialism, and French Romanticism,* 85–144.

59. Moses, "'Difference' in Historical Perspective: Saint-Simonian Feminism," in Moses and Rabine, *Feminism, Socialism, and French Romanticism,* 72.

60. *La Femme de l'avenir. Apostolat des femmes,* no. 3, p. 7.

61. *La Tribune des femmes,* vol. 2, p. 104.

62. Ibid., p. 140.

63. *La Femme libre,* no. 1, p. 5.

64. Charles Marchal, *Physiologie de la fille sans nom* (Paris: Charles La-Chapelle, n.d.), 30–31.

65. This thesis was elaborated by Alain Corbin in his work *Les filles de noces* and applied more specifically to the grisette in the work of Joëlle Guillais-Maury. See especially her article cited in n. 13.

66. A good overview of the changes in the publishing world can be found in John Lough, *Writer and Public in France: From the Middle Ages to the Present Day* (Oxford: Clarendon Press, 1978). On the changing reading public in the nineteenth century, see James Smith Allen, *In the Public Eye: A History of Reading in Modern France, 1800–1940* (Princeton: Princeton University Press, 1991). On the press during the July Monarchy, see René de Livois, *Histoire de la presse française,* vol. 1, *Des origines à 1881* (Lausanne: Editions Spes, 1965); Claude Bellanger et al., *Histoire générale de la presse française,* 4 vols. (Paris: Presses universitaires de France, 1964); and César Graña, *Modernity and Its Discontents: French Society and the French Man of Letters in the Nineteenth Century* (New York: Harper and Row, 1964).

67. Marc Martin, "Journalistes parisiens et notoriété (vers 1830–1870): Pour une histoire sociale du journalisme," *Revue historique* 266:1 (1981): 53.

68. Livois, *Histoire de la presse française,* 218. For those who resisted, see Irene Collins, *The Government and the Newspaper Press in France, 1814–1881* (Oxford: Oxford University Press, 1959), 82–89.

69. Lenore O'Boyle, "The Image of the Journalist in France, Germany, and England, 1815–1848," in Clive Emsley, ed., *Conflict and Stability in Europe* (London: Croom Helm, 1979), 20.

70. Lucienne Frapier-Mazur, "Publishing Novels," in Denis Hollier, ed., *A New History of French Literature* (Cambridge, Mass.: Harvard University Press, 1989), 693–98.

71. Pierre Bourdieu, "The Link Between Artistic and Literary Struggles," in Peter Collier and Robert Lethbridge, eds., *Artistic Relations: Literature and the Visual Arts in Nineteenth-Century France* (New Haven: Yale University Press, 1994), 30–39.

72. This is not to say that eighteenth-century journalists were not dependent upon market forces. Some writers consciously strove to make money writing for the public; others, deprived of opportunities for patronage, found themselves necessarily dependent upon the market. For an example of the first, see Jeremy Popkin, "Un journaliste face au marché des périodiques à la fin du dix-huitième siècle: Linguet et ses 'Annales politiques,'" in *La Diffusion et la lecture des journaux de langue française sous l'Ancien Régime* (Amsterdam: Holland University Press, 1988), 11–19. Robert Darnton has eloquently described the situation of the second group in *The Literary Underground of the Old Regime* (Cambridge, Mass.: Harvard University Press, 1982).

73. Lough, *Writer and Public in France*, 334.

74. Girardin began accepting such advertisements in *La Presse* in 1836, and other newspapers quickly followed suit. This was a new form of advertisement for newspapers, although both medical and personal advertisements did appear in the eighteenth-century press. Colin Jones, "The Great Chain of Buying: Medical Advertisement, the Bourgeois Public Sphere, and the Origins of the French Revolution," *American Historical Review* 101:1 (February 1996): 13–14; Jennifer Jones, "Personals and Politics: Courting *La Citoyenne* in Revolutionary Paris" (paper presented at the 110th meeting of the American Historical Association, Atlanta, 1996).

75. Frapier-Mazur, "Publishing Novels," 695.

76. Charles-Augustin Saint-Beuve, "La littérature industrielle," quoted in Lough, *Writer and Public in France,* 317.

77. Honoré de Balzac, *Illusions perdues* (Paris: Presses Pockets, 1991), 276.

78. The obsession with credit and debt that permeates Balzac's work is common to the majority of the work produced by writers and journalists during the July Monarchy. On Balzac, see V. S. Pritchett, *Balzac* (New York: Knopf, 1973); on Paul de Kock, see Ellen Constans, "'Votre argent m'intéresse': L'argent dans les romans de Paul de Kock," *Romantisme* 16:53 (1986): 71–82. On the role of money in nineteenth-century French and British realist literature, see John Vernon, *Money and Fiction: Literary Realism in the Nineteenth and Early Twentieth Centuries* (Ithaca: Cornell University Press, 1984).

79. William M. Reddy, *The Invisible Code: Honor and Sentiment in Postrevolutionary France, 1814–1848* (Berkeley: University of California Press, 1997); and "Condottieri of the Pen: Journalists and the Public Sphere in Postrevolutionary France (1815–1850)," *American Historical Review* 99:5 (December 1994): 1546–70.

80. Judith Wechsler, *A Human Comedy: Physiognomy and Caricature in Nineteenth-Century Paris* (Chicago: University of Chicago Press, 1982), 82.

81. Louis Huart and Charles Philipon, "Varin," in *Galerie de la presse, de la littérature et des beaux arts* (Paris: Aubert, 1839–40), n.p. "Varin" was the pen name of Charles-Victor Voirin.

82. Jules Janin, "La Grisette," in *Les Français peints par eux-mêmes: Encyclopédie morale du dix-neuvième siècle* (Paris: L. Curmer, 1841), 1:12.

83. *Histoire véritable d'une Grisette Contemporaine qui du fille de Portier est devenue femme de perruquier, puis femme Entretenue, et est aujourd'hui baronne!!!!* (n.p., n.d.).

84. Alphonse Esquiros, *Les Vierges folles* (1840; reprint, Paris: E. Dentu, 1873), 83.

85. *Les Bamboches amoureuses des grisettes de Paris: Histoires, aventures, moeurs et galanteries de ces demoiselles* (Paris: Chez les marchands de nouveautés, 1840), 10.

86. Janin, "La Grisette," 1:10.

87. Huart and Philipon, "Félix Pyat," n.p.

88. Ibid., "Jules Janin," n.p.

89. *Les Bamboches amoureuses*, 6.

90. Margaret Waller, *The Male Malady: Fictions of Impotence in the French Romantic Novel* (New Brunswick, N.J.: Rutgers University Press, 1993).

91. On the influence of Catholicism among opponents to the July Monarchy, see Edward Berenson, *Populist Religion and Left-Wing Politics in France, 1830–1852* (Princeton: Princeton University Press, 1984); and on the cult of Mary, see Stéphane Michaud, *Muse et Madone: Visages de la femme de la Révolution française aux apparitions de Lourdes* (Paris: Seuil, 1985).

92. Louis Huart, *Physiologie de la grisette* (Paris: Aubert, n.d.), 12.

93. Arago, *Physiologie de la femme entretenue* (Brussels: Chez tous les libraires, 1841).

94. Huart, *Physiologie de la grisette*, 46–47.

95. Clébule Liabour, *Le Journalisme et les journaux* (Paris: Albert Frères, 1848), 55.

96. Bert, "La Presse parisienne," *Nouveau tableau de Paris au dix-neuvième siècle* (Paris: Madame Charles-Bechet, 1835), 5:144.

97. Ibid., 143.

98. Adolphe de Liancourt, *Le Rideau levé sur les mystères de Paris* (Paris: B. Renault, 1845), 2:25–26.

99. Janin, "La Grisette," 1:14; Honoré de Balzac, *Monographie de la presse parisienne* (Paris: Au Bureau central des publications nouvelles, 1842), 78; L'Héritier, *Les Mystères de la vie du monde, du demi-monde et du quart du monde, ou les moeurs d'aujourd'hui. Scènes épisodiques et anecdotiques prises dans tous les rangs et conditions de la société* (Paris: Charlieu frères et Huillery, 1868–69), 1:13.

100. Emile de Girardin, quoted in Eugène Hatin, *Histoire du journal en France, 1631–1853* (Paris: P Jannet, 1853), 177.

101. Alfred de Musset, "Mademoiselle Mimi Pinson. Profil de grisette," in *Le Diable à Paris. Paris et les parisiens. Moeurs et coutumes, caractères et portraits des habitants de Paris, tableau complet de leur vie privée, publique, politique, artistique, littéraire, industrielle, etc., etc.* (Paris: J. Hetzel, 1845–46), 1:343.

102. *Les Bamboches amoureuses*, 84.

103. Huart, *Physiologie de la grisette*, 28.

104. Lynn Hunt, "The Imagery of Radicalism," in *Politics, Culture, and Class in the French Revolution* (Berkeley: University of California Press, 1984).

105. These strategies are discussed in William Reddy, *The Invisible Code;* and G. R. Searle, *Morality and the Market in Victorian Britain* (Oxford: Clarendon Press, 1998).

106. See Janice Bergman-Carton, *The Woman of Ideas in French Art, 1830–1848* (Hew Haven: Yale University Press, 1995), for an extended discussion of the bluestocking.

107. Frédéric Soulié, "Le Bas bleu," in *Le Lion amoureux, Oeuvres complètes,* rev. ed. (Paris: Michel Lévy, 1870), 183.

108. Albéric Second, "Le Débutant littéraire," in *Les Français peints par eux-mêmes,* 1:167.

109. Huart and Philipon, "Frédéric Soulié," n.p.

TWO Work, Wages, and Citizenship in the 1840s

1. Artisans had not been completely shielded from the market economy before the French Revolution. According to Michael Sonenscher, for example, a "bazaar economy" existed parallel to the regulated, guild-based economy in the eighteenth century in which many of the practices associated with the economic transformations of the nineteenth century, such as subcontracting, could already be found. At the same time, however, the legal recognition of collectivities before the Revolution afforded artisans a means to protect themselves that they no longer had once the individual became the primary legal unit of society. Michael Sonenscher, *Work and Wages: Natural Law, Politics, and the Eighteenth-Century French Trades* (Cambridge: Cambridge University Press, 1989).

2. Jules Burgy, *Présent et avenir des ouvriers. Par un typographe* (Paris: Chez les marchands de nouveautés, 1847), 24–25.

3. The literature on the development of a politically active and self-conscious working class in France is quite extensive. For a good overview, see Roger Magraw, *A History of the French Working Class*, 2 vols. (Oxford: Basil Blackwell, 1992). Most scholars now agree that artisans played a pivotal role in the development of working-class identity. However, politically active artisans most commonly referred to themselves as "workers," and thus I have used this term as well as the term "working class" throughout the chapter. In addition to reflecting the terminology of the period, the use of the term "working class," rather than the term "popular classes" used elsewhere, highlights the increasing importance of work as a constituent component of political, and perhaps personal, identity among these individuals.

4. The role of family imagery in the development of working-class politics in France has received little attention. An exception is Michael Hanagan, *Nascent Proletarians: Class Formation in Post-Revolutionary France* (Oxford: Basil Blackwell, 1989). Hanagan argues for the importance of claims based on the needs of the family in working-class politics, but assumes that the male breadwinner image reflected a reality of working-class life. While this may be accurate for the miners and metalworkers he studied, it was not the case in Paris. Susan Pedersen, on the other hand, argues that the persistence of large numbers of women in the workforce in France made the male-breadwinner wage norm less well established. Susan Pedersen, *Family, Dependence, and the Origins of the Welfare State: Britain and France, 1914–1945* (Cambridge: Cambridge University Press, 1993). In this chapter, I argue that the male breadwinner image was created for political purposes and so did not need to reflect the economic realities of working-class life. Thus despite women's long-standing participation in the workforce, French labor organizations in the nineteenth century did not usually welcome or recruit women. See, for example, Patricia Hilden, *Working Women and Socialist Politics in France, 1880–1914: A Regional Study* (Oxford: Oxford University Press, 1986). For French debates concerning the family wage in the late nineteenth and early twentieth centuries, see Laura L. Frader, "Engendering Work and Wages: The French Labor Movement and the Family Wage," in Laura L. Frader and Sonya O. Rose, eds., *Gender and Class in Modern Europe* (Ithaca: Cornell University Press, 1996), 142–64.

5. Eugène Buret, *De la misère des classes laborieuses en Angleterre et en France* (Paris: Chez Paulin, 1840), 1:17.

6. D——S., *Aperçu sur la condition des classes ouvrières en France et en Angleterre et critique de l'ouvrage de M. Buret sur la misère des classes laborieuses, etc.* (Paris: Chez Bureau, 1844).

7. Buret, *De la misère des classes laborieuses*, 1:318, 343–44.

8. Louis-René Villermé, *Tableau de l'état physique et moral des ouvriers*

employés dans les manufactures de coton, de laine et de soie (Paris: Union générale d'éditions, 1971), 74.

9. Buret, *De la misère des classes laborieuses*, 1:415.

10. H.-A. Frégier, *Des Classes dangereuses de la population dans les grandes villes, et des moyens de les rendre meilleures* (Paris: J.-B. Ballière, 1840), 1:11, 99.

11. Elinor Accampo, *Industrialization, Family Life, and Class Relations: Saint-Chamond, 1815–1914* (Berkeley: University of California Press, 1989); Gay Gullickson, *Spinners and Weavers of Auffay: Rural Industry and the Sexual Division of Labor in a French Village, 1750–1850* (Cambridge: Cambridge University Press, 1986); Tessie P. Liu, *The Weaver's Knot: The Contradictions of Class Struggle and Family Solidarity in Western France, 1750–1914* (Ithaca: Cornell University Press, 1994).

12. Lynn Hunt has demonstrated the way in which the family can operate, on a cultural level, as a metaphor for the organization of society in *The Family Romance of the French Revolution* (Berkeley: University of California Press, 1992).

13. Frégier, *Des Classes dangereuses*, 1:88.

14. Villermé, *Etat physique et moral des ouvriers*, 58.

15. Katherine A. Lynch discusses the importance of budgeting to reformers in *Family, Class, and Ideology in Early Industrial France: Social Policy and the Working-Class Family, 1825–1848* (Madison: University of Wisconsin Press, 1988).

16. *La Ruche populaire*, December 1839, p. 27.

17. The effects of competition in tailoring are discussed in Christopher H. Johnson, "Economic Change and Artisan Discontent: The Tailor's History, 1800–1848," in Roger Price, ed., *Revolution and Reaction: 1848 and the Second French Republic* (London: Croom Helm, 1975). Casey Harison discusses competition in the building trades in "An Organization of Labor: Laissez-Faire and *Marchandage* in the Paris Building Trades through 1848," *French Historical Studies* 20:3 (summer 1997): 357–80.

18. *L'Atelier*, December 1840, p. 25.

19. *La Ruche populaire*, July 1841, p. 7.

20. Ibid., October 1841, p. 6.

21. Women did participate in *La Ruche populaire* in significant numbers. Cécile Dufour, a millinery worker, was a member of the editorial board. Women seemed to have written the majority of letters to the newspaper; they also were the authors of articles and poems. *L'Atelier*, by contrast, did not include any women on its staff. It did, however, in the early 1840s, call for women's participation in the improvement of the working class.

22. Susan K. Grogan, *French Socialism and Sexual Difference: Women and the New Society, 1803–1844* (New York: St. Martin's Press, 1992), 86–87.

23. On associations, see K. Steven Vincent, *Pierre-Joseph Proudhon and the Rise of French Republican Socialism* (New York: Oxford University Press, 1984).

24. William H. Sewell Jr., *Work and Revolution in France: The Language of Labor from the Old Regime to 1848* (Cambridge: Cambridge University Press, 1980).

25. I use the term "communal" to differentiate it from the extended family, made up of members related to each other through blood or marriage. Studies that address this type of family organization in eighteenth- and nineteenth-century France include: Victoria Thompson, "Urban Renovation, Moral Regeneration: Domesticating the *Halles* in Second Empire Paris," *French Historical Studies* 20:1 (winter 1997): 87–109; Arlette Farge, *Fragile Lives: Violence, Power, and Solidarity in Eighteenth-Century Paris*, trans. Carol Shelton (Cambridge, Mass.: Harvard University Press, 1993); Rachel Fuchs, *Poor and Pregnant in Paris: Strategies for Survival in the Nineteenth Century* (New Brunswick, N.J.: Rutgers University Press, 1992); the forum "Women, Social Relations, and Urban Life," with contributions by Roderick Phillips, Georg'ann Cattleona, Leslie Page Moch and Rachel Fuchs, and Elinor Accampo, in *French Historical Studies* 18:1 (spring 1991): 1–64; and David Garrioch, *Neighborhood and Community in Paris, 1740–1790* (Cambridge: Cambridge University Press, 1986). For similar practices in England, see Ellen Ross, *Love and Toil: Motherhood in Outcast London, 1870–1918* (New York: Oxford University Press, 1993).

26. This strategy would have obvious appeal for workers whose families were longtime inhabitants of the capital, but even migrant workers or newly arrived immigrants could understand the value of the communal family. Although middle-class observers stressed their lack of family ties, historians have shown how family networks helped integrate new arrivals into the life of the city. On migrant workers, see Leslie Page Moch, *Paths to the City: Regional Migration in Nineteenth-Century France* (Beverly Hills: Sage Publications, 1983); and Alain Corbin, *Archaïsme et modernité en Limousin au dix-neuvième siècle* (Paris: M. Rivière, 1975).

27. Adeline Daumard, *Les Bourgeois et la bourgeoisie en France depuis 1815* (Paris: Aubier Montagne, 1987), 45.

28. Frégier, *Des Classes dangereuses*, 1:357–58.

29. Lynch, *Family, Class, and Ideology in Early Industrial France*, 61.

30. Edward Berenson, *Populist Religion and Left-Wing Politics in France, 1830–1852* (Princeton: Princeton University Press, 1984), 43.

31. Iorwerth Prothero, *Radical Artisans in England and France* (Cambridge: Cambridge University Press, 1997), 133.

32. Buret, *De la misère des classes laborieuses*, 1:431. Buret explicitly refers to the work of Parent-Duchâtelet in making this observation.

33. Ibid., 2:491.

34. Frégier, *Des Classes dangereuses,* 386.

35. *La Ruche populaire,* August 1847, p. 165.

36. Both William Sewell and Jacques Rancière have argued that during the July Monarchy, workers developed a political program and class identity through interaction with, and incorporation of, bourgeois ideals and language. Sewell, *Work and Revolution in France;* Jacques Rancière, *La Nuit des prolétaires: Archives du rêve ouvrier* (Paris: Fayard, 1981).

37. The complexity of Coutant's use of middle-class discourse tends to refute the work of scholars who have argued that the working class blindly adopted standards of middle-class morality during the nineteenth century. The most influential proponent of this thesis has been Michel Foucault, who argued that during the July Monarchy the bourgeoisie was able to impose its ideas about sexuality and the family on the working class and that this was an important step in its mastery of French society. Foucault, *The History of Sexuality,* vol. 1, *An Introduction,* trans. Robert Hurley (New York: Random House, 1980), 121–22.

38. Louis Blanc, *L'Organisation du travail* (Paris: Prévot, 1840), 18, 37.

39. *La Ruche populaire,* August 1847, pp. 162, 163.

40. The male breadwinner ideal has received greater attention in the historiography of the English labor movement than in that concerning France. See, for example, Deborah Valenze, *The First Industrial Woman* (New York: Oxford University Press, 1995); Sonya O. Rose, *Limited Livelihoods: Gender and Class in Nineteenth-Century England* (Berkeley: University of California Press, 1992); and Wally Seccombe, "Patriarchy Stabilized: The Construction of the Male Breadwinner Wage Norm in Nineteenth-Century Britain," *Social History* 11:1 (January 1986): 53–76. Although he doesn't use the term "male breadwinner," Louis Devance does discuss the importance of male mastery in the family among French workers in 1848 in "Femme, famille, travail et morale sexuelle dans l'idéologie de 1848," *Romantisme* 13/14 (1976): 79–103.

41. *L'Atelier,* February 1841, p. 47; December 1842, p. 32.

42. *La Ruche populaire,* July 1841, p. 26.

43. *L'Atelier,* October 1841, p. 12.

44. Similarly, Jacques Rancière has identified the desire to escape the toil of the workplace expressed in working-class writings of the 1830s as proof of a need to be considered as "humans" rather than as "workers." Rancière, *La Nuit des prolétaires.*

45. Grignon, *Réflexions d'un ouvrier tailleur sur la misère des ouvriers en général* (Paris: n.p., 1833), 2, 3.

46. Jules Janin, "La Grisette," *Les Français peints par eux-mêmes: Encyclopédie morale du dix-neuvième siècle* (Paris: L. Curmer, 1841), 1:11.

47. *Le National,* quoted in *L'Atelier,* January 1845, p. 50.

48. *L'Atelier,* January 1845, p. 51.

49. *La Ruche populaire*, December 1839, p. 11.

50. Joan Scott, "'L'Ouvrière! Mot impie, sordide . . .': Women Workers in the Discourse of French Political Economy, 1840–1860," *Gender and the Politics of History* (New York: Columbia University Press, 1988), 139–63.

51. Magraw, *A History of the French Working Class*, 1:74–75; Armand Cuvillier, *Un Journal d'ouvriers: "L'Atelier" 1840–1850* (Paris: Alcan, 1914).

52. *Journal des débats*, quoted in *L'Atelier*, January 1841, p. 36.

53. *L'Atelier*, January 1841, 36; December 1842, p. 32.

54. Ibid., June 1841, p. 77; January 1841, p. 36; and June 1841, pp. 76–77.

55. Ibid., December 1842, p. 32.

56. Ibid., June 1845, p. 144.

57. *La Ruche populaire*, August 1847, p. 67.

58. *L'Atelier*, June 1845, p. 142.

59. Ibid., December 1847, p. 39.

60. *La Ruche populaire*, August 1847, pp. 165, 167.

61. *L'Atelier*, 30 September 1849, p. 405.

62. Sewell has argued that treating workers as children (another dependent state) served much the same purpose. *Work and Revolution in France*, 196.

63. *L'Atelier*, July 1845, p. 160; January 1844, pp. 76–77.

64. Ibid., April 1847, p. 482.

65. Ibid., September 1847, p. 570.

66. *Le Charivari*, 10 March 1848, no. 70, p. 1.

67. *La Voix des femmes*, 20 March 1848, no. 1, p. 1.

68. Reine Garde, *Essais poétiques* (Paris: Garnier frères, 1851).

69. Jeanne Strallen, *La Voix des femmes*, 21 April 1848, no. 29, p. 1.

70. *La Voix des femmes*, 14 April 1848, no. 23, p. 1.

71. Ibid., 31 March 1848, no. 11, p. 1; 21 April 1848, no. 29, p. 2.

72. Ibid., 28 March 1848, no. 8, p. 3.

73. Deroin's paper was renamed *L'Opinion des femmes* following the June Days; she continued publication until August 1849. On Deroin see Joan Wallach Scott, *Only Paradoxes to Offer: French Feminism and the Rights of Man* (Cambridge, Mass.: Harvard University Press, 1996), chap. 3.

74. *La Voix des femmes*, 22 March 1848, no. 2, p. 3.

75. Ibid., 6 April 1848, no. 16, p. 3

76. Ibid., 16 April 1848, no. 25, p. 2; 9 April 1849, no. 18, p. 1.

77. Ibid., 8–10 June 1848, no. 42, p. 1.

78. Julie-Victoire Daubié, *La Femme pauvre au dix-neuvième siècle* (1866; reprint, Paris: Côté Femmes, 1992), 1:37–38.

79. *La Voix des femmes*, 23 April 1848, no. 31, p. 4.

80. Laura S. Strumingher, "The Vésuviennes: Images of Women Warriors in 1848 and Their Significance for French History," *History of European Ideas* 8:4–5 (1987): 452.

81. Reproduced in *La Voix des femmes,* 18 April 1848, no. 26, p. 3.

82. *La Voix des femmes,* 10–13 June 1848, no. 43, p. 1.

83. Ibid., 29 April 1848, no. 36, p. 3.

84. On the June Days and the reaction to them, see Roger Price, ed., *Revolution and Reaction: 1848 and the Second French Republic* (New York: Barnes and Noble, 1975); and Price, *The French Second Republic: A Social History* (Ithaca: Cornell University Press, 1972).

85. Ernest Desprez, "Les Grisettes à Paris," in *Paris ou le livre des cent-et-un* (Paris: Ladvocat, 1832), 6:213.

86. Alfred Delvau, *Grandeur et décadence des grisettes* (Paris: A. Desloges, 1848), 93.

87. Eugène Bruncamp, *Nos idées, nos moeurs, nos caractères* (Paris: Hachette, 1866), 163.

88. Henry de Kock, *Le Guide de l'amoureux à Paris . . . d'après le manuscrit original de Mme la Baronne de C.* (Paris: A. Faure, 1865), 86.

89. Maximillien Perrin, *La Fleur des grisettes,* 2 vols. (Paris: Louis Chappe, 1861).

90. Jules Simon, *L'Ouvrière* (Paris: Hachette, 1861), 14, 83, 38.

91. Judith F. Stone, "The Republican Brotherhood: Gender and Ideology," in Elinor A. Accampo, Rachel G. Fuchs, and Mary Lynn Stewart, eds., *Gender and the Politics of Social Reform in France, 1870–1914* (Baltimore: Johns Hopkins University Press, 1995), 28–58.

92. A thorough bibliography on the social policies of the Third Republic and their impact on the working class can be found in Accampo et al., *Gender and the Politics of Social Reform.*

93. Joan W. Scott, "A Statistical Representation of Work: *La Statistique de l'industrie à Paris, 1847–1848,*" in *Gender and the Politics of History.*

94. Chambre de Commerce de Paris, *Statistique de l'industrie à Paris, résultant de l'enquête faite par la Chambre de Commerce pour les années 1847–1848* (Paris: Chez Guillaumin et Cie, 1851), 1:49.

95. Certain trades, such as textile manufacturing, had by the 1840s moved out of Paris to escape high overhead costs, thereby diminishing work opportunities for women. While exact statistics do not exist, increased opportunities for women in clothing and printing probably helped to offset these losses.

96. Hunt, *Family Romance,* chaps. 2 and 3.

97. On the valuation of the paternal figure in the second half of the century, see Robert A. Nye, *Masculinity and Male Codes of Honor in Modern France* (New York: Oxford University Press, 1993); and Yvonne Knibehler, *Les Pères aussi ont une histoire* (Paris: Hachette, 1987).

98. See Judith Coffin, *The Politics of Women's Work: The Paris Garment Trades, 1750–1915* (Princeton: Princeton University Press, 1996).

THREE Policing the Free Market

1. See Donald J. Olsen, *The City as a Work of Art: London, Paris, Vienna* (New Haven: Yale University Press, 1986); and David Harvey, *Consciousness and Urban Experience: Studies in the History and Theory of Capitalist Urbanization* (Baltimore: Johns Hopkins University Press, 1985).

2. Louis Chevalier has traced the growing fear of the poor during the July Monarchy in *Classes laborieuses et classes dangereuses à Paris pendant la première moitié du dix-neuvième siècle* (Paris: Hachette, 1984).

3. André Jardin and André-Jean Tudesq, *Restoration and Reaction, 1815–1848*, trans. Elborg Forster (Cambridge: Cambridge University Press, 1983), 93.

4. Harvey, *Consciousness and Urban Experience*, 67.

5. A good overview of the general transformation of the capital in the first half of the nineteenth century can be found in the series *La Nouvelle histoire de Paris*, in particular the volumes by Guillaume Berthier de Sauvigny, *La Restoration. 1815–1830* (Paris: Hachette, 1977); and Philippe Vigier, *Paris pendant la Monarchie de Juillet (1830–1848)* (Paris: Hachette, 1991). For the Second Empire, one of the most comprehensive works remains Jeanne Gaillard, *Paris la ville, 1852–1870; L'Urbanisme à l'heure d'Haussmann* (Paris: H. Champion, 1976).

6. Jennifer Jones, "*Coquettes* and *Grisettes:* Women Buying and Selling in Ancien Régime Paris," in Victoria de Grazia, with Ellen Furlough, *The Sex of Things: Gender and Consumption in Historical Perspective* (Berkeley: University of California Press, 1996), 25–53.

7. Michelle Perrot, *Femmes publiques* (Paris: Textuel, 1997), 7.

8. APP DA/222 "Rapport de l'Officier de la paix, service actif du dispensaire," 19 June 1841.

9. APP DA/222 "Enquête sur une scene scandaleuse survenue le 18 juin 1841 entre les marchandes tenant des comptoirs au Palais Royal, et sur les habitudes et la conduite de ces marchandes," 9 July 1841, testimony of Sr. Robert, *surveillant*, 1.

10. "Enquête," testimony of Sr. Perot, *limonadier*, 6.

11. "Enquête," testimony of Robert, 1. In the report of the officer of the peace filed 19 June, it said that they were pursued by the crowd itself.

12. The first made the Palais Royal and the boulevards in the area of the théâtres Royal, des Italiens, and de l'Opéra off-limits to prostitutes; the second forbad prostitution in boutiques.

13. APP DB/257 Ordinance of 1 October 1830.

14. These areas had also been centers of agitation in 1789 and throughout the nineteenth century. Insurrections broke out in the area around the *halles*, for example, in 1830, 1832, 1834, June 1848, and December 1851. This part of

the city was thus repeatedly designated off-limits for street merchants, and police regulations were issued in October 1832, October 1851, and December 1859. See APP DB/257. For an interesting discussion of popular control of the urban landscape during the 1848 revolution, see Françoise Paul-Lévy, *La ville en croix: De la révolution de 1848 à la rénovation haussmannienne* (Paris: Librairie des Méridiens, 1984). On insurrections in the neighborhood of the *halles*, see M. Vimont, *Histoire de la rue Saint-Denis: De ses origines à nos jours*, vol. 3, *De la Révolution à nos jours* (Paris: Les Presses Modernes, 1936).

15. J. C. Maldan, *Les Embarras de Paris*, 3d ed. (Paris: Chez l'éditeur, 1840).

16. Honoré de Balzac, "Les Boulevards de Paris," in *Le Diable à Paris. Paris et les parisiens. Moeurs et coutumes, caractères et portraits des habitants de Paris, tableau complet de leur vie privée, publique, politique, artistique, littéraire, industrielle, etc., etc.* (Paris: J. Hetzel, 1845–46), 2:101–2.

17. This fear of crowds persisted throughout the century. See Susanna Barrows, *Distorting Mirrors: Visions of the Crowd in Late Nineteenth-Century France* (New Haven: Yale University Press, 1981).

18. APP DB/257 circular issued by Girod de l'Ain, 1 October, 1830, 2; Ordinance of 6 October 1851, art. VIII.

19. AN F7 3893 General Police: Paris Bulletins, 26 February 1825, 2.

20. *Nouveau tableau de Paris, ou observations sur les moeurs et usages des parisiens au commencement du dix-neuvième siècle.* (Paris: Pillet-Ainé, 1828), 1:179–80.

21. The council concluded that the rumor was untrue. APP, *Rapports généraux sur les travaux du Conseil de Salubrité*, reports for the year 1841, 134.

22. APP DB/257 circular of 27 January 1837.

23. APP DB/257 circular of 11 August 1837; circular of 26 October 1837.

24. Théodore de Banville, *Les Parisiennes de Paris* (Paris: Michel Lévy, 1867), rev. ed., 314.

25. APP DA/222 "Enquête," testimony of Sr. Baudin, hairdresser, 2; testimony of Sr. Mack, merchant tailor, 4.

26. On the cholera outbreaks in Paris, see Catherine J. Kudlick, *Cholera in Post-Revolutionary Paris: A Cultural History* (Berkeley: University of California Press, 1996); and François Delaporte, *Disease and Civilization: The Cholera in Paris, 1832*, trans. Arthur Goldhammer (Cambridge, Mass.: MIT Press, 1986).

27. Eugène Roch, *Paris malade. Esquisses du jour* (Paris: Moutardier, 1832), 1:10; 2:361.

28. M. Sabatier, *Histoire de la législation sur les femmes publiques et les lieux de débauche*, rev. ed. (Paris: Gagniard, 1830), 221.

29. Elie Frebault, "Curiosités parisiennes: Les Industries de la rue," part 3, *L'Histoire*, 28 May 1870, n.p.

30. APP DA/222 "Enquête," testimony of Sr. Sigfeldt, *surveillant*, 8; testimony of Sr. Sevestre, *tabletier*, 9–10.

31. L. A. Berthaud, "Halles et marchés," in *Nouveau Tableau de Paris au dix-neuvième siècle* (Paris: Chez Madame Charles-Béchet, 1834–35), 5:269.

32. Aside from a small number of luxury boutiques, the department stores established during the Second Empire were the first to set fixed prices; bargaining was still the norm in markets such as the *halles* during this period. On the department store in France, see Michael Miller, *Le Bon Marché: Bourgeois Culture and the Department Store, 1869–1920* (Princeton: Princeton University Press, 1981); Rosalind H. Williams, *Dream Worlds: Mass Consumption in Late-Nineteenth-Century France* (Berkeley: University of California Press, 1982).

33. APP DA/257 circular of Delessert, 10 September 1845.

34. Edmond Texier, *Tableau de Paris* (Paris: Paulin et Le Chevalier, 1852), 1:145.

35. APP DB/257 circular of Delavaux, 28 April 1825, 1; circular, 24 September 1825.

36. APP DA/222 "Enquête," testimony of Sr. Joffee, 3; testimony of Sr. Robert, 2.

37. APP DA/222 "Rapport de l'Officer de la Paix," Dispensary Service report, 21 July 1841.

38. *Code Napoléon; or, The French Civil Code. Literally Translated from the Original and Official Edition, Published in Paris, in 1804. By a Barrister of the Inner Temple* (1804; reprint, Baton Rouge: Claitor's Book Store, 1960), 60.

39. G.-T. Doin and Ed. Charton, *Lettres sur Paris* (Paris: Imprimerie de Crapelet, 1830), 95.

40. *La Gazette des femmes*, 1 September 1836, no. 3, p. 75; and 1 May 1837, no. 5, 102. This paper appeared from July 1836 to March of 1838.

41. Alexandre Privat d'Anglemont, *Paris anecdote. Les Industries inconnues, la Childebert, les oiseaux de nuit, la villa des chiffonniers* (Paris: P. Jannet, 1854), 16.

42. Ibid., 25.

43. Ibid., 213.

44. APP DA/222 "Enquête," testimony of Sr. Baudin, *coiffeur*, 2; testimony of Sr. Sigfeldt, *surveillant*, "Enquête," 8.

45. APP DA/222 report of 6 August 1841.

46. APP DA/222 letter to the general intendant of the civil list, 14 August 1841.

47. APP DA/222 testimony of Marie-Florence Langlois, 14 November 1842.

48. APP DA/222 petition of the Femme Rey (Jacquin) to the prefect of police, 9 August 1841.

49. APP DA/222 report of the commissioner of the Palais Royal district, 24 October 1845.

50. Jean-Michel Baruch-Gourden, "La police et le commerce ambulant à Paris au *dix-neuvième* siècle," in Philippe Vigier et al., *Mantien de l'ordre et polices en France et Europe au dix-neuvième siècle* (Paris: Créaphis, 1987). See also "Les petits metiers parisiens et leurs fonctions au dix-neuvième siècle: L'exemple des marchands des quatre saisons" (doctoral thesis, University of Paris VII, 1983).

51. APP DB/257 circular of Girod de l'Ain, 20 January 1832.

52. APP DB/257 circular of Caussidière, 31 March 1848.

53. APP DB/257 police ordinance, 19 June 1830; circular of Carlier, 13 October 1851.

54. [T. Delord, A. Frémy, E. Texier], *Les Petits paris par les auteurs des Mémoires de Bilboquet: Paris gagne-petit* (Paris: Librairie d'Alphonse Taride, 1854), 91.

55. Emile Zola, *Le Ventre de Paris* (Paris: Librairie Générale Française, 1984), 30.

56. When Claude introduces Florent to the Méhudin women, both fish merchants, he compares the younger to "a virgin of Murillo, all blonde in the middle of her carps and eels," Zola, *Le Ventre de Paris*, 31.

57. Ibid.

58. On the renovation of the *halles*, see Bertrand Lemoine, *Les Halles de Paris. L'Histoire d'un lieu, les péripéties d'une reconstruction, la succession des projets, l'architecture d'un monument, l'enjeu d'une 'cité'* (Paris: L'Equerre, 1980); Pierre Lavendan, *La Question du déplacement de Paris et du transfert des Halles au Conseil Municipal sous la Monarchie de Juillet* (Paris: n.p., 1969); Jeanne Hugueney, "Les Halles centrales de Paris au dix-neuvième siècle," *La Vie urbaine: Urbanisme-Habitation. Aménagement du territoire* 2 (April–June 1968): 81–130.

59. APP DA 379 Lanquetin, *Question du déplacement de Paris*, Préfecture de la Seine, committee on the halles, documents for study, no. 4 (April 1840), 13.

60. APP/DA 379 Lanquetin, *Observations sur un travail de l'administration municipale de Paris intitulé "Etudes sur les Halles,"* Préfecture de la Seine, committee on the halles, documents for study, no. 6 (20 March 1841), 6.

61. APP DA/379 Préfecture de la Seine, committee on the halles, documents for study, no. 3, *Projet Daniel* (6 July 1842), 4.

62. APP DA/379 Halles centrales, "Réponse à la note du 8 juillet 1850. Rapport de l'architecte—Commissaire de la petite voirie," 5 November 1850, 10.

63. Ironically, this decision didn't meet either of its objectives. Luxury commerce continued to move to the northwestern area of the city, while the

destruction of many popular neighborhoods during the Second Empire meant that the popular classes tended to move out of the area around the *halles*.

64. The first pavilion, built in 1851, was immediately demolished after critics complained that it looked like a fortress designed to control the people. Baltard, the original architect, came up with new plans inspired by the *gare de l'est* and with the help of Haussmann had them approved by the emperor in 1853. Hugueney, "Les Halles centrales," 111–22.

65. Lemoine, *Les Halles de Paris*, 190.

66. Philippe Perrot, "Splendeur et déclin du marché du Temple," *L'Histoire* 33 (April 1981): 15.

67. It is interesting to note in this context that whereas one of the principles of American commerce is caveat emptor, "let the buyer beware," the French Civil Code placed the responsibility for transactions upon the seller.

68. Jurisdiction over the *halles* was shared by the Paris police and the Department of the Seine. The prefect of police, the prefect of the Seine, and the emperor were the three actors most directly involved in the renovation and regulation of the market.

69. APP DA/379 Lenoir, "Projet de Grande Halle," 1831, 1.

70. *Nouveau tableau de Paris au dix-neuvième siècle* (1834), 5:274, 254, 232.

71. Rene S. Marion, "*Les Dames de la Halle*: Women and Community in Late Eighteenth-Century Paris," *Proceedings of the Annual Meeting of the Western Society for French History* 17 (1990): 140–48; Jehanne d'Orliac, *Les Dames de la Halle, 1181–1939* (Paris: Editions Francex, 1946).

72. L. Montigny, *Le Provincial à Paris. Esquisses des moeurs parisiennes* (Paris: Ladvocat, 1825), 2:291.

73. Gaetan Niépovié, *Etudes physiologiques sur les grandes métropoles de l'Europe occidentale. Paris* (Paris: Librairie de Charles Gosselin, 1840), 186, 187.

74. Ibid.

75. Texier, *Tableau de Paris*, 1:149.

76. APP DA/379 Senard, 25.

77. Charles Paul de Kock, *La Grande ville. Nouveau tableau de Paris comique, critique, et philosophique* (Paris: Marescq, 1844), 1:146.

78. *Le Diable à Paris. Paris et les parisiens. Moeurs et coutumes, caractères et portraits des habitants de Paris, tableau complet de leur vie privée, publique, politique, artistique, littéraire, industrielle, etc., etc.* (Paris: J. Hetzel, 1845–46), 2:xxv.

79. Victor Fournel, *Ce qu'on voit dans les rues de Paris* (Paris: Adolphe Delahays, 1858), 323.

80. APP DA/378 Storez, "Mémoire sur la Construction des Halles de Paris," June 1853, 9.

81. APP DA/380 "Lettre de marchands de volaille à l'Inspecteur-Général des Halles et Marchés," n.d.

82. APP DA/723 "Pétition des Marchands du Temple à Sa Majesté l'Empereur," 16 April 1866, 2.

83. APP DA/723 prefect of police to prefect of the Seine, 7 May 1864.

84. APP DA/723 letter of the inspector of the Temple market to the prefect of police, 17 May 1865.

85. APP DA/380 report of the inspector of the Innocents Market to the director of provisioning, 9 March 1857.

86. APP DA/380 petition to the prefect of police, 9 October 1857.

87. APP DA/380 prefect of the Seine to prefect of police, 13 June 1856.

88. APP DB/371 decision of 25 October 1854.

89. APP DA 723 note to prefect of police, 28 March 1842.

90. APP DA 723 petition of stall-holders at Temple to prefect of police, 12 March 1842.

91. APP DA 723 petition of *chiffon* merchants to prefect of police, 7 April 1843.

92. According to the police ordinance of 11 June 1829.

93. APP DA 380 decree issued by prefect of the Seine, 2 July 1868. In 1868 the concession of places in the market was transferred from police to departmental authorities.

94. *Moniteur universel,* 17 November 1868.

95. Ibid.

96. APDS, V^2 F^4 article 3: Marchands au petit-tas; questions de place; letter of 7 July 1869.

97. APP DA/723 inspector of Temple market to prefect of police, 18 April 1843.

98. APP DA/723 Petition of *chiffon* merchants to prefect of police, 7 April 1843.

99. APP DA/380 analysis of prefect of police, 14 June 1853.

100. Ordinance sur les marchés publics, 1865, articles 58, 56, 57.

101. Paul de Musset, *Paris et les parisiens* (Paris: Morizot, 1856), 440.

102. Anicet-Bourgeois and Michel Masson, *La Dame de la halle. Drame en sept actes* (Paris: Michel Lévy, 1852), 106

103. Texier, *Tableau de Paris,* 1:139.

104. Hector Horeau, *Assainissement, embellissement de Paris. Edilité urbaine mise à la portée de tout le monde* (Paris: A. Morel, 1868), 44.

105. Louis Lazare, *Revue municipale et gazette réunies* 267 (10 August 1858): 309.

106. BN, MSS n.a.f. 10338, Emile Zola, "Notes Préparatoires. *Le Ventre de Paris,*" 58.

107. "Une visite aux halles centrales," *Magasin pittoresque* 30 (January 1862): 27.

FOUR The Lorette

1. On John Law, see Jacques Cellard, *John Law et la Régence* (Paris: Plon, 1996). On the stock market, Roger Sitri, *"J'ai" ou "Je prends": La Bourse des valeurs et la compagnie des agents de change à travers les âges* (Paris: La Pensée universelle, 1979).

2. Léon Epsztein, *L'Economie et la morale aux débuts du capitalisme industriel en France et en Grande Bretagne* (Paris: Armand Colin, 1966), 40.

3. Judith Wechsler, *A Human Comedy: Physiognomy and Caricature in Nineteenth-Century Paris* (Chicago: University of Chicago Press, 1982), 85.

4. Nestor Roqueplan, *Nouvelles à la main* (20 January 1841) (Paris: Rue d'enghien, 1841), 70.

5. Arago, *Physiologie de la femme entretenue* (Brussels: Chez tous les libraires, 1841), 15.

6. The convention that the lorette wore masculine clothes may have come from her association with the theater since during the mid-nineteenth century it was common for female actors to play male roles. Lenard R. Berlanstein, "Breeches and Breaches: Cross-Dress Theater and the Culture of Gender Ambiguity in Modern France," *Comparative Studies in Society and History* 38:2 (April 1996): 338–69. For a general overview of the cultural significance of cross-dressing, see Marjorie Garber, *Vested Interests: Cross-Dressing and Cultural Anxiety* (New York: Routledge, 1992).

7. Maurice Alhoy, *Physiologie de la lorette* (Paris: Aubert, n.d.), 90.

8. Mary Louise Roberts, *Civilization Without Sexes: Reconstructing Gender in Postwar France, 1917–1927* (Chicago: University of Chicago Press, 1994).

9. Alfred Delveau, *Grandeur et décadence des grisettes* (Paris: Alfred Desloges, 1848), 72.

10. This paragraph and the next draws heavily on the following works: Philip T. Hoffman, Gilles Postel-Vinay, and Jean-Laurent Rosenthal, "Private Credit Markets in Paris, 1690–1840," *Journal of Economic History* 52:2 (June 1992): 293–306; and William Chester Jordan, *Women and Credit in Pre-Industrial and Developing Societies* (Philadelphia: University of Pennsylvania Press, 1993).

11. Eleanor S. Riemer, "Women, Dowries, and Capital Investment in Thirteenth-Century Siena," in Marion A. Kaplan, ed., *The Marriage Bargain: Women and Dowries in European History* (New York: Haworth Press, 1985), 64.

12. Jordan, *Women and Credit,* 78.

13. On the importance of women in neighborhood networks during the eighteenth century, see Arlette Farge, *Fragile Lives: Violence, Power, and Solidarity in Eighteenth-Century Paris,* trans. Carol Shelton (Cambridge, Mass.: Harvard University Press, 1993); and David Garrioch, *Neighborhood and Community in Paris, 1740–1790* (Cambridge: Cambridge University Press, 1986).

14. Hoffman et al., "Private Credit Markets," 305; see also by the same authors, "Information and Economic History: How the Credit Market in Old Regime Paris Forces Us to Rethink the Transition to Capitalism," *American Historical Review* 104:1 (February 1999): 69–94.

15. David Landes discusses the history of these projects in "Vieille banque et banque nouvelle: La Révolution financière du dix-neuvième siècle," *Revue d'Histoire Moderne et Contemporaine* 3 (1956): 204–22.

16. Hoffman et al., "Private Credit Markets," 294.

17. Or in Balzac's 1844 article for *Le Diable à Paris*, in which he painted Madame la Ressource with a much less lighthearted touch. Honoré de Balzac, "Une Marchande à la toilette, ou Madame la Ressource en 1844," in *Le Diable à Paris. Paris et les parisiens. Moeurs et coutumes, caractères et portraits des habitants de Paris, tableau complet de leur vie privée, publique, politique, artistique, littéraire, industrielle, etc., etc.* (Paris: J. Hetzel, 1845–46), 271–77. Emile Zola, *La Curée* (Paris: 1871).

18. Honoré de Balzac, *Splendeurs et misères des courtisanes* (Paris: Garnier-Flammarion, 1968), 398.

19. M. and Françis Girault, *Les Abus de Paris* (Paris: Breteau, 1844), 78.

20. According to Edmond Texier, the Temple had a long association with money lending. Texier stated the Knights Templar were the "first bankers of Europe" and that before the Revolution of 1789 the Temple was a site of asylum for bankrupts seeking to avoid debtor's prison. Edmond Texier, *Tableau de Paris* (Paris: Paulin et le Chevalier, 1852), 1:146.

21. F. D'Antonelle, "Le Marché aux vieux linges," in *Nouveau tableau de Paris au XIXe siècle* (Paris: Mme Charles-Béchet, 1834–35), 1:355.

22. *Moeurs des lorettes. La Pêche aux anglais par la Reine Pomaré, oeuvre posthume, exhumée et revue par Julia Fleur-des-Près* (Paris: Librairie de Jules Labitte, 1847), 18–19.

23. Alain Plessis, *The Rise and Fall of the Second Empire, 1852–1871,* trans. Jonathan Mandelbaum (Cambridge: Cambridge University Press, 1985), 67.

24. Alfred Delvau, *Grandeur et décadence des grisettes* (Paris: Desloges, 1848), 57.

25. Félix Mornand, *La Vie de Paris* (Paris: Librairie nouvelle, 1855), 200, 201.

26. Gabriel Pélin, *L'Enfer des femmes. Etudes réalistes sur les grandes dames, dames, bourgeoises, boutiquières, femmes d'employés, ouvrières, servantes, lorettes et femmes tolérées. Leur position et leurs misères dans la bonne ville de Paris* (Paris: L'Ecrivain et Toubon, 1861), 78.

27. Ibid., 77.

28. Henry de Kock, *Le Guide de l'amoureux à Paris. D'après le manuscrit original de Mme la Baronne de C.* (Paris: A. Faure, 1865), 84.

29. Jules Noriac, *Journal d'un flâneur* (Paris: Michel Lévy, 1865), 255.

30. Delvau, *Grandeur et décadence des grisettes,* 7.

31. *Les Bamboches amoureuses des grisettes de Paris. Histoires, aventures, moeurs et galanteries de ces demoiselles* (Paris: Chez les marchands de nouveautés, 1840), 85.

32. Arnould Frémy, *La Révolution du journalisme* (Paris: Librairie centrale, 1866), 228.

33. Edmond Texier, *Le Journal et le journaliste. Physionomies parisiennes* (Paris: A. Le Chevalier, 1868), 9, 118–19.

34. J. F. Vaudin, *Gazettes et gazetiers. Histoire critique et anecdotique de la presse parisienne* (Paris: E. Dentu, 1863), 265–66.

35. Léon Rossignol, *Nos petits journalistes* (Paris: Librairie Gosselin, 1865), 8, 13.

36. Frémy, *La Révolution du journalisme,* 84.

37. Henry de Kock, *Le Guide de l'amoureux à Paris,* 84.

38. Pélin, *L'Enfer des femmes,* 75.

39. In 1832, republican insurgents were killed by the army and national guard at the Cloister of Saint-Merri. Antonio Watripon, *Souvenirs du quartier latin. Les Lolottes. Histoire de Carmagnole* (Paris: L. Marpon, 1861), 49–50, 54.

40. *Paris-Vivant, par des hommes nouveaux.* Vol. 9: *La Fille* (Paris: Chez tous les libraires, 1858), 45.

41. Quoted in Plessis, *The Rise and Fall of the Second Empire,* 64. Other works concerning the change in financial markets and institutions during this period include Pierre Dupont-Ferrier, *Le Marché financier de Paris sous le Second Empire* (Paris: Félix Alcan, n.d.); Landes, "Vieille banque et banque nouvelle"; and Guy P. Palmade, *Capitalisme et capitalistes français au dix-neuvième siècle* (Paris: Armand Colin, 1961).

42. Marcel Marion, *Histoire financière de la France depuis 1715,* vol. 5, *1819–1875* (Paris: Rousseau et Cie, 1928), 367.

43. Iowerth Prothero, *Radical Artisans in England and France* (Cambridge: Cambridge University Press, 1997), 155.

44. David I. Kulstein, *Napoleon III and the Working Class: A Study of Government Propaganda under the Second Empire* (n.p.: California State Colleges, 1969), 170–79.

45. Palmade, *Capitalistes français,* 150; Shepard Bancroft Clough, *France: A History of National Economics* (New York: Octagon Books, 1970), 176.

46. According to Tom Kemp, Paris was second only to London in foreign investment during the Second Empire. *Economic Forces in French History* (London: Dennis Dobson, 1971), 164.

47. Charles Duvivier, *La Bourse* (Lyon: Chez Méra, 1854), 4.

48. *La Bourse ou la vie. Argent et échange. Par un converti* (Paris: Chez Dentu, 1856), 10, 14.

49. Cham [Amédée de Noé], *La Bourse illustrée* (Paris: Au Bureau du Journal *le Charivari*, 1853), n.p.

50. Oscar de Vallée, *Les Maniers d'argent. Etudes historiques et morales. 1720–1857* (Paris: Michel Lévy, 1857), 356.

51. Eugène de Mirecourt, *La Bourse et les signes du siècle* (Paris: E. Dentu, 1863), 344–45.

52. Pierre-Joseph Proudhon, *Manuel du spéculateur à la bourse* (Paris: Garnier frères, 1854), 9, 31.

53. Ibid., 144.

54. *Boursicotiérisme et lorettisme, ou Flibusterie, vice et paresse. Etude de moeurs parisiennes. Par le Juif-Errant* (Paris: Bibliothèque historique du Juif-Errant, 1858), 12.

55. A. G. de Mériclet, *Nouveau tableau de la Bourse de Paris. Conseils aux spéculateurs* (Paris: E. Dentu, 1855), 182.

56. Epsztein, *L'Economie et la morale*, 33.

57. Article 5, Ordinance of 1 Thermidor Year IX (20 July 1801), Gabriel Delessert, ed., *Collection officielle des ordonnances de police depuis 1800 jusqu'à 1844* (Paris: Librairie administrative de Paul Dupont, 1844–74), 93.

58. *Le Charivari*, 8 August 1848, no. 221, p. 2.

59. Henry de Kock, *Les Femmes de la Bourse* (Paris: Alexandre Cadot, 1858), 301.

60. Ibid., 302.

61. Eugène de Mirecourt, *La Bourse. Ses Abus et ses mystères* (Paris: Chez l'auteur, 1858), 149.

62. [T. Delord, A. Frémy, E. Texier], *Paris-Boursier* (Paris: Librairie d'Alphonse Taride, 1854), 60–61.

63. Amédée Matagrin, "Un Coin de Paris: La Bourse des femmes," *L'Illustration, Journal universel* 17:428 (10 May 1851): 302.

64. Mirecourt, *La Bourse: Ses Abus*, 93. The *coulisse* did have its defenders; for example, the 1859 brochure *La Coulisse devant l'opinion publique* (Paris: Castel, 1859) argued that the "true territory [of the *coulisse*] was that of liberty" (26). It was, however, this very liberty of the *coulisse* that made it so worrisome to many.

65. At the same time, the *coulisse* was implicitly recognized as legitimate when the commissioner of police of the stock exchange (a separate division of the general Parisian police force) ordered his agents to draw up a list of *coulissiers* so that they could be taxed. See *La Coulisse devant l'opinion publique*, 9; also APP DB 188, "La Bourse."

66. APP DB 188 note of public prosecutor to prefect of police, 13 September, 1851, 1, 2.

67. APP DB 188 report of the commissioner of the stock exchange police to the prefect of police, 17 September, 1851, 1.

68. APP DB 188 prefect of police to the superintendents of police, for the sections des Italiens and de la Bourse, and to the head of the municipal police, 22 September 1851; letter to public prosecutor, 22 September 1851.

69. APP DB 188, prefect of police to the superintendent of police, section des Italiens, 10 December 1852.

70. APP DB 188 report to prefect of police, 13 December 1852.

71. Marion, *Histoire financière de la France*, 5:378.

72. *La Bourse de Paris. Chronique de la semaine* (Paris: Gustave Havard, 1857), 33–34.

73. Auguste Vitu, *Le Constitutionnel*, 24 November 1861.

74. Ibid.

75. APP DB 188 report submitted by the prefect of the Seine to the prefect of police, 21 March 1857.

76. APP DB 188 prefect of police to superintendent of police, section des Italiens, 21 May 1856.

77. APP DB 188 report of superintendent of police, 2d arrondissement, section des Italiens, 25 March 1857.

78. Report of officer of the peace, municipal police to head of municipal police, 27 April 1857.

79. Vitu, *Le Constitutionnel*, 24 November 1861.

80. APP DB 188, imperial decree of 22–24 November 1861.

81. "Bulletin hébdomadaire de la Bourse de Paris," *Le Constitutionnel*, 25 November 1861.

82. J.-J. Weiss, *Journal des débats*, 25 November 1861. See also the articles by Rousset, "Bulletin financier," *Le Siècle*, 26 November 1861; and Vitu, *Le Constitutionnel*, 24 November 1861.

83. See Sharon Marcus, *Apartment Stories: City and Home in Nineteenth-Century Paris and London* (Berkeley: University of California Press, 1999), especially chap. 4.

84. Honoré de Balzac, *César Birotteau* (Paris: Gallimard, 1975), 397.

85. Vitu, *Le Constitutionnel*, 24 November 1861, 1.

86. Craig Muldrew, *The Economy of Obligation: The Culture of Credit and Social Relations in Early Modern England* (New York: St Martin's Press, 1998), 156.

87. Buying on margin means buying on credit, for example, using the anticipated returns from a stock to pay off the loan you took out to buy the stock in the first place. Trading in options entails speculating on the rise or fall of a stock that you may or may not own. If the stock moves in the opposite direction you anticipated, you have to pay the difference. Since both require little initial outlay of capital, the integrity of the person engaging in either method is of paramount importance.

88. *La Coulisse devant l'opinion publique*, 29.

89. The role of honor in the formation of middle-class masculinity has been studied by William M. Reddy, *The Invisible Code: Honor and Sentiment in Postrevolutionary France, 1814–1848* (Berkeley: University of California Press, 1997); and Robert Nye, *Masculinity and Male Codes of Honor in Modern France* (New York: Oxford University Press, 1993).

90. Alexandre Dumas, fils, *La Question d'argent* (Paris: Charlieu, 1857), 126.

91. *La Bourse* (Paris: Michel Lévy, 1866), 35. Such fears resulted in regular demands to forbid the practice of selling before liquidation and to limit the ability of people to buy on credit. See, for example, M. Boboeuf, *La Bourse et la loi. Pétition adressée au Sénat pour rendre obligatoires les marchés à terme* (Paris: E. Dentu, 1863).

92. *Boursicotiérisme et lorettisme*, 27, 29.

93. George V. Taylor, "The Paris Bourse on the Eve of the Revolution, 1781–1789," *American Historical Review* 67:4 (July 1962): 955, n. 13.

94. Daniel Dessert, *Argent, pouvoir et société au Grand Siècle* (Paris: Fayard, 1984), 86.

95. Le vicomte d'Arlincourt, "Le Spéculateur," *Les Français peints par eux-mêmes* (Paris: L. Curmer, 1841), 1:378.

96. Dumas fils, *La Question d'argent.*

97. Henry de Kock, *Les Femmes de la Bourse*, 75.

98. Ernest Feydeau, *Un Coup de bourse. Etude dramatique en cinq actes* (Paris: Michel Lévy, 1868), 148.

99. E. Pellisson, review of Eugène de Mirecourt, *La Bourse: Ses Abus et ses mystères* (Paris: Imprimerie Walder, 1858), 3.

100. Mirecourt, *La Bourse: Ses Abus,* 218

101. David Cohen, *La Promotion des Juifs en France à l'époque du Second Empire (1852–1870)* (Paris: CNRS, 1980), 2:651. See also Pierre Birnbaum, "Anti-Semitism and Anti-Capitalism in Modern France," in Frances Malino and Bernard Wasserstein, eds., *The Jews in Modern France* (Hanover, N.H.: University Press of New England, 1985), 215.

102. Over 60 percent of the Jews who died before 1870 were paupers. Robert F. Byrnes, *Antisemitism in Modern France*, vol. 1, *The Prologue to the Dreyfus Affair* (New York: Howard Fertig, 1969), 97.

103. Ibid., 118–19.

104. Cohen, *La Promotion des Juifs,* 2:446.

105. Ibid., 449.

106. *Le Figaro,* 1 February 1863, quoted in Cohen, *La Promotion des Juifs,* 2:465. Although the Baron James Rothschild was also Jewish, his role as defender of the "high bank" against the Périeres as well as his opposition to the new methods of raising capital, which he said encouraged speculation, made him less of a target for anti-Semites.

107. Ibid.

108. Georges Duchêne, *La Spéculation devant les tribunaux* (1867), cited in Cohen, *La Promotion des Juifs*, 655.

109. Ernest Feydeau, *Mémoires d'un coulissier* (Paris: Librairie nouvelle, 1873), 247.

110. Frédéric Soulié, "La Bourse," in *Deux séjours. Province et Paris* (Paris: Hippolyte Souverain, 1836), 2:318.

111. *La Bourse de Paris. Chronique de la semaine*, 137.

112. *La Bourse* (Paris: Michel Lévy, 1866), 26.

113. Dandelot, "Bulletin financier," *Journal des économistes* 48:144 (15 December 1865): 477.

114. Alexandre Durant, *La Bourse et les emprunts étrangers* (Paris: Aux Bureaux de L'Indépendant Français, 1868), 12.

115. Feydeau, *Un Coup de bourse*, 21.

116. *Physiologie de l'argent. Par un débiteur* (Paris: Desloges, 1841), 50.

117. [Delord et al.], *Paris-Boursier*, 72. See also, for example, *La Bourse de Paris*, 47–50, 80–82, 114; Henry de Kock, *Les Femmes de la Bourse*, 228, 303; Mirecourt, *La Bourse et les signes du siècle*, 250; Feydeau, *Memoirs d'un coulissier*, 245–47.

118. Feydeau, *Memoirs d'un coulissier*, 248–49.

119. Pélin, *L'Enfer des femmes*, 79.

120. *Boursicotiérisme et lorettisme*, 10.

121. Ernest Feydeau, *La Comtesse de Chalis ou les moeurs du jour* (Paris: Michel Lévy, 1868).

122. "Opinion de M. le Procureur Général Dupin sur le luxe effréné des femmes à l'occassion d'une pétition contre la prostitution," 22 June 1865, reproduced in Ernest Feydeau, *Du Luxe, des femmes, des moeurs, de la littérature, et de la vertu* (Paris: Michel Lévy, 1866), 200–204.

123. Feydeau, *Du Luxe, des femmes*, 53.

124. Constance Aubert, *Encore le luxe des femmes. Les Femmes sages et les femmes folles* (Paris: Dentu, 1865), 4–5.

125. *La Gazette des femmes*, 1 July 1836, no. 1, p. 6.

126. Julie-Victoire Daubié, *La Femme pauvre au dix-neuvième siècle* (Paris: Guillaumin et Cie, 1866).

127. Amélie Bosquet, "Types Masculins. Don Juan," *Le Droit des femmes*, 17 July 1869, no. 15, pp. 3–4.

128. Richer expressed his frustration that critics interpreted the paper's call for the "enfranchisement" of women as a demand for "free love" in 25 December 1869, no. 35, p. 2.

129. *Le Droit des femmes*, 11 September 1869, no. 23, p. 1.

130. Matt K. Matsuda, *The Memory of the Modern* (New York: Oxford University Press, 1996), 45–46; APP DB 188, "La Bourse."

Conclusion

1. Jean-Baptiste Say, *Olbia* (1800), cited in R. R. Palmer, *J.-B. Say: An Economist in Troubled Times* (Princeton: Princeton University Press, 1997), 37.

2. Viviana A. Zelizer, *The Social Meaning of Money* (New York: Basic Books, 1994). See especially her introduction for the theoretical basis of her argument.

3. Ibid., 21.

4. G. R. Searle, *Morality and the Market in Victorian Britain* (Oxford: Clarendon Press, 1998), 164.

5. On the attempt to establish the regulatory system in England, see Judith Walkowitz, *Prostitution and Victorian Society: Women, Class, and the State* (New York: Cambridge University Press, 1980).

6. J. Jeannel, *De la prostitution dans les grandes villes au dix-neuvième siècle et de l'extinction des maladies vénériennes* (Paris: J.-B. Ballière et fils, 1868), 136, 140.

7. Chambre de Commerce de Paris, *Statistique de l'industrie à Paris, résultant de l'enquête faite par la Chambre de Commerce pour l'année 1860* (Paris: Chambre de Commerce, 1864), xliii.

8. Ibid., 296.

9. Ibid., 292.

10. Ibid., 402.

11. Eugène Scribe and Ernest Legouvé, *Les Doigts de fée. Comédie en cinq actes* (New York: Henry Holt and Co., 1864).

12. Ibid., 105.

13. *Le Charivari*, 20 October 1869, reprinted in *Le Droit des femmes*, 6 November 1869, no. 28, p. 1.

14. *Le Droit des femmes*, 6 November 1869, no. 28, p. 2.

15. Reprinted in *Le Droit des femmes*, 24 April 1869, no. 3, p. 2.

16. Whitney Walton, *France at the Crystal Palace: Bourgeois Taste and Artisan Manufacture in the Nineteenth Century* (Berkeley: University of California Press, 1992), 53.

17. Leora Auslander, "The Gendering of Consumer Practices in Nineteenth-Century France," in Victoria de Grazia, with Ellen Furlough, eds., *The Sex of Things: Gender and Consumption in Historical Perspective* (Berkeley: University of California Press, 1996), 98.

18. On female shoplifters in Paris, see Michael B. Miller, *The Bon Marché: Bourgeois Culture and the Department Store, 1869–1920* (Princeton: Princeton University Press, 1981), 197–206.

19. The debate over whether consumerism empowered women or increased their subservience to men is an interesting one that is far from being resolved, as indicated in the thoughtful essay by Mary Louise Roberts, "Gender, Con-

NOTES TO PAGES 177–178

sumption, and Commodity Culture," *American Historical Review* 103:3 (June 1998): 817–44.

20. Ann-Louise Shapiro makes this connection in *Breaking the Codes: Female Criminality in Fin-de-Siècle Paris* (Stanford: Stanford University Press, 1996).

21. Vanessa Schwartz studies the potential of mass culture to create a unified community in *Spectacular Realities: Early Mass Culture in Fin-de-Siècle Paris* (Berkeley: University of California Press, 1998).

22. This interpretation of the novel appears in Rosalind H. Williams, *Dream Worlds: Mass Consumption in Late-Nineteenth-Century France* (Berkeley: University of California Press, 1982), 135.

23. APP DB 188 reported in *Paris-Jour,* 15–16 April 1967.

24. APP DB 188 article in *L'Aurore,* 3 March 1967.

25. T. Delord, A. Frémy, and E. Texier, *Les Petits Paris, par les auteurs des Mémoires de Bilboquet. Paris-boursier* (Paris: Librairie d'Alphonse Taride, 1854), 54.

Select Bibliography
of Primary Sources

Archival and Manuscript Sources

Archives Nationales (AN)

F/7   Police générale
  3893
  9305

Archives de Paris et du Département de la Seine (APDS)

D/1/P/4	Registres du cadastre
D/6/U	Justice de paix
D/22/U/1	Simple police
VI/1	Service des sergents de ville
V2/F/4	Halles et marchés

Archives de la Préfecture de Police (APP)

DA/221	Répression de la prostitution
DA/222	Service des moeurs: prostitution
DA/300	Halles centrales
DA/378	Halles centrales
DA/379	Halles centrales
DA/380	Halles centrales
DA/677	Marchands des quatres saisons
DA/696	Marché du Temple
DA/723	Reconstruction du marché du Temple
DB/58	Travestissement (autre que pour le carnival)
DB/129	Ouvriers/travail
DB/188	Bourse
DB/190	Maisons de jeu

DB/193   Brocanteurs
DB/195   Marchands ambulants
DB/199   Marchands en étalage, marchands ambulants
DB/225   Lavoirs
DB/257   Embarras de la voie publique (autre que travaux)
DB/371   Marché du Temple
DB/393   Marchands ambulants

Bibliothèque Nationale de France (BN)

Zola, Emile. Notes for *La Curée*. BN: Nouvelles acquisitions françaises 10282 (microfilm 3104, f. 209–469).

Books, Articles, and Pamphlets
Anonymous Works

Les Bamboches amoureuses des grisettes de Paris. Histoires, aventures, moeurs et galanteries de ces demoiselles. Paris: Chez les marchands de nouveautés, 1840.

La Bourse. Paris: Tous les marchands de nouveautés, 1826.

La Bourse. Paris: Michel Lévy, 1866.

La Bourse est un marché libre? Paris: Imprimerie de Schiller ainé, 1860.

La Bourse ou la vie. Argent et échange. Par un converti. Paris: Chez Dentu, 1856.

Boursicotiérisme et lorettisme, ou Flibusterie, vice et paresse. Etude de moeurs parisiennes. Par le Juif-Errant. Paris: Bibliothèque historique du Juif-Errant, 1858.

Code Napoléon; or, The French Civil Code. Literally Translated from the Original and Official Edition, Published in Paris, in 1804. By a Barrister of the Inner Temple. Reprint, Baton Rouge: Claire's Book Store, 1960.

La Coulisse devant l'opinion publique. Paris: Castel, 1859.

Le Diable à Paris. Paris et les parisiens. Moeurs et coutumes, caractères et portraits des habitants de Paris, tableau complet de leur vie privée, publique, politique, artistique, littéraire, industrielle, etc., etc. 2 vols. Paris: J. Hetzel, 1845–46.

Dictionnaire anecdotique des nymphes du Palais Royal et autres quartiers de Paris, par un homme de bien. Paris: Les Marchands de nouveautés, 1826.

Doléances des filles de joie de Paris à l'occassion de l'ordonnance qui leur défend de se montrer en public. Paris: Chez les librairies du Palais-Royal, 1830.

Les Etudiants et les femmes du quartier latin en 1860. Par un étudiant. Paris: Chez tous les libraires, 1860.

Les Français peints par eux-mêmes. Encyclopédie morale du dix-neuvième siècle. 2 vols. Paris: L. Curmer, 1841.

The Gentleman's Night Guide. The Gay Women of Paris and Brussels, commonly called cocottes or lorettes. 2d ed. Paris: Published for the Author, 1869.

La Grisette à Paris et en province. Sa vie, ses moeurs, son caractère, ses joies, ses espérances, ses tribulations, ou les vicissitudes de la fille du peuple entre l'amour et la coquetterie. Paris: Renault, 1843.

Histoire véritable d'une grisette contemporaine qui, de fille de portier est devenue femme de perruquier, puis femme entretenue et est aujourd'hui baronne!!!. n.p.: n.d.

Moeurs des lorettes. La Pêche aux anglais par la Reine Pomaré, oeuvre posthume, exhumée et revue par Julia Fleur-des-Près. Paris: Librairie de Jules Labitte, 1847.

Nouveau tableau de Paris au dix-neuvième siècle. 7 vols. Paris: Chez Mme Charles-Béchet, 1834–35.

Nouveau tableau de Paris, ou Observations sur les moeurs et usages des parisiens au commencement du dix-neuvième siècle. 2 vols. Paris: Pillet-ainé, 1828.

Paris-Guide, par les principaux écrivains et artistes de la France. 2 vols. Paris: Librairie Internationale, 1867.

Paris, ou le livre des cent-et-un. 2d ed. 15 vols. Paris: L'advocat, 1832.

Paris-Vivant, par des hommes nouveaux. Vol. 9, *La Fille.* Paris: Chez tous les libraires, 1858.

Physiologie de l'argent. Par un débiteur. Paris: Desloges, 1841.

Physiologie de la presse. Biographie des journalistes et des journaux de Paris et de la province. Paris: Aubert, 1841.

Physiologie des demoiselles de magasin, par un journaliste. Paris: Lachapelle, 1842.

Physiologie des quartiers de Paris. Paris: Desloges, 1841.

Physionomies parisiennes. Les joueuses, Paris, Bade, Ems, Hambourg et Monaco. Par une joueuse. Paris: A. LeChevalier, 1868.

Réponse de M. le Préfet à toutes les pétitions et réclamations des filles publiques de Paris. Paris: Chez les Librairies du Palais Royal et les Marchands de Nouveautés, 1830.

"Une Visite aux halles centrales." *Magasin pittoresque* 30 (January 1862): 26–30.

Works with Author(s) Listed

Alhoy, Maurice. *Physiologie de la lorette.* Paris: Aubert, n.d.

Ambs-Dalès, J.-B. *Amours et intrigues des grisettes de Paris, ou Revue des*

Belles dites de la petite vertu . . . le tout rédigé d'après les renseignements donnés par une grisette sur le retour. 3d ed. Paris: Roy Terry, 1830.

Arago. *Physiologie de la femme entretenue.* Brussels: Chez tous les libraires, 1841.

Aubert, Constance. *Encore le luxe des femmes. Les Femmes sages et les femmes folles.* Paris: Dentu, 1865.

Balzac, Honoré de. *Monographie de la presse parisienne.* Paris: Au Bureau central des publications nouvelles, 1842.

Banville, Théodore de. *Les Parisiennes de Paris.* Rev. ed. Paris: Michel Lévy, 1867.

Bargemont, Alexandre de. *Les Halles.* Collection: Paris historique, pittoresque et anecdotique. Paris: Gustave Havard, 1855.

Bayard, Henri. *Mémoire sur la topographie médicale du quatrième arrondissement de Paris, recherches historiques et statistiques sur les conditions hygiéniques des quartiers qui composent cette arrondissement.* Paris: J. B. Ballière, 1842.

Bazin, M. A. *L'Epoque sans nom. Esquisses de Paris, 1830–1833.* 2 vols. Paris: A. Mesnier, 1833.

Béraud, Antony, and P. Dufey. *Dictionnaire historique de Paris.* 2d ed. 2 vols. Paris: Chez J.-N. Barba, 1828.

Blanc, Louis. *L'Organisation du travail.* Paris: Prévot, 1840.

Boboeuf, M. *La Bourse et la loi. Pétition adressée au Sénat pour rendre obligatoires les marchés à terme.* Paris: E. Dentu, 1863.

Bruncamp, Eugène. *Nos idées, nos moeurs, nos caractères.* Paris: Hachette, 1866.

Buret, Eugène. *De la misère des classes laborieuses en Angleterre et en France.* Paris: Chez Paulin, 1840.

Burgy, Jules. *Présent et avenir des ouvriers. Par un typographe.* Paris: Chez les marchands de nouveautés, 1847.

Cham [Amédée de Noé]. *La Bourse illustrée.* Paris: Au Bureau du Journal le Charivari, 1853.

Chambre de Commerce de Paris. *Statistique de l'industrie à Paris, résultant de l'enquête faite par la Chambre de Commerce pour les années 1847–1848.* Paris: Guillaumin, 1851.

———. *Statistique de l'industrie à Paris, résultant de l'enquête faite par la Chambre de Commerce pour l'année 1860.* Paris: Chambre de Commerce, 1864.

Collomb, A.-B. *La Vérité sur le sort des ouvriers en France.* Paris: n.p., 1842.

Conseil de Salubrité. *Rapports généraux sur les travaux du Conseil de Salubrité.* Paris: Boucquin, 1817–94.

Cottu, Louis. *Du Sort des travailleurs, en réponse à M. le Baron Charles Dupin.* Paris: Delaunay, 1841.

Dairnvaell, Georges [Satan]. *Organisation du travail. Les Ecrivains ouvriers de la pensée. Ont-ils le droit de vivre? Lettre à M. Louis Blanc.* Paris: Chez Georges Dairnvaell, 1848.

———. *Physiologie des étudiants, de grisettes et des bals de Paris.* Paris: Chez Georges Dairnvaell, 1849.

Dash, Comtesse. *Les Femmes à Paris et en province.* Paris: Michel Lévy, 1868.

Daubié, Julie-Victoire. *La Femme pauvre au dix-neuvième siècle.* Paris: Guillaumin et Cie, 1866.

Décembre-Alonnier. *Les Merveilles du Nouveau Paris.* Paris: Bernardin-Béchet, 1867.

Delord, Taxile. *La Parisienne. Physiologies parisiennes.* Paris: Aubert, 1850.

Delord, T., A. Frémy, and E. Texier. *Les Petits Paris, par les auteurs des Mémoires de Bilboquet. Paris-boursier.* Paris: Librairie d'Alphonse Taride, 1854.

———. *Les Petits Paris, par les auteurs des Mémoirs de Bilboquet. Paris-gagne-petit.* Paris: Librairie d'Alphonse Taride, 1854

———. *Les Petits Paris, par les auteurs des Mémoires de Bilboquet. Paris-grisette.* Paris: Librairie d'Alphonse Taride, 1854.

———. *Les Petits Paris, par les auteurs des Mémoires de Bilboquet. Paris-journaliste.* Paris: Librairie d'Alphonse Taride, 1854.

———. *Les Petits Paris, par les auteurs des Mémoires de Bilboquet. Paris-lorette.* Paris: Librairie d'Alphonse Taride, 1854.

Delvau, Alfred. "Alexandre Privat d'Anglemont." In *Paris-Inconnu.* Paris: Delahays, 1861.

———. *Grandeur et décadence des grisettes.* Paris: Desloges, 1848.

Delvau, Alfred, et al. *Paris qui s'en va, Paris qui vient.* Paris: Les éditions de Paris, 1985 [1859–60].

Doin, G.-T. and E. Charton. *Lettres sur Paris.* Paris: Imprimerie de Crapelet, 1830.

D. S. *Aperçu sur la condition des classes ouvrières en France et en Angleterre et critique de l'ouvrage de M. Buret sur les misères des classes laborieuses.* Paris: Chez Bureau, 1844.

DuCamp, Maxime. *Paris, ses organes, ses fonctions et sa vie dans la seconde moitié du XIXe siècle.* 6 vols. Paris: Hachette, 1869–75.

Dulaure, Jacques. *Histoire physique, civile et morale de Paris depuis 1821 jusqu'à nos jours.* 2 vols. Paris: Librairie des écoles, 1835.

Dumas, Alexandre. *Filles, lorettes et courtisanes.* Paris: Dolin, 1843.

Dumas, Alexandre, et al. *Paris et les Parisiens au dix-neuvième siècle. Moeurs, arts et monuments.* Paris: Morizot, 1856.

Duvant, Alexandre. *La Bourse et les emprunts étrangers.* Paris: Aux Bureaux de l'Indépendant Français, 1868.

Duvivier, Charles. *La Bourse.* Lyon: Chez Méra, 1854.

Egron, A. C. *Le Livre de l'ouvrier, ses devoirs envers la société, la famille, et lui-même.* Paris: P. Mellier, 1844.

Esquiros, Adèle. *Les Marchandes d'amour.* Paris: E. Pick de l'Isère, 1865.

Esquiros, Alphonse. *Les Vierges folles.* Paris: A. le Gallois, 1840.

———. *Les Vierges sages.* Paris: P. Delavigne, 1842.

Feydeau, Ernest. *Du Luxe, des femmes, des moeurs, de la littérature, et de la vertu.* Paris: Michel Lévy, 1866.

———. *Mémoires d'un coulissier.* Paris: Librairie nouvelle, 1873.

Fix, Théodore. *Observations sur l'état des classes ouvrières.* Paris: Guillaumin, 1846.

Forster, Charles de. *Quinze ans à Paris (1832–1848). Paris et les parisiens.* 2 vols. Paris: Firmin Didot frères, 1848–49.

Fournel, Victor. *Ce qu'on voit dans les rues de Paris.* Paris: Adolphe Delahays, 1858.

Frébault, Elie. "Curiosités parisiennes: Les Industries de la rue." *L'Histoire* 28 (May 1870): n.p..

Frégier, H.-A. *Des Classes dangereuses de la population dans les grandes villes, et des moyens de les rendre meilleures.* 2 vols. Paris: Ballière, 1840.

Frémy, Arnould. *La Révolution du journalisme.* Paris: Librairie centrale, 1866.

Germain, A. *Martyrologue de la Presse, 1789–1861.* Paris: H. Duminéray, 1861.

Gisquet, Henri-Joseph. *Mémoires d'un préfet de police, 1830–1840.* Paris: Marchant, 1840.

Goncourt, Edmond de, and Jules de Goncourt. *La Lorette.* Paris: Dentu, 1853.

Hatin, Eugène. *Bibliographie historique et critique de la presse périodique française.* Paris: Firmin Didot, 1866.

———. *Histoire du journal en France, 1631–1853.* 2d ed. Paris: P. Jannet, 1853.

Horeau, Hector. *Assainissement, embellissement de Paris. Edilité urbaine mise à la portée de tout le monde.* Paris: A. Morel, 1868.

Huart, Louis. *L'Etudiant.* Paris: Aubert, 1850.

———. *Le Flâneur.* Paris: Aubert, 1850.

———. *La Grisette.* Paris: Aubert, 1850.

———. *Muséum parisien. Histoire physiologique, pittoresque, philosophique et grotesque de toutes les bêtes curieuses de Paris et de la banlieue pour faire suite à toutes les éditions des Oeuvres de M. de Buffon.* Paris: Beauger et Cie, 1841.

———. *Physiologie de la grisette.* Paris: Aubert, n.d.

Huart, Louis, and Charles Philipon. *Galerie de la presse, de la littérature et des beaux arts.* Paris: Aubert, 1839–40.

Izambard, Henri. *La Presse parisienne. Statistique bibliographique et alphabétique de tous les journaux revues et canards périodiques nés, morts, ressucités ou métamorphosés à Paris depuis le 22 février 1848 jusqu'à l'empire.* Paris: P.-H. Krabbe, 1853.

Jeannel, J. *De la prostitution dans les grandes villes au dix-neuvième siècle et de l'extinction des maladies vénériennes.* Paris: J.-B. Ballière et fils, 1868.

Jolicoeur, Cyprien. *Histoire amusante des jolies femmes; les amours et aventures galantes des grisettes; détails intéressans sur les Brodeuses, les Blanchisseuses, les Chamarreuses, les Brocheuses, les Brunisseuses, les Danseuses, les Modistes, les Fleuristes, les Passementières, les Mercières, les Culotières, les Cuisinières, les Lingères, les Coutourières, les Dames de la halle, les Figurantes de l'Opéra, de la Porte-Saint-Martin, de l'Ambigu et des principaux théâtres; le nom des endroits où elles se réunissent. Le tout écrit avec l'encre de la Petite Vertu.* Paris: Imprimerie de Herhan, 1834.

Jouy, E. de. *L'Hermite de la Chaussée d'Antin ou Observations sur les moeurs et les usages parisiens au commencement du dix-neuvième siècle.* 5 vols. Paris: Pillet, 1813–19.

Kock, Charles Paul de. *La Grande ville. Nouveau tableau de Paris comique, critique, et philosophique.* 2 vols. Paris: Marescq, 1844.

———. *Un homme à marier, suivi de recette pour faire un mariage, un tour de grisette, etc.* Paris: Gustave Barba, 1843.

Kock, Henry de. *Les Femmes de la Bourse.* Paris: Alexandre Cadot, 1858.

———. *Le Guide de l'amoureux à Paris. D'après le manuscrit original de Mme la Baronne de C.* Paris: A. Faure, 1865.

Lanfranchi, Louis-Ranier. *Voyage à Paris, ou Esquisses des hommes et des choses dans cette capitale.* Paris: Veuve Lepetit, 1830.

L'Héritier. *Les Mystères de la vie du monde, du demi-monde et du quart du monde, ou les moeurs d'aujourd'hui. Scènes épisodiques et anecdotiques prises dans tous les rangs et conditions de la société.* 2 vols. Paris: Charlieu frères et Huillery, 1868–69.

Liabour, Clébule. *Le Journalisme et les journaux, par un ministre d'hier.* Paris: Albert Frères, 1848.

Liancourt, Adolphe de. *Le Rideau levé sur les mystères de Paris.* 2 vols. Paris: B. Renault, 1845.

Luchet, Auguste. *Les Moeurs d'aujourd'hui.* Paris: Coulon-Pineau, 1854.

———. *Paris, esquisses dédiées au peuple parisien et à M. J.-A. Dulaure.* Paris: J. Barbezat, 1830.

M. et Girault, Françis. *Les Abus de Paris.* Paris: Breteau, 1844.

Marchal, Charles. *Physiologie de la fille sans nom.* Paris: Charles LaChapelle, n.d.

Massy, Jules Robert de. *Des Halles et marchés du commerce des objets.* Paris: n.p., 1862.

Matagrin, Amédée. "Un Coin de Paris: La Bourse des femmes." *L'Illustration, Journal universel* 17:428 (10 May 1851): 301–2.

Mathieu, E. *Rapport sur les marchés publics de Londres.* Paris: n.p., 1861.

Mercier, Louis-Sébastien. *Tableau de Paris.* 1782–83. Reprint, Paris: Pagnerre, 1853.

Méreuil, Georges. *Sur le trottoir.* Paris: Librairie Cournol, 1863.

Mériclet, A. G. de. *Nouveau tableau de la Bourse de Paris. Conseils aux spéculateurs.* 2d ed. Paris: E. Dentu, 1855.

Mirecourt, Eugène de. *La Bourse. Ses Abus et ses mystères.* Paris: Chez l'auteur, 1858.

———. *Sur le mercantilisme littéraire.* Paris: E. Duverger, 1845.

Montigny, L. *Le Provincial à Paris. Esquisses des moeurs parisiennes.* 3 vols. Paris: Ladvocat, 1825.

Mornand, Félix. *La Vie de Paris.* Paris: Librairie nouvelle, 1855.

Musset, Paul de. *Paris et les parisiens.* Paris: Morizot, 1856.

Nettement, Alfred. *Histoire politique, anecdotique et littéraire du Journal des Débats.* Paris: Aux Bureaux de l'Echo de France, 1838.

Neufville, Etienne de. *Physiologie de la femme.* Paris: Aubert, 1842.

Neuville, Gerard de. *Les Joyeuses dames de Paris.* Paris: Chez tous les libraires, 1867.

Niépovié, Gaetan. *Etudes physiologiques sur les grandes métropoles de l'Europe occidentale. Paris.* Paris: Librairie de Charles Gosselin, 1840.

Noriac, Jules. *Journal d'un flâneur.* Paris: Michel Lévy, 1865.

Paoli, Toussaint. *La Bourse et ses tripots.* Paris: Arnauld de Vresse, 1864.

Parent-Duchâtelet, A.-J.-B. *De la prostitution dans la ville de Paris, considérée sous le rapport de l'hygiène publique, de la morale, et de l'administration.* 2 vols. 2d ed. Paris: J.-B. Ballière, 1837.

Pélin, Gabriel. *L'Enfer des femmes. Etudes réalistes sur les grandes dames, dames, bourgeoises, boutiquières, femmes d'employés, ouvrières, servantes, lorettes et femmes tolérées. Leur position et leurs misères dans la bonne ville de Paris.* Paris: L'Ecrivain et Toubon, 1861.

———. *Les Laideurs du Beau Paris. Histoire morale, critique et philosophique des industries, des habitants, et des monuments de la capitale.* Paris: Lécrivain et Toubon, 1861.

Pellisson, E. *Eugène de Mirecourt. La Bourse. Ses Abus et ses mystères.* Paris: Imprimerie Walder, 1858.

Pigeory, Félix. "Les Halles centrales, quai de la Mégisserie." Parts 1–4. *Revue des Beaux-Arts.* May 15, June 1, June 15, and July 1, 1851.

Préfecture de Police de Paris. *Recueil officiel des circulaires émanées de la Préfecture de Police.* 2 vols. Paris: Imprimerie Chaix, 1882.

Privat d'Anglemont, Alexandre. *Paris anecdote. Les Industries inconnues, la Childebert, les oiseaux de nuit, la villa des chiffoniers.* Paris: P. Jannet, 1854.

———. *Paris inconnu.* Paris: Adolphe Delahays, 1861.

Proudhon, P.-J. *Manuel du spéculateur à la bourse.* Paris: Garnier frères, 1854.

Robert, Clémenc, et al. *Le Boudoir d'une coquette.* Paris: P.-H. Krabe, 1845.

Roch, Eugène. *Paris malade. Esquisses du jour.* 2 vols. Paris: Moutardier, 1832–33.

Rochefort, Henri. *La Grande Bohême.* Paris: Librairie centrale, 1867.

Rossignol, Léon. *Nos petits journalistes.* Paris: Librairie Gosselin, 1865.

Sabatier, M. *Histoire de la législation sur les femmes publiques et les lieux de débauche.* Rev. ed. Paris: Gagniard, 1830.

Simon, Jules. *L'Ouvrière.* Paris: Hachette, 1861.

Soulié, Frédéric. "L'Agent de Change." *Le Lion Amoureux.* Paris: Michel Lévy, 1870.

———. "Le Bas bleu," *Le Lion amoureux.* Paris: Michel Lévy, 1870.

———. "La Bourse." *Deux séjours. Province et Paris.* Vol. 2. Paris: Hippolyte Souverain, 1836.

———. *L'Homme de lettres.* Brussels: Société typographique Belge, 1838.

Surrel, Louis. *Les Petits mystères du Temple. Esquisse de Moeurs, Us et Coutumes.* Paris: Redond, 1854.

Texier, Edmond. *Les Choses du temps présent.* Paris: Collection Hetzel, 1862.

———. *Histoire des journaux.* Paris: n.d.

———. *Le Journal et le journaliste. Physionomies parisiennes.* Paris: A. Le Chevalier, 1868.

———. *Tableau de Paris.* 2 vols. Paris: Paulin et le Chevalier, 1852.

Tristan, Flora. *L'Union ouvrière.* Paris: Prevot, 1843.

Trollope, Mme. *Paris et les parisiens en 1835.* 3 vols. Paris: H. Fournier, 1836.

Vallée, Oscar de. *Les Maniers d'argent. Etudes historiques et morales 1720–1857.* Paris: Michel Lévy, 1857.

Vaudin, J. F. *Gazettes et gazetiers. Histoire critique et anecdotique de la presse parisienne.* Paris: E. Dentu, 1863.

Véron, Pierre. *Le Pavé de Paris.* Paris: Librairie centrale, 1865.

Vidal, François. *Vivre en travaillant! Projets, voies et moyens de Réformes Sociales.* Paris: Capelle, 1848.

Villars, Emile. *Le Roman de la parisienne.* Paris: Librairie centrale, 1866.

Villermé, Louis-René. *Tableau de l'état physique et moral des ouvriers employés dans les manufactures de coton, de laine et de soie.* 2 vols. Paris: J. Renousad, 1840.

Viret, Frédéric. *Des Femmes, ou Quelques mots sur leur position morale et matérielle et plus particulièrement sur celle de la fille du peuple dans l'organisation sociale actuelle.* Paris: P. Martinon, 1850.

Watripon, Antonio. *Souvenirs du quartier latin. Les Lolottes. Histoire de Carmagnole.* Paris: L. Marpon, 1861.

Zurgy, Jules. *Présent et avenir des ouvriers, par un typographe.* Paris: Chez les marchands de nouveautés, 1847.

Periodicals

L'Artisan. Paris. 1830.

L'Atelier. Paris. 1840–50.

La Bourse de Paris. Chronique de la semaine. Paris. 1857.

Le Charivari. Paris. 1832–93.

Le Droit des femmes. Paris. 1869–70.

La Femme libre. Paris. 1830–33.

La Gazette des femmes. Paris. 1836–37.

La Gazette des femmes. Paris. 1840–44.

L'Opinion des femmes. Paris. 1848–49.

La Politique des femmes. Paris. 1848.

Revue municipale et gazette réunies: La Revue municipale: Journal adminis-tratif et historique. Paris. 1852–62.

La Ruche populaire. Paris. 1839–49.

La Voix des femmes. Paris. 1848.

Novels and Plays

Anicet-Bourgeois and Michel Masson. *La Dame de la Halle. Drame en Sept actes* (1852).

Balzac, Honoré de. *César Birotteau* (1837).

———. *La Cousine Bette* (1846).

———. *La Fille aux yeux d'or* (1835).

———. *Illusions perdues* (1837–43).

———. *Splendeurs et misères des courtisanes* (1838–47).

[Dumas, Alexandre]. *Le Roman de Violette* (1864).

Dumas, Alexandre, fils. *La Dame aux camélias* (1848).

———. *La Question d'argent* (1857).

Feydeau, Ernest. *La Comtesse de Chalis ou les moeurs du jour* (1868).

———. *Un Coup de Bourse. Etude dramatique en cinq actes* (1868).

Flaubert, Gustave. *Education sentimentale* (1869).

Hugo, Victor. *Les Misérables* (1862).

Kock, Charles Paul de. *Mon Voisin Raymond* (1822).

Legouvé, Ernest, and Eugène Scribe. *Les Doigts de fée* (1864).

Luchet, Auguste, and Desbuards. *La Marchande du Temple. Drame en cinq actes* (1856).

Murger, Henry. *Scènes de la vie de bohème* (1850).

Perrin, Maximillien. *La Fleur des grisettes* (1861).

———. *La Marchande du Temple* (1850).

———. *Soirées d'une grisette en l'attendant!* (1835).

———. *Vierge! et Modiste* (1840).

Sue, Eugène. *Les Mystères de Paris* (1842–43).

Zola, Emile. *L'Argent* (1891).

———. *L'Assomoir* (1876–77).

———. *La Curée* (1869–71).

———. *Nana* (1879–80).

———. *Le Ventre de Paris* (1873).

Index